Coming Together?

Coming Together?

MEXICO–UNITED STATES RELATIONS

Barry Bosworth,
Susan M. Collins, *and*
Nora Claudia Lustig, Editors

Brookings Institution Press
Washington, D.C.

Copyright © 1997 by
THE BROOKINGS INSTITUTION
1775 Massachusetts Avenue, N.W.
Washington, D.C. 20036

Library of Congress Cataloging-in-Publication data

Coming together?: Mexico–United States relations / Barry Bosworth,
    Susan M. Collins, and Nora Claudia Lustig, editors.
        p.   cm.
    Papers from a conference sponsored by the Brookings Institution on
July 25, 1996.
    Includes bibliographical references and index.
    ISBN 0-8157-1028-3 (alk. paper). — ISBN 0-8157-1027-5 (pbk. :
alk. paper)
        1. United States—Relations—Mexico—Congresses. 2. Mexico—
Relations—United States—Congresses. 3. Mexican-American Border
Region—Environmental conditions—Congresses. I. Bosworth, Barry,
1942–   . II. Collins, Susan Margaret. III. Lustig, Nora.
IV. Brookings Institution.
E183.8.M6C63 1997
327.72073—dc21   97-4738
                                                              CIP

9 8 7 6 5 4 3 2 1

The paper used in this publication meets the minimum requirements of American
National Standard for Information Sciences—Permanence of Paper for Printed
Library Materials, ANSI Z39.48-1984.

Typeset in Times Roman

Composition by AlphaWebTech
Mechanicsville, Maryland

Printed by R. R. Donnelley and Sons Co.
Harrisonburg, Virginia

Foreword

In mid-1997 the Clinton administration must present Congress with a three-year review of the North American Free Trade Agreement (NAFTA). This will reignite the debate on the agreement's benefits that occurred during its negotiation and ratification. The review is coming at a time of increased tensions between the Mexican and U.S. governments—tensions that are likely to contribute to a decline in public support for expanding the economic and social links between the two countries.

The 1995 economic collapse in Mexico complicated the issues. Although not caused by NAFTA, the sharp recession in Mexico contributed to a surge of illegal immigration into the United States. Contrary to expectations when NAFTA was approved, the U.S. trade balance with Mexico has slid into substantial deficit—fueling claims that NAFTA has destroyed jobs and depressed wages in the United States. Furthermore, many politicians blame foreigners for the American drug problem. As a result, Mexico has come under increasing focus as a major conduit for the flow of drugs into the United States.

Unfortunately, debates on Mexico–U.S. issues are often based on misinformation. To contribute to a more balanced and informed debate, the Brookings Institution held a conference on July 25, 1996. The purpose of the conference was to evaluate recent development in the U.S.–Mexico relationship with the participation of researchers from the two countries. Five papers were presented at the conference, each concentrating on a particular subject: bilateral trade flows, movements of financial capital, immigration, drug trafficking, and environmental issues. This book includes revised versions of those papers, together with the remarks of the commentators on each paper and a summary of the discussion that followed. The introductory chapter presents a brief overview of the main issues and summarizes the five chapters and discussion. Because of time constraints, the book was not subjected to the formal review and verification procedures established for research publications at Brookings.

The book was edited by Steph Selice, and Lin Lin and James J. Prescott assisted with the research. Evelyn Taylor and Mark Steese provided administrative assistance. Brookings gratefully acknowledges the financial support of the Ford Foundation for this project.

The views expressed in this book are those of the individual authors and should not be ascribed to any of the persons or organizations whose assistance and support is acknowledged above, or to the trustees, officers, or other staff members of the Brookings Institution.

MICHAEL H. ARMACOST
President

April 1997
Washington, D.C.

Contents

Tables

Figures

1 Introduction

Barry Bosworth, Susan M. Collins, and Nora Claudia Lustig

THE signing of the North American Free Trade Agreement (NAFTA) in November 1993 represented a historic point of reference in relations between Mexico and the United States. NAFTA was expected to bring about a substantial expansion of trade among the three member countries and to give a strong boost to economic growth in Mexico.[1] It also represented a recognition of efforts, extending over the prior decade, to modernize and open up the Mexican economy to the global trading system. But above all, it was to be the basis for a new closer relationship between Mexico and the United States.

Since NAFTA's ratification, however, events have not gone completely as planned. The Mexican economy entered into a severe depression triggered by the financial crash of December 1994. Large inflows of foreign capital, which had previously been highlighted as emblematic of Mexico's growing integration with the global economy, suddenly reversed, draining Mexico of foreign exchange reserves and forcing a massive devaluation of the currency. The crisis also affected the relationship between Mexico and the United States, causing a drop in public support for expanding the economic and social links between the two countries.

The economic collapse in Mexico sharply curtailed its ability to finance rapid economic growth and led to increased pressures on illegal immigration into the United States. Moreover, increased competition from and migration of workers in low-wage countries, such as Mexico, is often advanced as an explanation for the decline of wages for low-skilled U.S. workers. Contrary to expectations at the time of NAFTA's approval, the U.S. trade balance with Mexico has fallen into substantial deficit—fueling claims that NAFTA has destroyed jobs in the United States. Even worse, the United States had to lend Mexico $13.5 billion in 1995 (which has been repaid) as part of an international financial rescue package to prevent the

---

1. For an overview, see Lustig, Bosworth, and Lawrence (1992).

Mexican economy's collapse.[2] Mexico has also attracted increasing attention as a major conduit for the flow of drugs into the United States.

Nevertheless, it is possible to point to several areas showing positive gains. Thanks to the trade liberalization embodied in NAFTA, trade between the United States and Mexico held up far better than that with non-NAFTA countries during the crisis of 1995.[3] The Mexican government has become more vigorous in its efforts to suppress drug traffic. And, despite the fiscal austerity following the crisis, the Mexican government is making serious efforts to curb environmental hazards in the border region.[4] Furthermore, and in contrast with the past, the Mexican authorities are willing to cooperate in preventing illegal migrants from crossing the border.

NAFTA is symbolic of the increased effort both countries are making to find cooperative solutions to bilateral problems. Since the early 1980s, a binational commission has been holding meetings to discuss a wide range of issues at the highest level of both governments. Since 1990, there has been an effort to develop a cooperative approach to the migration issue through a working group within the Binational Commission. Furthermore, the ratification of NAFTA created new institutions to deal with trade disputes and environmental and labor-related issues.[5] There is no doubt that the setting for a more constructive relationship is in place, especially in comparison with the last sixty years.

However, NAFTA is also interesting for what it is not. It is not a customs union, and certainly not a European-style political community. It is only an agreement to form a free trade region. Citizens of both the United States and Mexico are highly nationalistic and have little interest in integration beyond the economic sphere. In fact, large factions within both countries are concerned that pressures for greater economic integration threaten their sense of national identity. Despite NAFTA, the relationship will continue to be highly asymmetrical. Americans tend to be self-absorbed, and when they do look beyond their own borders no one country dominates: Mexico is only one among many nations competing for the attention of U.S. policymakers. Mexicans, in contrast, are far more focused on the bilateral rela-

---

2. In February 1995, the United States pledged a contribution of U.S.$20 billion to the almost $50 billion international rescue package, but only U.S.$13.5 billion were actually disbursed. By early 1997, the loan had been fully repaid. For a detailed discussion of the 1995 financial rescue package, see Lustig (1996).

3. See chapter 2.

4. See chapter 4.

5. See chapters 2 and 4.

tionship and resentful of what they regard as heavy-handed and unwarranted U.S. interference with their internal affairs.

Examples of U.S. heavy-handedness abound. Every year, the U.S. government issues a statement of "certification" for major drug-producing and transit countries, Mexico included. Although Mexico has been "certified" for several years, the process is always accompanied by extremely negative hearings in the U.S. Congress. (Some Mexicans believe that it is the United States that should be "decertified" for its failure to control drug usage, at great cost to Mexican society.) Some U.S. states are building walls to keep migrants out, and there have been incidents of police brutality against immigrants. Similarly, Mexicans resent U.S. efforts to impose environmental standards (and have Mexico bear the costs) that the United States accepted only after accumulating substantial wealth.

Finally, during the first two years of NAFTA's implementation, there were continued conflicts over trade. The United States used the threat of "antidumping" measures to coerce Mexican growers to agree to fix a minimum price for imports of tomatoes. The United States has also refused to carry through with the provision allowing Mexican trucks passage into the United States after 1995. For its part, Mexico has also sought to limit the participation of foreigners in the ownership of petrochemical firms and pension-fund management, contrary to NAFTA provisions.

This book is the result of a conference sponsored by the Brookings Institution on July 25, 1996. The purpose of the conference was to evaluate developments in the Mexico–U.S. relationship with the participation of researchers from both sides of the border. The conference focused on five areas of interest: trade flows, movements of financial capital, immigration, drug trafficking, and environmental issues. For each subject, authors were asked to provide an overview of the basic issues and a summary of recent academic research on the issue. This book consists of revised versions of those five papers, together with the discussants' comments. The remaining portions of this introduction provide a summary of the events that led up to the economic crisis of 1995, and a brief overview of the next five chapters.

The Opening of Mexico's Economy

For Mexico, NAFTA was the culmination of an extraordinary decade-long process of economic reform in which it shifted away from an inward-oriented development policy that emphasized import substitution and close regulation of commercial ties with other nations. Since the mid-1980s Mexico has promoted a policy of economic liberalization, sharply reducing restrictions on external trade and expanding the role of private markets. Even before NAFTA, it acted unilaterally to cut tariffs in half, to an average of about 12 percent, and the proportion of domestic output protected by import licensing was reduced from 75 to 20 percent.[6] Mexico joined the General Agreement on Tariffs and Trade (GATT) in 1986. In addition, controls on cross-border financial transactions were largely eliminated. In its macroeconomic policies Mexico emphasized fiscal consolidation and sharply lower rates of inflation. The inflation rate declined from an annual rate of 132 percent in 1987 to a low of 7 percent in 1994, and the budget balance swung from a deficit equal to 15 percent of gross domestic product (GDP) in 1987 to a surplus of 1.6 percent in 1992 (table 1-1). Mexico also embarked on an extensive program of privatization and deregulation of domestic economic institutions. Revenues from privatizations exceeded 7 percent of gross national product (GNP) in the 1991–94 period, and the previously nationalized banks were returned to private ownership.[7]

NAFTA was perceived by many of its advocates as a means of solidifying the reforms of the government of Mexico's President Carlos Salinas, locking them in against potential reversal by a future administration and reassuring potential foreign investors of the stability of the Mexican economy by tying it more tightly to its northern neighbors. The direct gains to Mexico in the form of lower trade barriers were marginal; the applicable tariffs of the United States and Canada were already low, and the nontariff barriers were to be phased out only gradually.

Mexico also wanted NAFTA as a means of constraining the arbitrariness of U.S. trade policy, guaranteeing access to a market that accounts for about 80 percent of Mexico's total exports. The United States is a huge economy with a pattern of emphasizing domestic considerations in the formulation of its trade policies. Changes in those policies can have devastating effects on the trade of smaller partner countries. Mexico was facing significant market-access problems in apparel, steel, and agricultural products. NAFTA includes a set of procedures for dispute resolution that would theoretically give Mexico greater input into decisions that affect bilateral trade. As mentioned earlier, that part of the agreement has not worked entirely as planned. On occasion the United States has ignored provisions of the agreement that interfered with domestic objectives.

The agreement also made sense for the United States, but for different reasons. The apparent stalemate of the Uruguay Round of multilateral

6. See chapter 2, table 2-3.
7. Further details of the reform program are provided in Lustig (1992).

Table 1-1. Macroeconomic Indicators for Mexico, 1980–95
Annual percentage change

Year	GDP	Consumer prices	Budget balance[a]	Current account[b]	Real exchange rate[c]	Non-oil exports	Imports
1980–86	2.2	60.6	−10.5	−1.1	93.2		
1987	1.9	131.8	−15.0	3.1	63.6	23.7	5.0
1988	1.2	114.2	−10.9	−1.4	77.4	15.2	36.7
1989	3.3	20.0	−5.0	−3.0	83.5	7.5	21.3
1990	4.5	26.7	−2.8	−3.2	83.0	12.0	18.8
1991	3.6	22.7	−0.5	−5.3	91.0	12.8	16.6
1992	2.8	15.5	1.6	−7.6	96.8	9.7	24.3
1993	0.6	9.8	0.7	−6.6	103.1	17.4	5.2
1994	3.5	7.0	−0.1	−7.9	97.2	20.4	21.5
1995	−6.9	35.0	0.1	−0.3	60.0	33.1	−8.6

Source: Banco de México (1996).
a. Economic balance, percent of gross domestic product (GDP).
b. Percent of GDP.
c. 1980 = 100, based on consumer prices.

negotiations made regionalism an attractive option. Moreover, the negotiation of freer trade with Mexico could be used to achieve other objectives, such as improved access and protection for U.S. investors and protection of intellectual property rights.

The results of Mexican economic reforms have been mixed. There was the obvious benefit of a lower rate of inflation; Mexico's trade with other nations also surged with the removal of the trade restrictions. However, the gains in real GDP growth were disappointing. The government came under increased political pressure to show that the economic sacrifices made at the beginning of the reform process were generating positive returns. Investment began to recover from the depressed levels of the mid-1980s, but it was accompanied by a sharp fall in domestic saving that necessitated growing reliance on foreign capital inflows.[8] The current account balance switched from a surplus of 3 percent of GDP in 1987 to a deficit of 8 percent in 1994. Furthermore, the amount of foreign direct investment was modest, averaging $4.5 billion per year in 1991–93 compared with $2.5 billion in 1986–88, with most of the inflow being highly volatile portfolio capital. The financial deregulation was also accompanied by a weak oversight system, excessive asset-market speculation, and problems of debt repayment.

Mexico began to encounter serious financial difficulties in 1994. The exchange rate-based stabilization policy resulted in a recurring real appre-

8. See Bosworth (1996).

ciation as the actual inflation rate consistently exceeded the target—albeit
by modest amounts (table 1-1). One consequence was a widening of the
current account deficit that was covered by increasingly large inflows of
foreign portfolio capital.[9] For a time, the inflows could be supported by the
optimism that surrounded the NAFTA agreement and a favorable interest
rate differential. However, the capital inflow began to dry up and was
reversed in early 1994. The Mexican government met the initial outflows
by drawing down reserves and issuing Tesobonos, bonds denominated in
pesos but indexed to the dollar. Between March and December 1994, the
outstanding stock of Tesobonos rose from $3 billion to $29 billion; international reserves fell from $26 billion in March to $6 billion by December.

With the exhaustion of its reserves, Mexico was forced to devalue its
currency. But the initial 15 percent realignment of the peso, rather than
stabilizing the market, led instead to a financial panic and an intensification
of capital outflows. Mexico abandoned the fixed exchange rate and let the
peso depreciate from 3.4 pesos to the dollar in November 1994 to 5.7 to the
dollar by the end of January 1995. The magnitude of the financial collapse
was a great surprise. Even those who had once argued for devaluation
agreed on the fundamental soundness of the Mexican economic situation,
and a modest currency realignment was expected to lower the current
account gap and lead to an "export-led" expansion. No one anticipated the
degree of panic—particularly on the part of American investors.

With the crisis, Mexico could no longer finance a current account deficit,
and that alone implied an enormous adjustment of trade flows. But Mexico
sought assistance from the United States and the international institutions to
head off an even larger net outflow of private funds.[10] In mid-January 1995
the Clinton administration proposed a $40 billion package of loan guaran-
tees to assist Mexico through what was widely seen as a short-term liquidity
crisis. That package encountered severe problems in the U.S. Congress,
whose members saw an opportunity to press Mexico on other issues such as
illegal immigration, environmental concerns, and drug trafficking. Fearing
that the proposal would be rejected, the Clinton administration developed
an alternative plan that avoided congressional involvement. The new financial package included up to $20 billion in U.S. loans and guarantees from
the Exchange Stabilization Fund, a $18 billion standby arrangement with
the International Monetary Fund (IMF), $1 billion from Canada, and a

9. Much of that capital inflow is believed to be repatriation of funds that had fled the
country in the early 1980s.

10. Lustig (1996).

potential $10 billion from the Bank for International Settlements. Mexico drew on $23 billion of that credit during 1995, but by mid-1996, it was in the process of repaying the loans. The outstanding balances with the United States and Canada were fullly repaid by early 1997, and the $8.2 billion of credits from the IMF is to be repaid over a five-year period.

Despite the efforts to contain the crisis, Mexican GDP fell by 7 percent in 1995, and income per capita is now 15 percent below its peak of the early 1980s. The economy leveled out in 1996, but the recovery is expected to stretch over several years. For Mexico, the 1980s were often referred to as the "lost decade." The 1990s now threaten to become a repeat.

Mexico's financial crisis was not an isolated event. This has been an all too common outcome for countries attempting a rapid deregulation of their financial markets without adequate attention to supervision and oversight responsibilities. Foreign capital inflows can be an attractive means of addressing the most critical barrier to higher incomes, the shortage of domestic capital. Yet if those funds are to be of value, they must be invested in highly illiquid physical plant and equipment. As a result, if the financial inflow is dominated by short-term portfolio capital, there is always the potential for a liquidity crisis brought on by a reversal of the inflow. In fact, several observers foresaw a substantial portion of Mexico's crisis based on what they viewed as an unsustainable magnitude of foreign capital inflows in 1993 and early 1994.[11]

Capital inflows, though frequently cited as a symbol of the success of reform, also create a vulnerability to failure because their sudden reversal can leave policymakers with little time to adjust. The United States and the international institutions have strongly encouraged countries like Mexico to open their financial markets to foreign investors. But there has been too little appreciation of the risks attached to such actions and, as was discovered in the Mexican case, little thought about how to respond if a crisis does occur. In light of these concerns, some countries have sought means of discouraging short-term capital inflows.

Did NAFTA contribute to the 1994–95 crisis? At least in the area of foreign capital inflows, the hype surrounding NAFTA may have helped generate unrealistic expectations, unsustainable inflows of financial capital, and an overvaluation of financial assets. It did attract a large number of unsophisticated investors from Wall Street who were quick to panic when Mexican prices turned down. However, most studies conclude that the crisis was triggered more by political shocks (such as the assassination of

11. See, for example, Dornbusch and Werner (1994).

Luís Donaldo Colosio, the Mexican presidential candidate) and caused more fundamentally by a misalignment of Mexico's macroeconomic policies.[12] Still, Mexico stands out for the severity of the penalty it paid for relatively minor transgressions of economic policies.

Beyond Trade and Financial Flows

The agenda of issues that affect Mexico–U.S. relations extends well beyond the economic arena. There have long been differences over immigration policies. Continued strong demand for illegal drugs in the United States has a powerful corrupting influence on Mexican society. Persistent environmental concerns have focused attention on potential problems of cross-border spillovers of polluted air and water. Each of these problems contributes to friction between the United States and Mexico, because perceptions of the basic causes of the problems differ sharply.

Mexicans represent the largest single source of both legal and illegal immigration into the United States. According to some estimates, the number of Mexican-born individuals residing in the United States increased from 2.5 million in 1980 to 4.5 million in 1990 and 6 million in 1995. Of the latter, it is estimated that about 2 million could be undocumented migrants. Between 1990 and 1995, the estimated average annual flow of permanent migrants was between 280,000 (as cited by Mexican sources) and 340,000 (as cited by U.S. sources).[13] About 90 percent of Mexican-born migrants reside in four states (California, Texas, Illinois, and Arizona).

As indicated in recent congressional elections and various voter referendums, the costs and benefits of immigration are becoming increasingly contentious issues. The lack of job opportunities in Mexico clearly adds to the pressures for immigration. However, Mexicans would also argue that U.S. producers and consumers are the primary beneficiaries through cheap labor and low-cost goods and services, and many Americans have encouraged the illegal immigration that others condemn. The issue has become more controversial in part because of a sharp widening of the wage distribution in the United States since 1973.[14] It is alleged that the decline in real wages of the least-skilled workers is partly due to a surge is the supply of unskilled immigrants. Furthermore, a focus on the costs to state and local

---

12. Leiderman and Thorne (1996); Calvo and Mendoza (1996); Lustig (1995).
13. Gomez de Leon and Tuiran (1996).
14. See Borjas and Friedman (1992); Burtless (1995).

governments that supply basic health care and education has led to a sharp debate over the net benefits of immigration.

Mexico also accounts for a growing portion of the flow of illegal drugs into the United States. Drug trafficking has a highly deleterious effect on the relationship between the two countries, because the United States has consistently held foreign suppliers rather than domestic users as primarily responsible for its drug problems. It pressures other countries to do more to restrict the production and flow of drugs into the United States rather than reducing internal demand. U.S. policies create the potential for enormous profits for drug traffickers operating out of Mexico; those profits have played a major role in the corruption of the Mexican political system. There is increased concern that Mexico could be headed for some of the same problems of intimidation and corruption that have plagued Colombia.

In addition, NAFTA discussions and the last GATT round have given witness to the growth of two other issues of potential conflict: labor and environmental standards. The linking of trade and social issues is a new and controversial aspect of international negotiations. In NAFTA those links are relatively weak. The signatories limited themselves to reaffirming past commitments and broadly shared goals; the trade and social policy agendas are largely separate, reflecting a concern that labor and environmental standards would be used to promote protectionist ends. But there are growing pressures for a more aggressive use of trade policies to influence the domestic social policies of trade partners. There is an oft-expressed concern that further steps to liberalize trade will initiate a competitive race to the bottom with respect to social policies.

These are potentially highly divisive issues. Even if the two countries agreed on the basic goals, they differ widely in the stages of their economic development and the resources that they can devote to solving these problems. Unless the United States is willing to provide significant financial assistance to achieve compliance, the labor and environmental standards cannot be fully harmonized. Mexicans are not indifferent to the benefits of higher standards—they simply cannot afford them.

Summary of the Chapters

The five papers presented at the conference deal with distinct features of the U.S.–Mexican relationship. The issue of trade is critical to the assessment of the initial impact of NAFTA, and inflows and outflows of financial capital played a critical role in the economic crisis of 1994–95. But some of the most difficult aspects of this bilateral relationship are concentrated in areas frequently viewed as outside the range of economic analysis: environmental concerns, drug trafficking, and immigration.

Emerging Patterns in Mexico–U.S. Trade

In chapter 2 J. Enrique Espinosa and Pedro Noyola analyze the evolution of trade flows since the passage of NAFTA. Their primary hypothesis is that the change in the bilateral trade balance is more a reflection of Mexican exchange rate policy than NAFTA's trade liberalization schedule. Although the average ad valorem tariff on Mexican imports fell from 4.3 percent to 1.5 percent between December 1993 and February 1995, the dollar–peso exchange rate declined by 52 percent. Nevertheless, they do find some important trends in bilateral trade that cannot be explained solely by exchange rate movements.

A brief review of some of the pre-1993 literature on the likely effects of NAFTA indicated that the agreement would probably be a positive-sum game for the three member countries. A number of studies predicted that wages and environmental protection in Mexico would improve, as would the efficiency of certain industries and regions in both the United States and Mexico. However, not all the reviews were positive. For example, some authors expressed concern over the slower liberalization schedule in the energy and financial sectors in Mexico as well as the trade diversion implied by restrictive rules of origin in textiles and automobiles.

Espinosa and Noyola doubt that NAFTA's impact on trade can be measured by the events of the first two years after its implementation. This seems even more true given that the Mexican economy fell into a sharp recession in 1995. Instead of the predicted rise, real manufacturing wages fell by a phenomenal 22 percent, and they continued to fall—albeit more slowly—in 1996. Mexico's trade deficit with the United States of $2.4 billion in 1993 became a surplus of $12.8 billion in 1995.

Nevertheless, there are some indications that NAFTA is making its imprint on both the magnitude and composition of bilateral trade flows. For example, the average rate of growth of Mexican exports to the United States was more than 10 percentage points higher after 1994 than in the 1991–93 period. The sectors showing the highest rates of growth were those in which regional integration was fairly advanced even before NAFTA: autos and auto parts, and textiles and apparel. Autos and auto parts have benefited from the negotiated rules of origin as well as improved access to the U.S. markets. Other sectors that saw a remarkable boost in Mexican exports were food and beverages and agriculture and cattle products.

Perhaps the most striking result presented by Espinosa and Noyola relates to the performance of U.S. exports to Mexico. Despite the large depreciation of the peso and the sharp recession in Mexico, U.S. exports grew at an average of 9 percent annually between 1993 and 1995, only slightly lower than the 11.5 percent growth rate of 1991–93. Moreover, although U.S. exports to Mexico fell by only 2 percent in the crisis year of 1995, those of non-NAFTA countries fell by 25 percent.

The authors argue that part of the difference in export performance might be attributed to the depreciation of the dollar vis-à-vis other major currencies in 1994. However, the larger portion must be ascribed to the expanded market access for U.S. exporters and the growing importance of intraindustry bilateral trade, both strengthened by NAFTA. Some participants at the conference also argued that the result reflected enactment of contingent protectionist measures by Mexico against non-NAFTA countries after the economic crisis erupted. Either way, NAFTA appears to have had an important payoff for the United States, shielding its trade from the brunt of the Mexican crisis and from a degree of temporary policy reversal.

The authors also point out that, in contrast with the crisis in 1983 when most goods were subject to import permits, Mexico has kept its open-economy policies in place. There has also been a large decline in the relative importance of maquiladora (in-bond industries) exports. In 1982, after a massive depreciation of the peso, maquiladora exports rose by 29 percent; however, nonmaquiladora, non-oil exports fell by nearly 6 percent the next year. In contrast, in 1995 nonmaquiladora exports rose by 37 percent while maquiladora exports increased by 30 percent.

Espinosa and Noyola conclude by arguing that the most important issue is whether NAFTA is contributing to a more efficient allocation of resources at the national, regional, and global levels. For this to happen, the authors believe that the three countries should continue to lower their tariff structures and modify the rules of origin and other trade rules (such as those on contingent protection, technical, health and safety standards, and competition policy) to make them more consistent with freer global trade. Moreover, the liberalization of services and investment under NAFTA is still incomplete, and NAFTA rules are not compulsory for local governments (in the area of procurement, for example). Developments in these areas are a litmus test of whether NAFTA is a building block to freer global trade.

Sherman Robinson agrees with Espinosa and Noyola that NAFTA appears to have contributed to "locking in" Mexican reforms, has been more "trade creating" than "trade diverting," and has made a major difference in economic sectors such as autos, auto parts, metal products, textiles and apparel, agriculture, and food products. However, Robinson also believes that some problems are emerging. The "rules of origin" are generating many complex disputes, and pressures for protection have interfered with implementation of the agreement in some sectors. To make NAFTA fully effective, Robinson argues for greater policy coordination across the three NAFTA countries in trade policy, particularly in agriculture.

Financial Capital Inflows

John Williamson in chapter 3 argues that at the root of the Mexican peso crisis was the buildup of a large current account deficit. However, since that deficit could not have been financed without large capital inflows into Mexico during the 1990s, Williamson notes that "the crisis was caused by the excessive size of capital inflow, which consisted both of foreign lending and a partial repatriation of the flight capital of the preceding years." However, given that Mexican authorities were using the exchange rate as a nominal anchor, a reduction in the flow of capital would have caused the economy to grow even more slowly than the 3 percent it increased on average over the 1990–94 period. Williamson asks whether Mexico could have followed an alternative strategy—that is, given the propensity of capital to flow, could a current account deficit of such magnitude have been avoided? He argues that if Mexico had followed macroeconomic policies similar to those of Chile and Colombia, the buildup of a current account deficit could have been avoided.

During the first half of the 1990s Chile, Colombia, and Mexico received large inflows of capital from abroad. In particular, Chile and Mexico received similar amounts as a percentage of GNP (5.9 percent and 5 percent, respectively). However, their economic performance was quite different. Although Chile's current account deficit averaged 1.9 percent of GDP over the 1990–94 period, Mexico's averaged 5.9 percent. Moreover, in Chile real growth rate averaged 5.2 percent, while in Mexico it equaled 3 percent. Mexico outperformed Chile in terms of reducing inflation, but at the cost of lower economic growth.

According to Williamson, the difference in economic performance must be ascribed to the differences in macroeconomic policies. Both Chile and Mexico had undertaken structural reforms such as trade liberalization, which should have raised the supply-side determinants of growth. Both were pursuing prudent fiscal policies, and their investment rates were similar. The only factor that explains the less buoyant growth in Mexico was the external sector. The current account deficit increased by 4.6 percent of GDP in Mexico while it fell marginally in Chile.

There are two possible explanations for the deterioration of the current account in Mexico: the appreciation of the currency and the liberalization of imports that started in the mid-1980s. Although Mexico's exports grew at healthy rates, imports grew even more. A rapid trade liberalization should be accompanied by a real depreciation of the exchange rate. But because Mexico used the exchange rate as an anchor, it allowed it to appreciate and financed the resulting current account deficit with capital inflows. Exchange rate policy was an area of critical difference between Mexico and Chile. Chile's policy was to devalue its currency in line with the inflation differential with its major trading partners, so as to maintain a target for the real exchange rate. The policy did imply more inflation than Mexico's, but the differences were minor. Starting from a similar rate of about 26 percent annually in 1990, Chile's inflation was 11 percent in 1994 compared with a 7 percent rate in Mexico.

Maintaining a competitive exchange rate has been a central feature of Chile's policy, where in 1982 a crisis similar to Mexico's caused GDP to fall by 14 percent. Three principal causes of the Chilean crisis have been identified:

—A process of financial liberalization not accompanied by an adequate system of prudential supervision;

—The adoption of a fixed exchange rate at a time when inflation rates were still quite high; and

—The deceleration of inflation impeded by a system tying wage increases to past rates of price increase.

When capital inflows revived in the early 1990s, Chile used those funds to increase its reserves from $3.6 billion in 1989 to $13.1 billion at the end of 1994. The bulk of the capital inflows was thus sterilized at an estimated cost of 0.5 percent of GDP. In addition, Chile introduced a number of supporting measures to dampen market expectations. Controls on capital outflows were also relaxed. Chile implemented a minimum holding period of one year for all equity-type investments and imposed a reserve requirement against foreign holdings of bank deposits and other interest-bearing claims. A small tax was also imposed on short-term external credits for a period of time.

Williamson concludes that it is the combination of these measures that helped restrain the pressures of capital inflows on the current account. Although the policy had its costs in the form of higher inflation and the costs of sterilization, its dividends were precious: "faster growth and avoidance of the risks that result from excessive foreign indebtedness."

Colombia, like Chile, also places a high priority on maintaining a competitive exchange rate. To that end, it modified its long-standing crawling peg by introducing a wider band for exchange rate fluctuations. In 1993, after a substantial liberalization of its capital account, it reintroduced controls on short-term capital inflows. Although Colombia's performance was less impressive than Chile's in terms of inflation, growth, and the current account deficit, the country's ability to withstand shocks has been demonstrated. In mid-1995, the Colombian president was accused of having knowingly accepted contributions from narcotraffickers for his election campaign.

Williamson suggests that Mexico should consciously target the current account deficit in the future. The principles used to guide this target should be feasibility and sustainability. The author recommends using a relatively simple rule of thumb to determine such a target. It should also take into account other factors—the initial stock of debt, the composition of borrowing, the consumption/investment mix, and supply constraints on growth. Although Williamson acknowledges that using rules of thumb may not be particularly appealing, he argues that the alternative—direct controls on capital flows—is even less so. Moreover, pursuing prudent fiscal and monetary policies, while sufficient in a world of perfect capital markets, may not be enough when capital markets seem so susceptible to herd behavior.

Enrique Mendoza disagrees with Williamson's interpretation of the Mexican crisis. Rather than being a crisis of trade flows, he interprets it as crisis of financial stocks. In his view, the crisis cannot be traced to the currency peg and its negative consequences on the real exchange rate, competitiveness, and the current account deficit. Although those were symptoms of a disease, the crisis was caused by runs on Mexican financial instruments. Moreover, the devaluation of the peso, far from correcting the problem, was followed by the worst Mexican crisis since the Great Depression. Although Mendoza does not agree with Williamson's explanation of the crisis, he subscribes to the chapter's policy recommendations: tight fiscal policy, careful management of capital inflows, and strict bank supervision.

Several conference participants suggested that, although the policy recommendations apply to developing countries in general, certain recurrent phenomena in the patterns of capital flows between the United States and Mexico might be worth exploring and are not discussed in Williamson's chapter. Both crises in Mexico—in 1982 and 1995—had been preceded by large inflows of private capital, particularly from the United States, where the flow came to a sudden stop. In the first instance, the capital came largely in the form of loans from U.S. commercial banks. In the second, portfolio investors bought Mexican bonds and invested in the Mexican equity market. In both cases, the United States had to contribute public funds to a financial rescue package for Mexico—bailing out its own banks in the 1980s and its portfolio investors in the 1990s. Furthermore, on both occasions, the trends in capital flows were affected by the evolution of interest rates in the United States. Given that U.S. macroeconomic policy has such an important bearing on Mexico's economic performance and that when Mexico runs into trouble the United States has to be brought in to rescue it from a collapse, there is a need to improve the monitoring, consultation, and coordination between the two countries. After all, macroeconomic stability in Mexico is a precondition to making progress on the other elements of the relationship between Mexico and the United States.

Environmental Concerns

Despite their "sudden" prominence in the late stages of the NAFTA negotiations, environmental concerns have a longer history in the relations between Mexico and the United States. In chapter 4, Juan Carlos Belausteguigoitia and Luis F. Guadarrama provide a historical perspective on the various bilateral agreements in the environmental sphere and summarize the major issues of concern. The agenda has been dominated by four broad issues: border pollution, pollution havens, common standards, and the impact of trade liberalization on the environment. The authors argue that significant progress has been made in the most important aspect, border pollution, and that concerns in the other areas are overstated.

The border region, defined as 100 kilometers on each side, has developed extremely rapidly, with the result that the increased population has produced severe strains on the environment. This is most evident in the area of water usage, which is scarce throughout the region, and inadequate waste treatment, particularly on the Mexican side of the border. The two countries negotiated their first agreement governing water use in 1944, while in the La Paz Agreement of 1983 they initiated programs to share in the costs of constructing waste treatment plants. These efforts are expanded in NAFTA by the creation of a development bank to assist in financing environmental infrastructure projects. Less progress has been made in the area of hazardous waste from the maquiladora plants, because this waste is not being returned to the United States for disposal, as required in the agreement governing plant operations.

The authors argue that issue of pollution havens is overstated. The costs of compliance with environmental standards are usually a small part of production costs and thus have a minor influence on deciding where to locate a plant. In addition, the environmental standards of Mexico are generally similar to those of the United States, with the greatest differences being in the area of enforcement. Private firms cannot be sure that differences in enforcement will persist and are therefore unlikely to be a major factor in decisions on facility location.

In addition, NAFTA explicitly allows each country to maintain its own health, safety, and environmental standards. The issue of standards actually arises most prominently for those governing process and production methods (PPM). In most situations, these standards are not significant for international trade, because the pollution effect does not extend beyond borders. But there are some exceptions, as witnessed by the dispute over tuna harvesting using nets unsafe for dolphins. Here, the authors argue that the issues are best resolved through cooperative efforts rather than coercion.

Finally, some environmentalists argue that freer trade is bad for the environment because it leads to increased economic activity and added pollution. However, the authors note that economic growth is often accompanied by increased concern about environmental consequences and greater efforts to reduce pollution. In effect, environmentalism is seen as a rich man's good, and higher incomes allow nations to devote more effort to avoiding environmental damage. They also note that economic growth often brings about a shift of production away from the most polluting products, and that Mexico's exports to the United States are not tilted toward heavily polluting products.

The authors go on to point to some of the problems inherent in developing common perspectives on environmental issues between the North and the South. The industrial countries often seek to define the standards or goals in marginal terms, using current levels of pollution as a baseline. But the developing countries argue that such standards favor the richer nations, which account for a disproportionate share of current pollution emissions, and the poorer nations seek some redistribution of existing resource use. The United States seeks a target for each country's future pollution that is marginally below today's level; Mexico favors a standard of equal per capita effluents.

In his comment on chapter 4, Peter Emerson echoes the importance of expanding the cooperative framework for resolving the environmental problems along the border. He also stresses the need to carry through with implementing the environmental measures that were agreed to in NAFTA. Emerson also argues that more effort should be devoted to involving private firms in the process of developing common benchmarks for auditing and performance evaluation.

Drug Trafficking

Peter H. Smith's chapter 5 concludes that drug traffic will remain an unpredictable and volatile source of conflict between the United States and Mexico, despite a shared concern over the devastating consequences of drug production, traffic, and consumption. Indeed, the U.S. State Department has stated that Mexico poses a greater narcotics threat to the United States than does any other country, while President Ernesto Zedillo identifies drug traffic as Mexico's greatest security threat.

The first section of chapter 5 summarizes Smith's assessment of how Mexico's drug industry has evolved over the past twenty-five years. In the 1970s, it was locally organized, though often supplying substantial shares of the U.S. markets for marijuana and heroin. U.S. pressures to reduce the flows in the mid-1970s led to a coordinated attack that was highly successful. Drug supplies from Mexico fell dramatically, although there was little evidence of a drop in U.S. consumption, and the flows have since recovered. Smith suggests that an unintended consequence of this crackdown was an increase in the concentration and power of remaining Mexican drug traffickers.

Smith argues that trends in Mexico's drug industry have had significant adverse effects on Mexico's political system. In his assessment, political authority has become less extensive and more decentralized in Mexico, with growing divisions within the ruling elite. He cites a variety of claims that the growing problems in the Mexican political system, including a number of recent political assassinations, have been linked with drug traffic. He suggests that the increasingly powerful drug industry has led to growing political corruption and more human rights violations. His stark conclusion is that drugs threaten Mexican national security, erode the ability of Mexican authorities to govern, and alienate Mexican society from its leadership.

Finally, Smith contrasts the different goals and approaches to addressing the drug problem in the United States and in Mexico. The U.S. focus is on reducing drug use and its implications, particularly for domestic crime. Since Ronald Reagan announced the "War on Drugs" in the early 1980s,

U.S. attention has focused inflexibly on reducing the supply of drugs from abroad, with a tendency to blame Mexico (and other suppliers) for drug-related problems. Despite the mounting cost of this drug policy effort and the growing evidence of its failure, Smith concludes that the basic approach is unlikely to change. Indeed, it has become increasingly unilateral. In this context, chapter 5 reviews recent episodes in which U.S. politicians debated "decertifying" Mexico for not cooperating fully with the U.S. antidrug efforts. Such a decertification could have implied an end to financial flows under the peso rescue plan.

In contrast, Mexicans tend to see U.S. problems as related to persistent U.S. demand. In Mexico, the main concern is not domestic drug consumption, but how to address the threats to national security and to maintain national sovereignty in light of a U.S. policy that at times violates international law. The response has been a search to improve the bilateral relationship while stepping up domestic antidrug activities in Mexico. Smith notes that drugs were not mentioned in the NAFTA treaty, which some see as a missed opportunity to reach a bilateral accord on drug policy. His review of existing evidence concludes that the free trade agreement is unlikely to have a major impact on cross-border drug shipments.

In her discussion of chapter 5, María Celia Toro concurrs with Smith's overall assessment, but not with all of his specific conclusions. She agrees that Mexican drug lords, like those elsewhere, have become more powerful. But she contests the claim that the Mexican industry is now more cartelized, arguing that it does not fix prices and that the industry appears to have become more disorganized over the past two decades. Toro shared Smith's concerns about the dire political implications of a war on drugs that relies on relatively weak Mexican institutions—the police and the judiciary. Combined with the significant increase in drug-related violence and corruption in Mexico, these conditions pose a major challenge to the state's ability to instill law and order. However, Toro questions his implicit assumption about the relative importance of drugs, suggesting that Mexico's political difficulties are largely related to other factors.

The overall assessment from chapter 5, Toro's Comment, and the general discussion is that drug traffic is likely to remain a contentious area of bilateral relations, with the potential to erupt into major conflict.

Immigration Policies

In chapter 6, George J. Borjas presents and assesses evidence on the economic impact of Mexican immigrants in the United States. He begins by documenting the significant increase in Mexican immigrants over the past two decades, both in absolute numbers and as a share of total immigration. The chapter also shows that Mexican immigrants are considerably less well educated than native-born Americans or other immigrants and that the gap has grown since 1970. This skill gap is partially attributable to the large numbers of illegal entrants, who tend to be less skilled than legal immigrants. The discussion then turns to three broad issues: the effect of Mexican immigrants on native-born American workers, the fiscal implications of the immigrant flow, and the likely overall impact of the flow on both the United States and Mexico. The two invited discussants, Jeffrey S. Passel and Marta Tienda, agree in their Comments that Borjas's chapter examines the central questions. They also concur that the U.S. policy debate is likely to focus increasingly on restricting admissions criteria and availability of social benefits. However, both disagree—at times quite strongly—with some of Borjas's conclusions. Passel, in particular, provides considerable additional evidence on key issues.

Borjas concludes that the influx of less-skilled immigrants has had an adverse effect on wages of Americans who did not complete high school, accounting for perhaps one-third of the decline in their relative wages that has occurred since 1980. Mexicans account for slightly more than half of all less-skilled immigrants. However, there is little evidence of a significant impact on relative wages of high school graduates relative to those with more than twelve years of schooling, and, as Borjas notes, the methodology on which these findings are based is controversial. An alternative approach to these national analyses has been to study implications of immigrants for local labor markets (such as the effect of the Mariel boat lift from Cuba on workers in Miami). These studies consistently find little if any effect. Borjas agrees with other recent studies that this approach is likely to be misleading, because metropolitan areas are essentially small, open economies. Standard international trade theory implies that changes in relative factor supplies may have no effect on relative factor earnings in economies already wide open to trade with outsiders. Borjas also notes that there may be significant outmigration by natives in response to increased immigration.

In contrast, neither Passel nor Tienda is convinced that Mexican immigrants have harmed American workers so severely. For example, Tienda cites evidence suggesting that most of the costs fall on previous immigrants to the United States, not on U.S. natives. Both also question the extent to which natives do migrate in response to an influx of new immigrants.

Borjas also assesses the fiscal impact of immigration. Are the many Americans who believe that immigrants do not "pay their way" correct? He argues that a greater proportion of Mexican immigrants than of either U.S. natives or non-Mexican immigrants receive social benefits (including both cash payments such as welfare and means-tested noncash benefits, such as medicaid). However, an overall assessment of whether immigrants impose a fiscal benefit or burden is difficult because it requires measures of the total taxes paid by immigrants, less the total value of the services they have received. Available studies are all over the map. Borjas finds fault with those that find a positive net impact as well as those that find a significant negative one, concluding that the net fiscal effect for the United States is negative, but perhaps small. He notes that there is considerably more agreement that immigration has imposed a fiscal burden on California— a state with a large (and predominantly Mexican) immigrant population— because many of the revenues accrue to the federal government.

Again, both Passel and Tienda take issue with Borjas's assessment. They argue that aggregate figures on benefit receipts present a highly misleading comparison of how Mexican immigrants fare relative to others. In particular, Passel advocates disaggregating by age and eligibility. Passel also suggests that the apparent recent fiscal burden in California may reflect political issues and a local recession, and that the situation in California has had an excessive influence on the national debate over immigration policy.

Finally, Borjas argues that the overall economic impact of Mexican immigrants on the United States is likely to be positive, though minor, but will involve significant amounts of redistribution. Borjas finds existing evidence on the overall impact for Mexico inconclusive. Although Passel concurs with this assessment for the United States, he argues that there may also be a gap between perception and reality with regards to redistribution. Immigrant-related costs may be more evident than immigrant-related benefits, such as lower prices on some goods and services. Passel also cites evidence consistent with the view that the overall effect on Mexico of migration to the United States is likely to have been positive.

The Future Agenda

The United States and Mexico have long had a contentious relationship. But in recent years they have made significant progress toward improving a bilateral relationship of increased importance to both countries. Clearly, in the economic sphere the two economies are becoming highly integrated. The liberalization of Mexico's trade regime and cross-border financial transactions has resulted in an extremely rapid expansion of the commercial link between the two countries. But NAFTA has not gone as far as some had hoped to reduce the economic issues of contention between the two countries.

Both governments have on occasion ignored the dispute resolution procedures and acted unilaterally to protect domestic interest groups. Furthermore, the 1994–95 financial crisis in Mexico was a huge setback, greatly lowering the magnitude of gains that were expected to accrue from trade over the next decade. However, the flow of trade between the two countries has held up surprisingly well compared with past crises. The trade structures of the two economies are still highly complementary, and the gains from the relationship will grow over time.

It is important that the two countries proceed with full implementation of the NAFTA agreement; but, as Espinosa and Noyola point out, further actions are needed if this is to truly serve as a building block for faster multilateral trade liberalization. The concern others share—that the agreement simply promotes trade diversion—could be most effectively dealt with by reducing the tariff structures for most favored nation status of the three countries and moving to a common external tariff. A common tariff would contribute directly to global trade liberalization, eliminating the need for the existing complex rules of origin.

In addition, the parties need to establish a common competition policy or find some other means of resolving disputes over trade practices. Recent events underscore the importance of finding ways to constrain the influence of powerful domestic lobbies. For example, the United States reneged on its prior agreement to allow passage of Mexican trucks into the United States, and Mexico has taken action to prevent foreign participation in the ownership of petrochemical firms. Nor have the member governments been able to limit the use of antidumping measures by domestic producer interests.

The 1995 financial crisis provides a heightened appreciation of the potential destabilizing effects of international financial flows. In the rush to open Mexico's financial markets to foreign investors, too little attention has been given to the need to coordinate market liberalization with effective oversight and regulation. These are still small markets easily overwhelmed by large and volatile flows.

Although there is substantial evidence of the value inflows of foreign direct investment have to the development process, the record on foreign portfolio capital is far more mixed. As argued by John Williamson, during periods of optimism financial markets are likely to offer more than it is prudent to accept, only to turn suddenly on the receipt of bad news. The inflows are of little value if they must be matched by large reserves against the possibility of capital flight. Yet capital controls are largely ineffective in limiting outflows, and fear of their imposition can convert temporary adversities into crises. As a result, primary attention should be directed toward discouraging the inflow of short-term portfolio capital. Williamson's chapter 3 outlines a set of measures currently being used in Chile and Colombia that effectively taxes short-term capital inflows while maintaining incentives for long-term investment in the domestic economy. Although it will limit the access of American investors, the United States should be supportive of such measures until Mexican financial markets can develop sufficient depth to withstand foreign shocks. These measures will reduce the probability of another crisis and the need for another bailout.

Moreover, the financial assistance package put together by the United States in early 1995 was effective in ending the external liquidity crisis that Mexico faced. The speed and magnitude of the response was a direct outgrowth of the expanded relationship between the two countries, and it would not have occurred without NAFTA. Yet, contrary to the claims of those who opposed the aid, the loan was fully repaid by early 1997.

In recent years, some of the more contentious aspects of the bilateral relationship have emerged in the noneconomic sphere. Policies towards immigration, drug trafficking, environmental pollution, and social policies have come to the forefront as areas of conflict. But once again, the lesson seems to be that it is important to focus on cooperation rather than confrontation.

As an example, the control of drug trafficking should be an area of easy cooperation, since both countries agree on the need to combat the production, sale, and use of illegal drugs. Yet it has been a source of repeated disagreements between the two countries. We suggest that it is imperative that the United States recognize the two-way nature of the problem. Although it blames others for an inability to control supply, the failure of the United States to control demand is imposing large costs on Mexico through the corruption that drug trafficking engenders. In this regard, the United States should abandon its drug certification program, which, by attempting to judge the effort of others to control drug trafficking, engenders only recriminations and conflict. Recently the two countries did announce an agreement to expand their cooperation, and Mexico has increased the resources directed against the drug traffickers. But without more effective U.S. efforts to contain demand, the result will only be higher drug prices and ever stronger incentives to take the risks of participating in the trade.

Immigration is another area of increased conflict. As shown by the discussion in George J. Borjas's chapter 6, in public discourse immigration is increasingly perceived as costly to the United States, both because of the low skill levels of recent immigrants and the potential burdens on local governments. However, the public discussion often fails to distinguish adequately between legal and illegal immigration, and public opinion has strongly affected by the economic recession California (the state with the largest immigrant inflow) experienced in the early 1990s.

The public support for immigration ebbs and flows with the state of the economy. It is worth noting that the measures taken to control illegal immigration have all failed; those who want to enter the United States can readily do so. But frustration with the various programs hardly justifies encouraging Mexico to detain individuals who have sought to leave the country. Over the near term, demographic trends in Mexico are likely to result in some lessening of the flow of immigration. Ultimately, however, the most effective limitation on immigration will be economic growth and job creation in Mexico. As Jeffrey S. Passel argued in his Comment on chapter 6, the potential gains to migrants and their families are probably well worth the effort of fostering greater tolerance in the United States.

Finally, the bilateral relationship must respond to a wide range of social concerns, such as the environment and labor standards. However, there should be no conflict between the goal of expanding the Mexico–U.S. economic interchange and acting to protect the environment or basic working conditions. Particularly in the environmental area, there are spillover effects that extend beyond national borders and necessitate joint actions.

The disagreement and concern arise at the level of threats to use access to the U.S. market to force Mexican compliance with U.S. interpretations of the required policies. This potential for conflict between proponents of open trade and the environment, or trade and labor standards, can best be met by a strong effort to develop a positive agenda for cooperative actions. In both of these areas, there is little difference in professed goals in the two countries, but there are dramatic differences in the resources that they can devote to achieving them. Local efforts along the border dealing with the environmental problems are representative of the type of interchange that should be promoted.

A common border more than 2,000 kilometers long, coupled with the growing interdependence of the two economies, have increased the importance of the bilateral relationship. Although some degree of conflict is inevitable, there are opportunities for expanded cooperation and coordination in both the economic and noneconomic spheres. NAFTA is a leading example of the achievements a cooperative approach can produce.

References

Banco de México. 1996. *The Mexican Economy.* Mexico City.

Borjas, George J., and Richard B. Freeman (eds). 1992. *Immigration and the Workforce: Economic Consequences for the United States and Source Areas.* University of Chicago Press.

Bosworth, Barry. 1996. "The Decline in Mexican Saving: A Cost of Reform." Washington: Country Department II, World Bank.

Burtless, Gary. 1995. "International Trade and the Rise in Earnings Inequality." *Journal of Economic Literature* 33 (June): 800–16.

Calvo, Guillermo A., and Enrique G. Mendoza. 1996. "Mexico's Balance of Payments Crisis: A Chronicle of Death Foretold." International Finance Discussion Papers No. 545. Washington, D.C: Board of Governors of the Federal Reserve.

Dornbusch, Rudiger, and Alejandro Werner. 1994. "Mexico: Stabilization, Reform, and No Growth." *Brookings Papers on Economic Activity* 1:253–97.

Gomez de Leon, José, and Rodolfo Tuiran. 1996. "La migración mexicana hacia Estados Unidos: Continuidad y cambio." Discussion Papers on U.S.–Mexican Relations. Washington: Brookings and Inter-American Dialogue, U.S.–Mexican Forum (October), p. 20 and table 2. (Executive Summary available in English)

Leiderman, Leonardo, and Alfredo E. Thorne.1996. "The 1994 Mexican Crisis and Its Aftermath: What Are the Main Lessons?" In *Private Capital Flows to Emerging Markets After the Mexican Crisis,* edited by Guillermo Calvo, Morris Goldstein, and Eduard Hochreiter, 1–43. Washington: Institute for International Economics.

Lustig, Nora. 1992. *Mexico. The Remaking of an Economy.* Brookings.

Lustig, Nora. 1995. "The Mexican Peso Crisis: The Foreseeable and the Surprise." Discussion Papers in International Economics No. 114. Brookings.

Lustig, Nora. 1996. "Mexico in Crisis, the U.S. to the Rescue: The Financial Assistance Packages of 1982 and 1995." Brookings (June).

Lustig, Nora, Barry Bosworth, and Robert Lawrence. 1992. *North American Free Trade: Assessing the Impact.* Brookings.

2 Emerging Patterns in Mexico–U.S. Trade

J. Enrique Espinosa and Pedro Noyola

EVER since the initiative to negotiate the North American Free Trade Agreement (NAFTA) was made public in 1990, questions have been raised regarding its effects on national, regional, and global welfare. Frequently, however, these questions have originated more on political considerations than on queries about NAFTA's effects on regional efficiency and competitiveness. This has been unfortunate for the quality of the debate, since the public discussion of NAFTA has often been shaped by special interests more than by objective analysis. Improving the quality of this debate is important, because the bilateral trade relation between Mexico and the United States (which is part of a broader and politically quite complex agenda) has had to resist rising protectionist pressures, especially in the United States.

Between 1990 and 1993, for example, during the negotiations and before the agreement entered into force, the opposition in the United States was often based on a diversity of environmental and labor market arguments. The underlying concern, however, was that a free trade agreement with Mexico would create permanent downward pressure on average wage rates for unskilled workers in the United States. This concern was particularly acute because the United States economy was confronting an economic recession and the nation faced a presidential election in 1992. Nonetheless, most of the independent economic studies conducted before NAFTA was enacted indicated that it was a positive-sum proposition. Fortunately, this opinion prevailed, and NAFTA was approved by the legislatures of the three countries in 1993.

More recently, protectionist pressures against NAFTA have surfaced again in the United States, in the wake of another presidential election. This

The authors are senior partners in SAI Law & Economics, a consulting firm in Mexico City. The views expressed in this chapter are solely those of the authors. They are grateful to Mauricio Solís for his research assistance.

time, traditional protectionism has been compounded with a growing uneasiness in the United States with other issues of the bilateral relation with Mexico. Given the state of the political debate in the United States during the last election year, it is important to identify the emerging bilateral trade patterns and explain their nature and consequences to evaluate how NAFTA is affecting the regional allocation of resources.

In contrast with the debate before NAFTA was enacted, today it is possible to analyze NAFTA's merits and limitations on the basis of observable data and not only on predictive modeling exercises. But isolating the effects of NAFTA is difficult. At the end of 1994 Mexico faced a severe financial crisis that entailed a large devaluation of the Mexican peso and therefore a sudden change in the relative prices of traded goods. An interesting question has since arisen: what were the relative effects of the devaluation of the peso and of NAFTA on the bilateral trade flows during 1995?

One hypothesis is that trade flows to date have not been greatly affected by NAFTA's trade liberalization schedule, which is still in an early stage. Under this view, the principal role in explaining bilateral trade performance in the last two years has been Mexico's exchange rate policy. The real appreciation of the peso up to early 1994 would explain the expansion of Mexico's import demand, whereas the real depreciation of the peso thereafter would explain Mexico's export performance since 1995.

Figure 2-1 presents some key indicators related to U.S. imports of Mexican manufactured goods. NAFTA's enactment reduced the average ad valorem tariff applied on Mexican imports to the United States from 4.3 to 1.5 percent, a 2.8 percentage point cut. This cut is quite significant in proportional terms but clearly overshadowed by the size of the recent exchange rate depreciation. From December 1993 to February 1995, the value of the Mexican peso in terms of dollars declined by 52 percent.

There are indications, however, that a pure exchange rate hypothesis may miss some important emerging trends in this bilateral trade relationship. In this chapter we argue that the most important structural effects experienced in the bilateral trade relationship over the last two years are a positive result of a comprehensive and ambitious effort at structural reform Mexico embarked on in the mid-1980s, and in which NAFTA is a major milestone. In particular, although we accept the notion that exchange rate policy had a strong impact on the magnitude of the bilateral trade flows in 1994 and 1995, we argue that even before 1994 economic agents allocated resources and took strategic decisions both in anticipation of NAFTA itself (and as a result of the unilateral reforms undertaken by Mexico since the

Figure 2-1. Key Indicators Related to U.S. Imports of Mexican Manufactured Goods

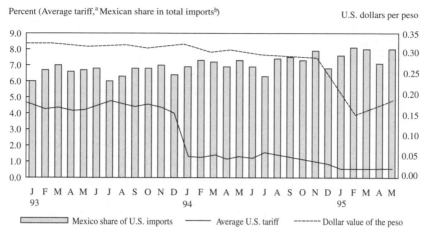

Percent (Average tariff,[a] Mexican share in total imports[b])   U.S. dollars per peso

☐ Mexico share of U.S. imports   ——— Average U.S. tariff   ------ Dollar value of the peso

Source: Tariff rate computed by Secretaría de Comercio y Fomento Industrial (SECOFI); trade data are from U.S. Department of Commerce, Bureau of Economic Analysis; and information on the exchange rate is from Banco de México.
a. Weighted average based on the structure of Mexican exports of manufactured goods to the United States.
b. Considering manufactured products only.

mid-1980s). Moreover, we believe that a pure exchange rate hypothesis belies the fact that during 1994 and 1995 there were substantial direct effects on trade flows in specific sectors that were subject to restrictive nontariff barriers until 1993.

In the first section of this chapter, we present the rationale of NAFTA for Mexico and the United States. We argue that, as a result of the unilateral reform program undertaken previously, stable access to the U.S. goods market became a major objective of Mexico's trade policy. In the United States, the rationale was somewhat different but complementary. The regional free trade initiative addressed several American concerns: the future of the General Agreement on Tariffs and Trade (GATT), national competitiveness vis-à-vis other industrial countries, and the access and protection of U.S. investments abroad. In the second section, we highlight the main features of the agreement. In the third and fourth sections, we discuss some of the studies carried out before 1994 and present an evaluation using 1994 and 1995 data, respectively. In the fifth section, we compare Mexico's economic structure before and after the exchange rate crisis of 1982, with the structure of the economy before and after the crisis of 1994. We argue that the prospects for the bilateral trade relation in 1983 were dramatically different from those in 1995 and after. In the final section we draw conclusions and present some policy recommendations.

The Rationale of NAFTA

In Mexico, the principal objective of the microeconomic reforms under-taken since the mid-1980s was to eliminate the antiexport bias of the economy and to induce a more efficient allocation of scarce resources. Trade and investment liberalization were two cornerstones of the reform program, complemented by internal market deregulation and the modern-ization of the legal framework to protect intellectual property rights. These reforms improved the performance of non-oil exports, whose share in the total merchandise export bill rose from 30 percent in 1983 to more than 70 percent in 1993. During this period, the dollar value of Mexican non-oil exports quintupled, and the annual direct foreign investment inflow tripled in absolute terms.

Notwithstanding the importance of unilateral reform in augmenting the level of efficiency in the Mexican economy, by 1990 it was evident that to consolidate structural change and propitiate adequate and sustained eco-nomic growth rates, it was necessary to support the model with stable market access for exported goods and services and with competitive condi-tions to attract continuous flows of foreign investment.

On the one hand, by 1990 Mexican exports faced severe access problems in its principal foreign markets, in particular the United States, which hindered Mexico's ability to fully benefit from unilateral reform. For exam-ple, apparel exports were heavily regulated by bilateral understandings established under the Multifiber Agreement and limited Mexican export potential precisely in the categories in which Mexico had proven to be competitive (for example, the cotton trousers category had to be ineffi-ciently rationed). Steel exports were subject to "voluntary" restraints, which also led to inefficient rationing. Agricultural exports were subject to tariff peaks and arbitrary nontariff border measures. Moreover, under the Gener-alized System of Preferences, the export potential of goods that benefited from tariff reductions was severely limited, because successful users of the system tended to lose their preferential status. On the other hand, Mexico faced increasingly stiff competition in its ability to attract foreign direct investment. In particular, the trend toward the formation of supranational trading areas, led by the European Community's drive to integrate central European economies and expand the European "space" to include the European Free Trade Agreement (EFTA) countries, highlighted the impor-tance of scale effects as a determinant of investment location.

By establishing a free trade area with its largest trading partner, Mexico could obtain market access to enhance the competitiveness of its export sector. It could concomitantly consolidate the conditions to make itself attractive for long-term foreign investment. The basic objectives Mexico pursued in the negotiations were to achieve long-term market access with the maximum reduction possible of tariff and nontariff restrictions for exports to the U.S. market, to introduce fair dispute settlement mechanisms, and to promote investment by inducing efficient complementarity between the two economies.

For the United States, free trade with Mexico was also consistent with its international trade agenda. By 1990, there were indications that an impasse of the Uruguay Round was affecting U.S. trade and investment interests. Moreover, the national debate over "national competitiveness" had made the American public sensitive to the fact that, through formal or informal integration schemes, Asian and European nations (particularly Japan and Germany) were overtaking the United States in terms of productivity and market scale.

In this context, the prospect of a trade agreement with Mexico, which complemented the one already in place with Canada, was perceived as an efficient strategy to follow. Such an initiative could help catalyze the Uruguay Round negotiations, especially in agriculture and the so-called "new topics." Regional free trade could also improve the competitiveness of the American economy by augmenting the size and scope of its regional economy and thus its ability to compete successfully with Japan's "flying geese" paradigm and with the European market unification. Finally, a comprehensive agreement with Mexico (covering not only trade in goods but also investment, services, and other related matters) could significantly improve the access and protection of U.S. investment in Mexico and provide a useful blueprint for other countries in the hemisphere.

Main Features of the Agreement

From the outset of the negotiations, it was deemed necessary to structure the agreement to minimize the possibility of trade diversion and its investment equivalent. Otherwise, NAFTA could become an obstacle to multilateral trade liberalization rather than a building block for it. In other words, NAFTA had to be consistent with GATT's article XXIV.

Based on this principle, the agreement consists of a set of rules on four themes: merchandise trade liberalization, deregulation and protection of foreign investment, liberalization of trade in services, and institutional framework and enforcement. The appendix to this chapter contains a schematic description of the components of NAFTA.

One of the most important implications of this comprehensive agreement is that it has locked in market-oriented policies in Mexico. This policy lock-in—plus the fact that regional trade and investment rules are explicit in a single, internationally enforceable document—are probably the two fundamental contributions of NAFTA to the long-term improvement of the bilateral trade relation.

Predicted NAFTA's Effects

Between 1990 and 1993, a relatively rich body of literature focused on the potential effects of NAFTA on global, regional, national, and even within-nation trade flows. Modeling North American integration became a topic of interest in academic and policy-oriented forums, inside and outside North America. It is not the purpose of this chapter to survey this literature; however, a brief reference to these studies can be useful analytical benchmarks for analysis and evaluation.

We concentrate on three references: an assessment of the text of the agreement by Gary Hufbauer and Jeffrey Schott, a compilation of general equilibrium models by Timothy and Patrick Kehoe, and a set of specific studies compiled by Peter Garber.[1]

The Hufbauer and Schott Study

Hufbauer and Schott analyze the agreement in three dimensions. First, they review the liberalization program in several sectors (energy, automotive goods, textiles and apparel, agriculture, financial services, transportation, and telecommunications). They then analyze NAFTA's fundamental trade and investment provisions (rules of origin, dumping and subsidies, safeguards, government procurement, dispute settlement, investment protection, and intellectual property rights). Finally, they evaluate the contextual obligations contained in NAFTA (environmental and labor issues and accession).

The authors believe that, on the whole, the agreement will lead to a substantial liberalization of regional trade and investment. Nonetheless, they express concern on two counts. On the one hand, they think the liberalization program of Mexico could have been deeper (for example, in the energy sector) and faster (for example, in the financial services sector). On the other hand, they believe the rules of origin are too restrictive and a

---

1. See Hufbauer and Schott (1992, 1993); Kehoe and Kehoe (1995); Garber (1993).

potential source of considerable trade diversion, especially in the automotive and textile sectors.

The Kehoe and Kehoe Study

The editors have compiled a series of studies that use general equilibrium models to predict the impact of NAFTA on the welfare of each member economy. General equilibrium analysis is undoubtedly the best analytical instrument to evaluate the long-term allocation effects of trade policy, and the Kehoe and Kehoe compilation provides useful benchmarks.

It is interesting that the authors of the models, which were built independently, reach a similar fundamental conclusion: NAFTA is a positive-sum proposition. However, gains of trade will be concentrated in Mexico, in some cases because of more efficient specialization (for example, in the automotive sector) and in other cases the result of scale effects likely to add little to those already achieved by the United States and Canada through their previous free trade agreement.

We can summarize the conclusions as follows. The three countries will tend to benefit from the agreement. In addition, the wage gap between Mexico and the United States will be reduced, and average costs will drop in many sectors throughout the region. These models are able to capture in detail most of the merchandise trade liberalization effects. However, they still need to be refined to fully capture the effects of some of the other features of NAFTA, such as the investment deregulation and protection provisions, or the liberalization of services.

The Garber Study

Garber has compiled a series of papers focusing on three questions: how wages and environmental standard differences will affect resource allocation in the region (Garber calls them "sources of comparative advantage"); how the agreement will affect location of production in the United States and Mexico; and how some specific sectors will be affected (such as agriculture, automotive goods, and financial services).

The studies show that NAFTA will improve conditions in Mexico in certain areas of concern for the United States and lead to regional efficiency gains. In particular, these studies conclude (as the general equilibrium models do) that NAFTA will likely increase relative wages in Mexico. As a result of real income gains, environmental quality will also probably improve in Mexico. Moreover, the studies indicate that the agreement will foster a more decentralized economy in Mexico and will likely consolidate efficient "clusters" in certain U.S. cities close to the Mexican border.

The sectoral studies are interesting because they analyze some of the indirect effects of the agreement on local economies. For example, some believe that liberalization of the agricultural sector will probably lead to more efficient use of water in California, as a result of regional specialization of production. Overall, the studies suggest that Mexico's small developing economy relative to that of the United States is a dominant factor in the prior analysis and that this fact will probably "push" the Mexican economy upward. Concerns that NAFTA will pull the U.S. economy down (as in Ross Perot's "giant sucking sound" theory) seem completely unwarranted.

Evaluating NAFTA's Effects More than Three Years Down the Road

Most economists and policymakers would agree that the full effects derived from the formation of a free trade area take time to develop. One reason for this is the structural adjustment to trade liberalization that each country must undertake. Capacity and employment need to be reduced in some sectors; in others, additional investments must be undertaken and new jobs filled with workers with new skills. Although this always takes time, the intensity of the adjustment will tend to be greater and may take longer the smaller, less developed, or more highly protected an economy was before the trade liberalization process. A second reason why the effects of trade liberalization are gradual is that some gradualism is deliberately built into the agreement itself. Phaseout periods are agreed upon for the full elimination of tariffs and the dismantling of nontariff barriers.

These considerations suggest that, although NAFTA has been in force for more than three years, it may still be to early to make a definitive judgment on its effects. Furthermore, Mexico's macroeconomic crisis (triggered by an abrupt devaluation of its currency in December 1994) has also affected trade flows between the NAFTA partners during this period. To evaluate the relative significance of NAFTA of U.S.–Mexico trade, we need to account for transition periods contained in the agreement as well as other factors when we analyze how such trade has evolved since January 1, 1994.

Overview of Mexico–U.S. Bilateral Trade

As expected, trade liberalization with the United States under the terms of NAFTA has reinforced that country's position as Mexico's main trading partner. Mexican exports to the United States grew at an average yearly rate of 24.6 percent, more than 10 percentage points above the average yearly rate observed between 1991 and 1993. Sales of manufactured goods grew at an average pace of nearly 26 percent per year—faster than mineral products, including oil (18.1 percent) and agriculture and animal products (17.4 percent).[2] However, between 1993 and 1995 the share of the United States in Mexico's total exports remained essentially unchanged at about 83 percent, whereas in imports its share increased from 69.3 to 74.3 percent.[3]

In 1995 a sharp change occurred in the bilateral trade balance. Mexico's sales of goods to the United States reached $66.6 billion, while its purchases of U.S.-made products totaled $53.8 billion. The surplus balance of nearly $12.8 billion contrasts dramatically with a $2.4 billion trade deficit observed in 1993. This turn in the bilateral trade balance undoubtedly has a lot to do with the gradual depreciation of the Mexican peso throughout 1994 and the abrupt devaluation at the end of that year. However, the sector-by-sector breakup of the trade data included in tables 2-1 and 2-2 also shows patterns that can only be explained by the particular liberalization program established by NAFTA.

Mexican Exports to the United States: Some Sectoral Highlights

Table 2-2 shows that two of the Mexican manufacturing industries with exceptionally high post-NAFTA rates of export growth were those where regional integration had progressed significantly even before the agreement entered into force: autos and auto parts (which are the lion's share of metal products and machinery), and textiles and apparel.

AUTOS AND AUTO PARTS.   The fact that this sector was singled out as particularly sensitive during the NAFTA negotiations is hardly surprising. From the Mexican perspective, it is not only the largest exporter and importer of manufactured goods but, as such, it is also a prime example of the kind of intraindustry trade that NAFTA was designed to boost. Free trade allows firms selling in the entire North American market to relocate their production facilities among the NAFTA countries to minimize costs and take full advantage of specialization and economies of scale.

2. Although exports of non-oil mineral products show a remarkable average yearly growth rate after NAFTA (28.4 percent), they represent only a tiny fraction of Mexico's total sales to the United States (barely 0.5 percent in 1995).

3. These shares can be compared with the trade shares with Canada and other non-NAFTA countries. In 1995, the former had a weight of 2.5 percent in Mexico's total exports and 1.9 percent in its total imports, while the shares of non-NAFTA countries were 14.1 and 23.8 percent, respectively.

Table 2-1. Mexico's Pre-NAFTA and Post-NAFTA Bilateral Trade with the United States
Millions of U.S. dollars

	Exports to the United States			Imports from the United States			Bilateral trade balance		
	1991 (A)	1993 (B)	1995 (C)	1991 (D)	1993 (E)	1995 (F)	1991 (G)	1993 (H)	1995 (I)
Total value of trade flows	32,817.9	42,850.9	66,573.3	36,465.2	45,294.7	53,829.6	68,647.3	62,443.8	12,743.7
Agriculture and animal products	2,115.9	2,457.4	3,386.4	1,448.0	1,673.4	1,784.9	667.8	784.0	1,601.5
Agriculture and forestry	1,404.1	1,660.9	2,286.2	1,165.0	1,469.8	1,684.5	239.1	191.0	601.7
Cattle breeding and bee products	362.5	452.9	543.6	271.6	170.2	87.5	91.0	282.7	456.1
Fisheries	349.3	343.6	556.6	11.5	33.4	12.9	337.7	310.2	543.7
Manufactured goods	25,989.0	35,909.4	56,927.4	34,742.6	43,310.3	51,530.4	−8,753.6	−7,400.9	5,397.0
Food, beverages, and tobacco	1,030.2	1,110.9	1,884.9	1,447.6	2,051.3	1,675.1	−447.4	−940.4	209.8
Textiles, apparel, and footwear	1,339.0	2,296.8	4,046.2	1,608.7	2,697.4	3,674.8	−269.7	−400.6	341.4
Wood products	481.0	532.1	552.7	457.4	602.5	342.7	23.6	−70.4	210.0
Paper and printed goods	391.1	579.5	721.8	1,425.2	1,968.3	2,576.3	−1,034.0	−1,388.8	−1,854.5
Chemicals, rubber, and plastics	1,982.2	2,612.4	3,607.5	5,836.0	7,689.9	9,492.1	−3,853.7	−5,077.5	−5,884.6
Nonmetallic mineral goods	560.9	715.4	899.3	295.8	438.2	451.7	265.1	277.2	447.6
Basic metal products	873.5	977.3	2,353.5	1,565.0	1,518.2	1,784.2	−691.4	−540.9	569.3
Metal goods and machinery	17,125.8	24,888.0	39,821.0	19,943.5	24,173.7	29,330.0	−2,817.7	714.4	10,491.0
Other manufactures	2,122.3	2,110.0	2,989.1	2,096.8	2,106.0	2,118.3	25.5	4.0	870.7
Nonclassified goods	82.9	86.9	81.5	36.7	64.9	85.2	46.2	22.1	−3.7
Mining industry goods	4,713.0	4,484.1	6,259.5	274.6	311.0	514.4	4,438.4	4,173.1	5,745.2
Crude oil and natural gas	4,338.2	4,301.9	5,959.3	31.0	90.4	105.8	4,307.2	4,211.5	5,853.5
Other minerals	374.8	182.2	300.2	243.6	220.6	408.6	131.2	−38.4	−180.4

Source: Secretaría de Comercio y Fomento Industrial (SECOFI).

Table 2-2. Evolution of Mexico's Pre-NAFTA and Post-NAFTA Bilateral Trade with the United States

Percent

| | Average percent change | | | | Structure | | | | X/M Ratio | |
| | Exports | | Imports | | Exports | | Imports | | | |
	1991–93 (A)	1993–95 (B)	1991–93 (C)	1993–95 (D)	1991 (E)	1995 (F)	1991 (G)	1995 (H)	1991 (I)	1995 (J)
Total value of trade flows	14.3	24.6	11.5	9.0	100.0	100.0	100.0	100.0	0.90	1.24
Agriculture and animal products	7.8	17.4			4.3	3.4	4.0	3.3	1.46	1.90
Agriculture and forestry	8.8	17.3	12.3	7.1	1.1	0.8	3.2	3.1	1.21	1.36
Cattle breeding and bee products	11.8	9.6	-20.8	-28.3	1.1	0.8	0.7	0.2	1.34	6.21
Fisheries	-0.8	27.3	70.0	-37.9			0.0	0.0	30.27	43.20
Manufactured goods	17.5	25.9	11.7	9.1	79.2	85.5	95.3	95.7	0.75	1.10
Food, beverages, and tobacco	3.8	30.3	17.8	-9.6	3.1	2.8	4.1	3.1	0.70	1.13
Textiles, apparel, and footwear	31.0	32.2	29.5	16.7	4.1	6.0	4.4	6.8	0.83	1.09
Wood products	5.2	1.9	14.8	-24.6	1.5	0.8	1.3	0.6	1.05	1.61
Paper and printed goods	21.7	11.6	17.5	14.4	1.2	1.1	3.9	4.8	0.27	0.28
Chemicals, rubber, and plastics	14.8	17.5	14.8	11.1	6.0	5.4	16.0	17.6	0.34	0.38
Nonmetallic mineral goods	12.9	12.1	21.7	1.5	1.7	1.4	0.8	0.8	1.90	1.99
Basic metal products	5.8	55.2	-1.5	8.4	2.7	3.5	4.3	3.3	0.56	1.32
Metal goods and machinery	20.6	26.5	10.1	10.2	52.2	59.8	54.7	54.5	0.86	1.36
Other manufactures	-0.3	19.0	0.2	0.3	6.5	4.5	5.8	3.9	1.01	1.41
Nonclassified goods	2.4	-3.2	33.0	14.6	0.3	0.1	0.1	0.2	2.26	0.96
Mining industry goods	-2.5	18.1	6.4	28.6	14.4	9.4	0.8	1.0	17.17	12.17
Crude oil and natural gas	-0.4	17.7	70.8	8.2	13.2	9.0	0.1	0.2	140.10	56.34
Other minerals	-30.3	28.4	-4.8	36.1	1.1	0.5	0.7	0.8	1.54	0.73

Source: SECOFI.

Today, several U.S.-assembled car models are sold in Mexico, and Mexico has become a major export location for American automakers as well as for non–North American car producers.[4] In addition, regional content requirements embedded in the NAFTA rules of origin have boosted imports of some auto parts, while others have benefited greatly from preferential access to the U.S. market under NAFTA.

The trend toward a more efficient regional integration in the auto industry is shared by other subsectors in the metal products and machinery division, where the $714 million bilateral surplus in 1993 had grown nearly fifteenfold by the end of 1995, to $10.5 billion.[5]

TEXTILES AND APPAREL.   The liberalization program agreed for this sector is based on a basic premise. From the point of view of the United States, whether or not quota restrictions were removed and tariffs eliminated on textile trade with Mexico, the more labor intensive activities (most notably apparel production) would inexorably continue to lose jobs in favor of low-wage countries, many of which were located in East Asia.

Moreover, to the extent those downstream activities moved away from North America, the more competitive segments of the U.S. textile complex (such as yarn and fabric production) would continue to face falling demand for their products. As more and more apparel producers relocated to Asia, they would seek non-U.S. input sources that, among other things, would allow them to save in transportation costs. Also, the anticipation that the Multifiber Agreement would be phased out as a result of the Uruguay Round meant that exempting Mexico from the U.S. quotas would amount to no more than giving it a head start vis-à-vis other suppliers of textiles and apparel to the U.S. market.

In turn, improved access to the United States market for its garments and textile products (including the full elimination of applicable quotas) was a major NAFTA goal for Mexico. The so-called Special Regime, by which Mexico-assembled apparel from U.S. formed-and-cut fabric was benefited with flexible quotas and the application of U.S. tariffs only on non-U.S. value added, had proven to be successful. Its intensive use by Mexican

---

4. The case of Chrysler's Ram Charger, which was exclusively produced in Mexico even before NAFTA, was recently replicated by Nissan's decision to transfer its entire North American production of its Sentra to its Aguascalientes facility in central Mexico.

5. Though autos and auto parts have a major share of the bilateral trade classified under "metal products and machinery," similar relocation and specialization trends have also taken hold for other items. For instance, Mexico has become the major supplier of TV sets, minibar refrigerators, and gas ranges to the United States, and it is a principal supplier of electronic equipment and components.

exporters in the years before 1994 had been the basis of a fast-growing garment industry and a source of jobs for low-skilled workers. An immediate elimination of quotas (coupled with substantial cuts on certain exceptionally high tariffs as the agreement entered into force) would build on this progress.[6] Its benefits would be expanded to Mexican fabric producers, who would become NAFTA-qualifying suppliers.[7]

After two years of textile trade under NAFTA, the performance of the sector indicates that these expectations were well founded. Mexican exports of these products grew at an average yearly rate of 32.2 percent in 1994 and 1995, reaching $4 billion by the end of 1995.[8] This extraordinary growth is enabling Mexico to catch up with China as the main foreign source of garments sold in the United States. Moreover, and despite the increased peso-cost of foreign yarn and fabric, imports of U.S. textiles, apparel, and footwear into Mexico kept growing at a rate of nearly 17 percent annually, on average.[9]

NAFTA reinforced the trends toward regional integration in autos and textiles that were previously present in the Mexico–U.S. bilateral trade relationship. The agreement also opened new opportunities in other sectors that shared some of the labor intensity competitive advantage of the garment industry and enjoyed additional advantages, such as abundance of quality domestic raw materials or favorable climatic conditions.

6. As illustrations of these "tariff peaks" consider the case of certain woven fabrics of synthetic filament yarn under headings 5407.92, 5407.93, 5408.33, 5404.34, 5515.13, 5515.22, 5515.92, 5516.31, and 5516.32, which were charged 38 percent ad valorem plus 48.5 cents per kilogram, and those of certain shirts knitted or crocheted blouses and shirts, sweaters, pullovers, sweatshirts, waistcoats, and similar articles under headings 6111.20, 6111.30, and 6111.90, which were charged 34.6 percent ad valorem. In fact, many items faced ad valorem tariffs with percentages in the high twenties to low thirties. In contrast, Mexico's maximum base tariff for NAFTA's liberalization schedule (including textiles and apparel) was 20 percent.

7. The basic rule of origin adopted under NAFTA was the so-called "yarn-forward" rule: to qualify for preferential treatment, textile goods would have to be made from North American spun or extruded yarn. This rule of origin was acceptable to Mexico because slightly more than half of Mexican fabric production was made by firms who also operated yarn-producing facilities.

8. Although footwear is lumped together with textiles and apparel in tables 2-1 and 2-2, the bulk of bilateral trade involves the latter two categories.

9. The positive conditions created by NAFTA for Mexico's apparel industry has also led to the establishment of new forms of production in the rural *ejidos*. Under the auspices of Mexican producer Compañía Manufacturera Libra, 15 *ejidatario*-owned and operated assembly plants have been opened on *ejidos* in the Mexican states of Coahuila, Durango, and Oaxaca, generating more than 2,000 jobs and selling competitively priced, quality garments to major retailers in the United States.

FOOD AND BEVERAGES.[10] Before NAFTA, Mexico's food and beverage industry had been fighting a losing battle vis-à-vis its foreign competitors, particularly those of the United States. A $448 million bilateral trade deficit for this sector in 1991 had ballooned to $940 million two years later. During that period, Mexican exports grew at a yearly rate of only 3.8 percent, while imports from the United States expanded at a pace of nearly 18 percent annually.

This competitive pressure, however, prompted strenuous efforts from Mexican producers to cut costs, boost productivity, and improve the quality of their products to international standards. Such efforts began to pay off at the onset of NAFTA, and their results were further amplified by a weak peso. In 1995, the trade deficit observed two years before turned into a $209 million surplus, with major U.S. supermarket chains moving such products as Mexican fruit juices and ready-to-eat foods, canned vegetables, candy, and even baked goods out of their ethnic-food counters to their regular food racks.[11]

AGRICULTURE AND ANIMAL PRODUCTS.   In line with the spirit that guided the Uruguay Round negotiations on this sector, NAFTA replaced standard quantitative restrictions with their tariff equivalents (the so-called "tariffication"). It also defined seasonal windows when U.S. supplies of certain goods (particularly fresh vegetables and fruit) is low. Within those seasonal openings, Mexico would be allowed to ship primary products to the United States at reduced or null tariffs, which would snap back to their normal levels when American growers entered the market. In exchange, Mexico would import predetermined amounts of grains (including corn) tariff free; surplus amounts would pay the tariffs that replaced the quantitative restrictions. Also, enhanced cooperation in the area of sanitary and phitosanitary measures would help to minimize the trade-restricting effects of these protective standards.

Under these NAFTA conditions, Mexican agricultural exports expanded from $2.1 billion in 1993 to $3.4 billion in 1995, nearly doubling its average

---

10. Although tobacco is included is included in the same industrial category as food and beverage products in tables 2-1 and 2-2, its weight in this sector is minor.

11. An initial primary equity placement for a new NAFTA-wide food growing and processing concern (Dallas-based UniMark) in the NASDAQ two years ago has produced impressive results for investors, with the price per share increasing from $3.50 to $16.50. UniMark has growing and processing facilties in several Mexican states, a processing plant in Los Angeles, and an additional one in Québec City, Canada. Although its largest market is the United States, the company has successfully penetrated the Japanese market as well.

rate of growth per annum (17.4 percent) as compared with the average growth they exhibited between 1991 and 1993.

BASIC METAL PRODUCTS. This sector has shown an exceptionally good export performance, but NAFTA has probably played a secondary role. The rapid expansion of Mexican exports attained by this group (55 percent on average during 1994–95) can be largely explained by the severe contraction of construction activity in Mexico during the recent crisis, as well as by a weaker peso. However, these circumstances would have had a much more limited effect if the so-called "voluntary restraint agreement" that remained in place until 1991 had been extended. Conversely, their effects would have been boosted if several steel products had not been subject later on to U.S. antidumping proceedings and remedial measures.[12]

Mexican Imports from the United States

Given the accumulated magnitude of the depreciation of the peso since NAFTA was enacted, the fact that Mexican imports from the United States continued to grow at an average yearly rate of 9.0 percent is striking.[13] In fact, that rate is only slightly lower than the one observed between 1991 and 1993 (11.5 percent). As figures 2-2 and 2-3 show, this general pattern is maintained for most sectors, except for three that jointly account for less that 6 percent in the total value of such imports: food, beverages, and tobacco; wood products; and animal fresh products.

As figure 2-4 shows, these numbers average out significant differences before and after the peso devaluation in December 1994. However, even when those differences are singled out, it is also clear that U.S. sales to Mexico were significantly less affected that those of non-NAFTA countries: in 1995, import from the United States declined by only 1.8 percent. This drop was more than offset by the rebound of 15.9 percent observed in the first quarter of 1996.

This difference could be partly explained by the fact that throughout most of 1994 the U.S. dollar experienced a significant depreciation vis-à-vis other major currencies, compounding the weakening of the Mexican peso and, therefore, increasing the relative cost of Mexican purchases of non-U.S. goods.[14] However, this trend reversed itself in 1995, so other

---

12. This sector is a veritable champion in terms of vocal advocacy (and systematic use) of trade remedy laws. For illustrations of this fact, see, for instance, Botluck and Litan (1991), chapter 1; Prusa (1995).

13. See table 2-2.

14. In 1994, the U.S. dollar depreciated by nearly 30 percent against the German mark and by almost 28 percent against the Japanese yen.

Figure 2-2. Growth of Imports from the United States to Mexico Before and After NAFTA: Agricultural and Animal Products

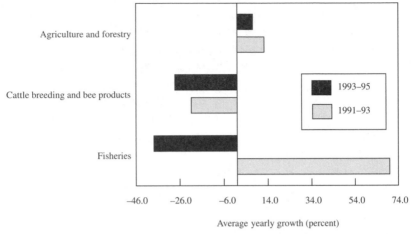

Average yearly growth (percent)

Source: SECOFI.

forces must also be at work. The expanded access acquired by American exports into the Mexican market as a result of NAFTA, and the growing importance of intraindustry bilateral trade that emerged even before NAFTA and was further enhanced by the agreement, certainly explain part of these dynamics.

As we discussed, this appears to be the case for sectors such as autos and auto parts, textiles and apparel, chemicals, and rubber and plastics, for which the rates of growth of trade flows before and after NAFTA are only modestly affected by currency fluctuations (see table 2-2).

The Mexican Economic Crisis: Has NAFTA Made a Difference?

Even before the negotiations were concluded and the details were disclosed to the public, the expectation of a complete elimination of trade barriers in North America prompted many business decisionmakers to incorporate this factor into their long-term planning, and to act accordingly.[15] Furthermore, the disciplines introduced by NAFTA provided cred-

15. In August 1992, at the Watergate Hotel in Washington, D.C., the trade ministers of the NAFTA Parties announced that the negotiation process had successfully concluded. However, close consultations with industry representatives of the three countries throughout the negotiations had kept business decisionmakers aware of the basic elements the agreement, as they were being crafted by the official negotiators.

Figure 2-3. Growth of Imports from the United States to Mexico Before and After NAFTA: Manufactured Products

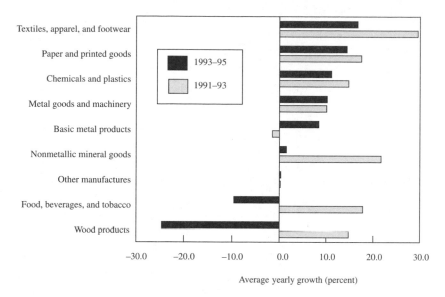

Average yearly growth (percent)

Source: SECOFI.

ible assurance that the fundamental reforms that Mexico had undertaken in the 1980s and early 1990s would remain in place over the long term. This perception, plus the perception of Mexican macroeconomic management as being intertemporally consistent and able to manage exogenous shocks, explains why the inflow of international funds into Mexico's capital markets between 1990 and 1993 was so substantial.

By 1994, however, and notwithstanding the importance of microeconomic reform on the expectations of economic agents, the perception of the ability of macroeconomic management to deal with exogenous shocks changed abruptly as a result of the combined effects of tragic and unprecedented events in Mexico's political arena, and a tightening of monetary policy in the United States.[16] These doubts generated mounting pressure on the exchange rate throughout 1994, which led to the abrupt devaluation of the peso at the end of that year and the ensuing contraction of output during 1995.

The fact that the devaluation occurred in the year of a presidential transition has nurtured the perception that the Mexican crisis of 1994 was

16. During 1994, the interest rate for six-month certificates in the United States more than doubled, rising from 3.32 percent to 6.51 percent.

Figure 2-4. Growth of Imports from the United States and Non-NAFTA Countries to Mexico

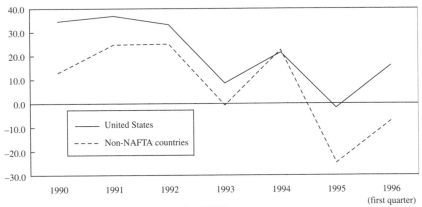

Yearly growth (percent)

Source: Computed by the authors on the basis of data from SECOFI.

largely a reprise of the one in 1982, which also occurred at the end of a presidential term and after interest rates in the United States had increased substantially. Therefore, a pertinent question is whether the policy responses were different from those adopted to face previous balance of payments crises (specifically, the 1982 crisis), and to what extent the observed differences in export and import performance after each crisis can be attributed to the structural reforms undertaken by Mexico after 1982, including NAFTA. More particularly, we should ask ourselves if export and import performance after each crisis was different, when such flows are analyzed considering separately the bilateral trade with the United States as compared with trade with non-NAFTA countries; and, if so, what this means for national, regional, and global welfare.

Although a detailed analysis of Mexico's current macroeconomic crisis is clearly beyond the scope of this chapter, we believe that a comparison of the 1982 and 1994 crises can shed light on the relative relevance of NAFTA during the last three years and, especially, on its role as new bilateral trade patterns emerge.

Basic Economic Policy: 1982 and 1994

Although the policy responses to the 1982 and 1994 balance of payments crises were quite similar (both involved large doses of fiscal and monetary austerity as well as real wage restraint), significant differences can be identified in three critical areas of macroeconomic management before the crises: fiscal, trade, and monetary policies. We refer to the selected indicators presented in tables 2-3 and 2-4.

Unilateral reforms (which gave the Mexican economy greater fiscal strength and a clear market orientation), coupled with the way in which Mexico has incorporated international disciplines into its domestic legal framework, are positive factors in the current recovery of the Mexican economy that were not present in the early 1980s.

FISCAL POLICY. The contrast could hardly be more striking. In 1981, the public sector was running a budget deficit equivalent to nearly 11 percent of GDP; in 1993, the fiscal balance showed a surplus equivalent to 1.5 percent of GDP. This turnaround liberated resources to reduce the relative size of the public debt and significantly increase the availability of funds for private firms to invest during the period of trade liberalization.

TRADE POLICY. By 1993, Mexico had made considerable progress with regard to trade liberalization. Its average tariff had been cut in half, to 12.6 percent, compared with the level prevailing in the early 1980s. With regard to import licenses, the main nontariff measure applied in Mexico in the early 1980s, and the share of total output protected by them had been reduced from more than 75 percent in 1981 to 20 percent in 1993. (The remaining licenses have been mostly concentrated in agriculture, petrochemical products, automotive goods, and some used manufactures.) Moreover, after joining GATT in 1987, Mexico became actively involved in the Uruguay Round negotiations. As a result of this change in policy, Mexican firms began the costly and protracted adjustment effort to an open trade regime. The counterpart to the adjustment was the expansion of non-oil exports, which expanded almost by a factor of five between 1981 and 1993, with a rising content of imported inputs.

MONETARY POLICY. The contrast in the conduct of monetary policy in the year preceding the 1994 crisis, as compared with the situation observed in 1981, is also impressive. Before the latest crisis, the monetary base was equivalent to only 0.3 percent of GDP; the domestic credit component of the base was negative in an amount equivalent to 1.5 percent of GDP. The central bank was clearly making an effort to sterilize the considerable inflows of foreign financial investment. The contraction of domestic credit also reflects the reduction in the domestic public debt. Comparable figures in 1981 were quite different—the size of the monetary base was nearly 4 percent of GDP, with

Table 2-3. Pre-Crisis Indicators in Two Crises in Mexico, 1982, 1994

	1981			1993		
	Value Millions of U.S. $[a]	*Share of GDP* Percent	*Structure*	*Value* Millions of U.S. $[a]	*Share of GDP* Percent	*Structure*
Gross domestic product	250,008	—	—	361,962	—	—
International trade						
Trade policy (percent)						
Average tariff	23.5	—	—	12.6	—	—
Domestic output protected by import licenses	75.2	—	—	20.0	—	—
Trade flows						
Global exports	23,053	9.2	100.0	51,832	14.3	100.0
Oil and gas	14,573	5.8	63.2	6,432	1.8	12.4
Non-oil mineral goods	686	0.3	3.0	307	0.1	0.6
Fresh plant and animal goods	1,482	0.6	6.4	2,564	0.7	4.9
Manufactured goods	6,312	2.5	27.4	42,529	11.7	82.1
Global imports	27,195	10.9	100.0	65,367	18.1	100.0
Consumer goods	2,808	1.1	10.3	7,902	2.2	12.1
Intermediate goods	16,813	6.7	61.8	46,332	12.8	70.9
Capital goods	7,574	3.0	27.9	11,134	3.1	17.0
Trade balance	-4,143	-1.7	—	-13,535	-3.7	—
Foreign investment						
DFI yearly inflow	1,701	0.7	—	4,901	1.4	—
Monetary policy						
Change						
Monetary base	9,726	3.9	100.0	1,084	0.3	100.0
Domestic credit	8,439	3.4	86.8	-5,530	-1.5	-510.2
FX reserves	1,103	0.4	11.3	5,991	1.7	552.8
Other	185	0.1	1.9	623	0.2	57.5
Fiscal policy						
Budget balance of the public sector	-27,352	-10.9	—	5,593	1.5	—
Foreign public sector debt						
Change in outstanding balance	19,148	7.7	—	2,992	0.8	—

Source: Compiled by the authors from Salinas de Gortari (1996); Zedillo Ponce de León (1995); Banco de México (1996); Instituto Nacional de Estadística, Geografía e Informática (INEGI) (1996); ten Kate (1990).
a. Unless otherwise specified.

Table 2-4. Key Indicators in Two Crises in Mexico, 1982, 1994

	1982		1983		1994		1995	
	Index 81	*Structure (percent)*	*Index 81*	*Structure (percent)*	*Index 93*	*Structure (percent)*	*Index 93*	*Structure (percent)*
Nominal variables								
Inflation	158.8	—	321.6	—	107.0	—	144.4	—
Peso value of U.S. dollar	233.3	—	613.2	—	108.4	—	206.1	—
Real aggregate demand and supply								
Aggregate demand	94.8	100.0	88.6	100.0	104.9	100.0	94.2	100.0
Domestic component	90.9	87.6	79.4	84.8	104.4	83.6	80.8	76.5
Private consumption	97.5	57.9	92.3	58.7	103.7	56.0	90.4	54.4
Public consumption	102.0	9.6	104.8	10.6	102.5	9.1	98.2	9.7
Gross capital formation	83.2	20.3	59.7	15.6	108.1	18.2	74.7	14.0
Change in inventories	-12.4	-0.3	-0.1	0.0	92.7	0.3	-405.8	-1.5
Export component (goods and services)	122.6	12.4	140.0	15.2	107.3	16.4	137.8	23.5
Aggregate supply	94.8	100.0	88.6	100.0	104.9	100.0	94.2	100.0
Domestic component	97.7	91.9	91.4	94.3	103.4	84.0	96.0	87.1
Import component (goods and services)	62.1	8.1	41.1	5.7	112.9	16.0	81.8	12.9
Gross domestic product	99.4	91.9	95.2	94.3	103.5	84.0	96.3	87.1
Merchandise-producing sectors	98.6	32.9	94.1	32.7	103.0	33.2	97.6	33.8
Other sectors	99.7	67.1	95.8	67.3	103.7	66.8	95.7	66.2

Source: Compiled by the authors from Salinas de Gortari (1996); Zedillo Ponce de León (1995); Banco de México (1996); INEGI (1996); ten Kate (1990).

the domestic credit component of the base having the largest share (3.4 percent of GDP).[17]

SUMMING UP. In 1993 all major policy instruments were aimed at supporting a stable, open, and deregulated market economy, whereas in 1981 the thrust of economic policy was expansionary and protectionist. Not surprisingly, these differences in the orientation of economic policy translated into quite different compositions of aggregate demand and aggregate supply.

Composition of Aggregate Demand and Aggregate Supply: 1982 and 1994

GROSS CAPITAL FORMATION. Clearly, the two crises had large and adverse effects on investment. However, such effect is milder in the most recent case. The average share of this variable in GDP between 1993 and 1995 fell 25.3 percentage points; between 1981 and 1993, the reduction reached 40.3 percentage points. This difference signals a stronger capacity for the economy to recover today than it had after the 1982 crisis.

PUBLIC CONSUMPTION. The effectiveness of the fiscal adjustment program in 1995 was higher than the program implemented in 1983. In the more recent case, one year after the balance of payments crisis, public consumption had been cut by nearly 2 percent of GDP, whereas in 1983 public consumption still increased by almost 5 percent of GDP. A stronger and better controlled fiscal position allowed the government in 1995 to act rapidly to compress current expenditures and contribute to a correction of the current account imbalance.

PRIVATE CONSUMPTION. To a large extent, this component of aggregate demand shows the most important short-term cost to the Mexican economy as a result of the two crises. This cost is higher in 1994. In the early 1980s few families had sizable debt outstanding; it was the public sector that had an debt overhang problem. By contrast, in 1994 many families and private companies had taken advantage of the larger credit availability brought about by the correction of the fiscal imbalance in the previous years. When credit was suddenly and severely tightened in 1995, the cuts in private consumption required to service debt (at extremely high real interest rates) were therefore substantial. These factors underscore the critical role of exports in a rebound in economic activity.

17. In assessing these differences, it is useful to keep in mind that inflation was 28.7 percent in 1981 and rising, while it was 8.0 percent in 1993 and falling.

EXPORTS. Although the rise in the GDP share of exports of goods and services in the two cases compared seems similar at first glance, the diminished importance of oil exports in the early 1990s should be borne in mind. In 1995, oil exports represented only 8.6 percent of total revenues in the current account of the balance of payments, whereas in 1983 their share in such revenues was 54.7 percent. Clearly, the export base Mexico can rely on today as the major driving force of the current recovery is much more diversified than the one it had in the early 1980s.

More significantly, the 86 percent devaluation that the Mexican peso had accumulated at the end of NAFTA's first year of operation prompted a more dynamic response from nonmaquiladora, non-oil exports than from those of in-bond or maquiladora plants. Nonmaquiladora sales abroad show a 37 percent surge in 1995, whereas maquiladora exports expanded by 30 percent. This dynamism of nonmaquiladora exports suggests a much deeper international integration of Mexico into the international economy than the one existing during the early 1980s. The 29 percent rise in maquiladora exports that followed a 466 percent depreciation of the Mexican currency in 1982 was not matched by nonmaquiladora, non-oil exports, which fell by nearly 6 percent in 1983.

In addition, it is interesting that the post-NAFTA surge in total merchandise exports to the United States and Canada, which show a 29 percent yearly increase in 1995, is significantly smaller than the one shown by total merchandise exports to non-NAFTA countries (46 percent). This pattern stands in contrast with the one observed in the immediate aftermath of the 1982 devaluation of the peso. In 1983, Mexican exports to the United States and Canada grew by more than 19 percent, but those directed to other countries actually decreased by 11.1 percent. Although a more detailed analysis is needed to elucidate the significance of these facts, they suggest that (when the situation prevailing in the early 1980s is taken as a benchmark) by the time NAFTA entered into force, the Mexican economy had achieved substantial gains in its global competitiveness.[18]

IMPORTS. The cutback in this component as a result of the 1994 devaluation of the peso has been substantially less severe that it was in 1982. Unlike the early 1980s, this time Mexico has maintained its commitment to free trade and, in general, to an economic policy blueprint designed

18. At a minimum, and given the significant decline observed since the early 1980s in the weight of oil among Mexico's total exports, an analysis by country of destination would require a distinction between oil and non-oil exports. Unfortunately, this breaking out of the export data at a country-by-country level is available only from 1989 on.

to restore price and foreign exchange stability. This policy stance has allowed a faster restoration of the country's access to international financial markets and will ultimately result in restoration of investor confidence. In fact, the expectation that NAFTA would lock in the structural reforms undertaken by Mexico in the late 1980s and early 1990s has been tested and has been proven justified.

There is a valid concern, however, that should not be overlooked. Some of NAFTA's bilateral trade effects may have possibly been the result of trade diversion rather than trade creation. This is an important issue that deserves a careful evaluation, which is clearly beyond the scope of this chapter. However, a comparison of the 1995 performance of Mexican imports by country of origin indicates that, at least for Mexico, the trade-diversion effects of NAFTA exist but do not appear to be inordinately large. As shown in figure 2-4, during 1995 Mexican imports from the United States fell much less than those originating in non-NAFTA countries, a fact that tends to support trade-diversion concerns. However, this pattern was also observed in the aftermath of the 1982 devaluation of the peso. In 1983, Mexican imports from the United States fell by 37 percent, while those originating in other countries decreased by 46 percent.

Concluding Remarks

The unilateral reforms carried out by Mexico over the last decade to structurally strengthen the fiscal balance (and, concomitantly, to subject the economy to efficient market signals through trade and investment liberalization) have modified the composition of aggregate demand and aggregate supply and have positively affected Mexican macroeconomic performance and prospects. This new composition implies that sustained economic growth in Mexico depends more heavily on the external sector than in the past, as illustrated by the dynamic growth rates of non-oil exports, imports, and foreign investment flows. This has important implications for the bilateral trade relation with the United States.

The prospect of North American economic integration, made public in 1990, further strengthened the outward-looking, more efficient orientation of the Mexican economy. Non-oil trade and direct foreign investment flows between 1991 and 1993 reflected the fact that economic agents had begun to anticipate NAFTA's effects on Mexican productivity and to allocate resources toward certain activities that took advantage of the relative competitiveness of the North American region, through production specialization and greater regional intraindustry trade in specific sectors.

The analysis of the emerging bilateral trade patterns needs to take these structural changes into account. Evidently, trade flows in 1994 and 1995 were affected by exchange rate policy, especially during 1995, after the accumulated depreciation of 1994. However, concentrating exclusively on the exchange rate appreciation observed between 1989 and 1993 to explain import demand expansion and the depreciation in 1994 and 1995 to explain export demand expansion would lead to an incomplete analysis. Bilateral trade flows during this period reflected resource allocation decisions, which were determined by Mexico's unilateral economic reforms, the anticipation of eventual North American economic integration, and (in some specific sectors) NAFTA's liberalization program in effect since January 1, 1994. A pure exchange rate explanation would severely underestimate the effect of these other factors.

We have used aggregate and sectoral data to show that structural change, and more specifically NAFTA, are in fact having strong effects on bilateral trade already, even though the agreement is still in the early phase of the transition to free trade. In some sectors such as automotive goods, textile and apparel, and basic metal products, NAFTA's effects are already quantitatively large.

We conclude with some food for thought. We have shown that NAFTA's effects are already relevant in terms of magnitude and composition of bilateral trade and aggregate investment flows. However, we do not believe this is the most important issue. In our view, determining if NAFTA is leading to a more efficient allocation of national, regional, and global resources or not is what really matters.[19]

To guarantee that NAFTA indeed contributes to multilateral trade liberalization and does not generate dominant trade diversion effects, special attention needs to be given to some of its critical building blocks.

TARIFFS. Competitive forces should begin to create downward pressures on the most favored nation (MFN) tariff structures of the three countries. These forces should lead, as soon as possible, to a minimum common external tariff schedule. Moreover, because bound MFN tariffs (that is, the tariff levels committed to the World Trade Organization [WTO]) are higher than applied tariffs in some goods, there is a danger that tariffs for final goods are increased to accommodate demands for effective

---

19. Consider an extreme scenario, in which bilateral trade increased dramatically but exclusively as a result of trade diversion. This would clearly be self defeating, not only because of its negative effects on global welfare, but also because it would lead to the eventual decline of the North American region's ability to compete with the rest of the world.

protection, instead of reducing those for intermediate inputs and capital goods.[20] It would therefore be desirable to bind all effective MFN rates.

RULES OF ORIGIN.   In most cases, the rules of origin that determine if a good is subject to preferential tariffs ("preferential rules of origin") reflect the previously existing degree of regional integration (that is, the status quo). However, the regional integration observed before 1994 was also a function of existing tariffs. If competitive pressures eventually lead to the lowering of MFN tariffs, the rules of origin chapter of NAFTA would no longer be consistent with such status quo rule. Undoubtedly, the rules of origin pose the greatest challenge in terms of avoiding trade diversion.

TRADE RULES.   The convergence of rules on contingent protection, technical, health and safety standards, and competition policy is a major challenge for the free trade region. For example, instead of having independent national trade remedy laws, which have been rationalized as substitutes for an international competition code, it would be more efficient and welfare enhancing to share a regional competition policy. Unfortunately, trade remedy laws, especially in the United States, are political enclaves of the most ferocious and protectionist special interests and lobbies.

LIBERALIZATION OF SERVICES AND INVESTMENT.   The liberalization program in the services sector is still incomplete. In part, this is because of the GATT-type negotiation process followed, which was based on the "mirror image" principle. For example, the Jones Act reservation of the United States, designed only to protect a politically powerful maritime transportation lobby, was matched by a similar reservation for Mexico. This type of negotiation is what got the Uruguay Round in trouble. It is necessary to analyze service liberalization with a completely different analytical methodology and to introduce different incentives in the negotiation process. Similarly, there are still too many access restrictions in the investment chapter.

SUBNATIONAL COVERAGE.   The application of many NAFTA disciplines is not compulsory for local governments (for example, government procurement and standards). This can lead to the erosion of the liberalization program.

As a concept since 1980 and as the law of the land since 1994, NAFTA has already played a major role in determining resource allocation in North

---

20. In 1995, Mexico raised the tariffs of footwear, textiles, and apparel from 20 percent to their bound rate (35 percent) as a result of protectionist pressures. From an economic point of view, this was clearly inefficient.

America. The policy challenge is to ensure that this new allocation leads to greater benefits for the region and the world.

Appendix to Chapter 2
NAFTA: Main Features

Trade in Goods

BASIC DISCIPLINES:

> Respect for all rights and obligations under GATT (WTO)
> —Most favored nation treatment
> —National treatment

TARIFF ELIMINATION SCHEDULES:

> Effective tariff bindings to avoid rollbacks and erosion of agreed-upon preferences
> —Gradual phaseout of tariffs to assure smooth transition to free trade
> Tariffication of import permits to eliminate quantitative controls and tariff rate–quota mechanisms to allow preferential access in goods with high initial tariffs and long transition periods
> Elimination of tariff peaks to maximize preferential benefits

RULES OF ORIGIN:

> Preferential rules of origin to determine which goods benefit from tariff preference
> Two alternative methods to determine origin of goods that do not originate in the region or are not produced wholly in the region:
> —Change in tariff classification (also called "tariff jump"), based on the Harmonized System of the Customs Cooperation Council; and
> —Regional content, based on the "transaction value" or net cost methods
> Transition to eliminate duty drawback for goods that satisfy rules of origin

TRADE RULES:

> Transparent procedural disciplines in the establishment of technical standards and sanitary and phitosanitary standards to eventually achieve regional harmonization:

—National treatment;
—Use of international references;
—Exchange of information, adequate notification, and
    procedural transparency
Liberalization of government procurement
Review mechanisms for antidumping and countervailing duty
    determinations to ensure adequate application of domestic laws
Strict regulations on the application of safeguards to avoid erosion
    of the trade liberalization program:
—Bilateral safeguards to temporarily suspend tariff reductions
    with compensation rules; and
—Global safeguards, under article XIX of GATT, with rules to
    exempt regional suppliers under certain conditions

SPECIAL SECTORAL LIBERALIZATION PROGRAMS:

—Textiles and apparel
—Automotive goods
—Energy
—Agriculture

TRADE AND COMPETITION POLICY:

Working group to consider relationship between trade and
    competition policies

Deregulation and Protection of Foreign Investment

COVERAGE:

All forms of ownership and interests in a business enterprise,
    tangible and intangible property, and contractual investment
    interests
No rule of origin, which means that an investor of any nationality
    can benefit from the protection of chapter XI as long as the
    investor has substantial business activities in the region
Explicit reservations with gradual liberalization schedules

STANDARD OF TREATMENT AND PERFORMANCE REQUIREMENTS:

National treatment
—Most favored nation treatment

Elimination of performance requirements, with a transition for
specific sectoral programs (for example, the automotive sector)

EXPROPRIATION:

Strict procedural disciplines for acts of expropriation
—Respect for due process
—Nondiscrimination
Prompt, adequate, and effective compensation at fair market value

TRANSFERS:

Free convertibility for earnings, proceeds of sales, loans,
repayments, and so on

DISPUTE SETTLEMENT:

Investor-state dispute settlement mechanism, which gives the
investor alternative forum selection (local tribunals or
international arbitration)

PROTECTION OF INTELLECTUAL PROPERTY RIGHTS:

Patent and copyright protection consistent with guidelines of World
Intellectual Property Organization

Trade in Services

CROSS-BORDER SERVICES:

National treatment
—Most favored nation treatment
—No residency requirements
—Possibility of agreeing on mutual recognition of professions
—Liberalization of government procurement

FINANCIAL SERVICES:

National treatment
—Most favored nation treatment
—Gradual liberalization
—Equal competitive opportunity

OTHER SERVICES:

Land transportation
—Construction

—Telecommunications

TEMPORARY ENTRY OF PERSONS:

Business visitors
—Traders and investors
—Intracompany personnel transfers
—Independent professionals

Institutional Framework and Enforcement

ADMINISTRATION OF THE AGREEMENT:

Creation of the NAFTA Free Trade Commission
—Working groups and committees

DISPUTE SETTLEMENT MECHANISM:

Consultation
—Intervention of the NAFTA Free Trade Commission
—Panel procedures

Comment by Sherman Robinson

I was pleased with this chapter, perhaps because it concurs with most of my prejudices. The authors consider the emerging bilateral trade patterns between the United States and Mexico after NAFTA was implemented and try to sort out what effect NAFTA had compared with other macroeconomic shocks. In particular, they seek to explain the relative impact of NAFTA versus the major swings in the exchange rate over the past two years on bilateral trade flows. They make the point that changes in relative prices due to changes in the exchange rate during this period have been much larger than changes resulting from trade liberalization under NAFTA.

Not surprisingly, the authors attribute the major shift in the trade balance between Mexico and the United States to the devaluation of the peso, gradually during most of 1994 and precipitously at the end of that year. However, they also find that NAFTA has made a major difference in a number of important sectors such as autos, auto parts, metal products, textiles, apparel, agriculture, and food products. They correctly argue that some of these changes, with significant increases in two-way trade at the sectoral level, began with the unilateral Mexican trade reforms in the mid-1980s. NAFTA continues this liberalizing trend. The authors' data indicate that producers on both sides of the border apparently see increased trade potential in the long run and discount short-run macroeconomic disturbances. During the debate on NAFTA ratification, many economists argued that its major impact would be to increase confidence on both sides of the border that the Mexican reforms would continue, and the early evidence they cite supports the view that this "lock-in" role has had a real impact.

In general, the empirical evidence the authors cite supports the view that NAFTA is "trade creating" rather than "trade diverting"—a view consistent with the results from the various computable general equilibrium (CGE) models used to simulate the effects of NAFTA. Although there is some trade diversion, trade creation is much greater. This result is interesting because it tends to support an optimistic view of other regional trading arrangements such as Mercosur, Asia Pacific Economic Cooperation (APEC), and a possible free trade area in southern Africa. Many trade economists argued that regional trading arrangements, including NAFTA, should not be pursued because they are potentially only trade diverting, lowering welfare.

These arrangements also divert policy attention from further global liberalization, which is the first-best goal. There is a growing body of evidence indicating that this view is incorrect. Results from multicountry

CGE simulation models of many such arrangements show trade creation far outweighing trade diversion, and similar results come from recent gravity models of international trade flows. It is also clear from experience both with the Uruguay Round and with recent free trade agreements (for example, NAFTA and Mercosur) that regional trading arrangements are much easier to negotiate than global liberalization under GATT. It seems to me that the burden of proof is now on those who argue against pursuing regional trade agreements to demonstrate their case empirically.

Increasing economic integration leads to more two-way trade and increasing indirect trade links. As the authors note, Mexico imports intermediate and capital goods to support its production for exports, so increased exports lead to increased import demand. Mexico is certainly not unique in this respect. Many semi-industrial countries were characterized by such increasing trade dependence as they successfully pursued an open development strategy. The problem is that such structural changes increase the sensitivity of the economy to macroeconomic shocks. It is harder to improve the balance of payments with a change in the exchange rate, because increasing exports requires additional imports. Not surprisingly, the authors find that the 1994 devaluation had a much larger impact on Mexican trade with non-NAFTA countries, where these indirect links were less significant. It also largely explains why Mexican imports from the United States continued to grow despite the dramatic devaluation.

Finally, the authors point out some emerging problems. NAFTA is not a customs union, only a free trade agreement. Each member country is free to pursue its own independent trade policy with respect to nonmember countries. Despite some fears expressed in the United States during the debate on ratification of NAFTA, the early evidence is that NAFTA will not turn Mexico into an "export platform" for other countries to gain access to the U.S. market. The "rules of origin" discussion in the NAFTA document, however, is quite lengthy and arcane and is generating many difficult disputes. There are still protectionist elements at work in both countries (but especially in the United States) that will exploit every opportunity to throw sand in the gears to hinder trade expansion. In the long run, it is hard to see how a free trade agreement can work without gradually evolving into a customs union.

Even in the short term, there is certainly a growing need for policy coordination across the three NAFTA countries. Agriculture provides some good examples of coordination problems. Florida tomato growers have used every protectionist tool possible, including antidumping laws, to keep out Mexican tomatoes. Under threat from an antidumping investigation in the U.S. Commerce Department that appears to be biased, Mexico reached a settlement with the Florida growers that certainly violates the spirit of North American economic integration. Canada and Mexico are especially sensitive to misuse of antidumping laws, with good reason, and favor NAFTA and World Trade Organization (WTO) institutions for resolving disputes. Increased regional integration requires institutional support, and NAFTA institutions will have to be strengthened if the experiment is to work.

The continued U.S. subsidization of agricultural exports under the Export Enhancement Program (EEP), which the United States has said it will continue to use as long as allowed under GATT, is simply incompatible with a unified North American market. The EEP program was instituted to allow the United States to subsidize exports, mostly of wheat, into markets where other countries were determined to be subsidizing their exports. In 1993, during the final stage of the NAFTA debate, the United States declared that because Canada was subsidizing east-west rail transport of wheat, the United States would subsidize wheat exports to the Mexican market. We declared one NAFTA partner to be an evil subsidizer and then disrupted the other partner's wheat market! The irony was that U.S. policymakers were then surprised to observe Canadian exports of wheat into U.S. markets (shipped by truck!). The Europeans understand that policy coordination is required if the goal is to maintain a price gap between domestic and world markets. Even with U.S. export subsidies finally eliminated, there will still be a need to coordinate agricultural support policies among the three countries.

General Discussion

Nora Lustig asked the authors whether the impact of the devaluation in 1995 was different from past devaluations in 1976 and 1982 in terms of the response of exports and imports—that is, was there evidence of a greater price elasticity exports and imports? The authors responded that the response to the price change did appear to be stronger in 1995, and they believed that it was a likely consequence of Mexico's ongoing structural change. Lustig also expressed some concern about the differential impact of the crisis on U.S. exports in comparison with those of other countries because it implied significant trade diversion, reflecting the differential treatment given to non-NAFTA trade partners. The authors agreed and mentioned the steep antidumping tariffs on Chinese imports as an example. John Williamson commented that he had heard of similar actions against other non-NAFTA trade partners and, although such an outcome was not directly related to NAFTA, it was an indirect consequence of the agreement that implied a much more careful treatment of the member countries.

Susan Collins asked whether, in light of what had been observed in the past two years, people believed that the eventual outcomes of NAFTA would be very different from what was predicted a couple of years ago. Zia Qureshi suggested that it would be useful to analyze the impact of NAFTA on productivity and domestic value added, and to distinguish between maquiladora and nonmaquiladora exports.

References

Banco de México. 1996. *The Mexican Economy.* Mexico City.

Boltuck, Richard, and Robert E. Litan. 1991. *Down in the Dumps: Administration of the Unfair Trade Laws.* Brookings.

Garber, Peter M. 1993. *The Mexico–US Free Trade Agreement.* MIT Press.

____. 1992. *North American Free Trade Issues and Recommendations.* Washington: Institute for International Economics.

Hufbauer, Gary C., and Jeffrey J. Schott. 1993. *NAFTA: An Assessment.* Washington: Institute for International Economics.

Instituto Nacional de Estadística, Geografía e Informática. 1996. *Banco de Datos* (computer diskettes). Mexico City: Instituto Nacional de Estadística, Geografía e Informática.

Kehoe, Patrick J., and Timothy J. Kehoe. 1995. *Modeling North American Economic Integration.* Dordrecht, The Netherlands: Kluwer Academic Publishers.

Prusa, Thomas J. 1995. "An Overview of the Impact of Unfair U.S. Trade Practices." In *Trading Punches: Trade Remedy Law and Disputes under NAFTA.* Edited by Beatriz Léycegui, William B. P. Robson, and S. Dahlia Stein. Washington: North American Committee.

Salinas de Gortari, Carlos. 1994. *Sexto Informe de Gobierno (Anexo).* Mexico City: Presidencia de la República.

Secretaría de Comercio y Fomento Industrial. 1992. *Description of the Proposed North American Free Trade Agreement.* Mexico City.

Ten Kate, Adriaan. 1990. "The Mexican Trade Liberalization of 1985–1987: Lessons of Experience." Washington: World Bank.

Zedillo Ponce de León, Ernesto. 1995. *Primer Informe de Gobierno (Anexo).* Mexico City: Presidencia de la República.

3 Mexican Policy toward Foreign Borrowing

John Williamson

ONE of the factors that has often been pointed to as a cause of the 1994–95 Mexican crisis is the current account deficit of almost 8 percent of gross domestic product (GDP) that had developed by 1994 (see table 3-1). Nothing on the horizon promised to reduce it except the possibility of growth becoming even more anemic than it had been over the 1990–94 period. My view was, and is, that this deficit created a situation in which the main question was not whether a crisis would occur but what would trigger it. I am not denying that the immediate cause of the crisis was the disparity between the stock of short-term, dollar-denominated claims and the limited reserves with which to meet a liquidation of those claims; I am arguing instead that a cumulative flow imbalance is likely to lead to precisely such a stock disequilibrium. But rather than devote time to yet another rehearsal of the arguments on the causes of the 1994 debacle, I propose to concentrate on a discussion of how to avoid a repetition, assuming it to be true that a current account deficit of that size will in due course make a country vulnerable.

Without this large capital inflow into Mexico during the 1990s, it would not have been possible to finance such a huge current account deficit. In that sense the crisis was caused by the excessive size of the capital inflow, which consisted both of foreign lending and a partial repatriation of the flight capital of the preceding years. But, given Mexico's macroeconomic policy, which was based on using the exchange rate as a nominal anchor to reduce inflation and ignoring the results of this policy in eroding competitiveness over time, a smaller capital inflow would have required the economy to grow even more slowly than it actually did (an average of 3.0 percent per year over the 1990–94 period). This was meager enough, given

The author acknowledges helpful comments on a previous draft from Enrique Mendoza and other participants in the conference and from Ricardo Ffrench-Davis and is indebted to Molly Mahar for her capable research assistance.

Table 3-1. The Mexican Economy, 1990–95
Percent (unless otherwise specified)

	Average 1986–89	1990	1991	1992	1993	1994	1995	Average 1990–94
Real GDP growth	0.6	4.5	3.6	2.8	0.7	3.5	-6.9	3.0
CPI inflation	82.6	26.6	22.7	15.5	9.7	6.9	35.0	16.3
Capital inflow (% GNP)	1.9	5.4	5.1	3.1	6.6	4.6	4.5	5.0
Current account deficit (% GDP)	0.6	3.0	5.1	7.3	6.4	7.6	-0.2	5.9
Real effective exchange rate (1968–89 = 100)[a]	100.0	113.0	124.0	131.7	140.3	131.7	81.2	128.1
Investment (% GDP)	18.8	18.4	19.2	20.5	20.0	20.3	16.3	19.7
Consumption (% GDP)	68.5	70.0	70.8	71.1	70.3	70.0	67.3	70.4
Export growth	82.5	33.5	10.4	7.4	9.1	15.5	138.6	14.8
Import growth	102.3	41.8	26.7	25.5	1.5	20.3	50.2	22.5
Percentage of capital inflow in form of FDI	130.8	22.3	36.4	46.6	22.0	47.4	35.0	34.9
Fiscal deficit (% GDP)	10.6	2.8	0.2	-1.5	-0.4	0.8	0.7	0.4
Terms of trade (1986–89 = 100)[b]	100.0	107.8	97.02	93.94	95.48	97.02	95.48	98.3

Source: World Bank (1996a, 1996b); International Monetary Fund (1996a, 1996b); Banco de México (1996).
a. Based on consumer prices (1993, 1994). An increase in the index represents an appreciation of the currency.
b. F.O.B./F.O.B.
n.a. = Not available.

the hopes that had been aroused by the reforms of the late 1980s. Eventually the slower inflation resulting from the buildup of slack in the economy would presumably have increased Mexican competitiveness and thus revived the economy. However, with inertial inflation—which Mexico surely had, as evidenced by the improvement in competitiveness since early 1995—the process would have been long and painful.

Did Mexico have an alternative strategy? That is, given the propensity of capital to flow into Mexico, could a current account deficit that transferred the inflow have been avoided? I argue that it could have been, had Mexico's policies emulated those of Chile and Colombia, two other Latin American countries that also experienced strong capital inflows but pursued a very different macroeconomic policy. In the first substantive section of the chapter I describe the policies that were pursued in Chile; in the next section I look much more briefly at the Colombian experience. I then discuss what would be involved in Mexico emulating their approach, with particular attention to the question of the size of the capital inflow that it would make sense to plan for.

Chilean Policies

I begin by describing Chilean policies because Chile articulates its policy stance with particular clarity. This discussion also draws a contrast with Mexico, going on to ask why Chile was driven to adopt its current policy stance and how it has succeeded in avoiding the outcomes that some apologists for Mexican policies aver were inevitable.

During the first half of the 1990s Chile experienced capital inflows that averaged 5.9 percent of gross national product (GNP) (table 3-2). Yet Chile's current account deficit averaged only 1.9 percent of GDP, somewhat less than the target of an average deficit of 3 percent of GDP that has been explicitly announced by the Central Bank of Chile. The deficit has not shown an increasing trend, despite a real appreciation of some 25 percent by 1994 from the average of 1986–89. Real growth over the period averaged 5.2 percent (this is actually somewhat below trend, as a result of the particular end points), while inflation fell from 26.0 percent in 1990 to 11.4 percent in 1994 (and has continued to decline since).

The comparable figures for Mexico, shown in table 3-1, were a capital inflow of 5.0 percent of GNP, a current account deficit that increased from 3.0 percent of GDP in 1990 to 7.6 percent in 1994 with an average of 5.9 percent, and an exchange rate that by 1993 had appreciated in real terms by 40 percent from the 1986–89 average (though it depreciated in 1994 as the

Table 3-2. The Chilean Economy, 1990–95

Percent (unless otherwise specified)

	Average 1986–89	1990	1991	1992	1993	1994	1995	Average 1990–94
Real GDP growth	7.2	2.1	6.0	10.4	6.0	4.9	7.0	5.2
CPI inflation	17.8	26.0	21.8	15.4	12.7	11.4	8.0	17.5
Capital inflow (% GNP)	5.9	8.6	4.1	4.3	4.5	8.2	n.a.	5.9
Current account deficit (% GDP)	3.8	2.2	–0.5	1.5	4.6	1.5	–1.0	1.9
Real effective exchange rate (1968–89 = 100)[a]	100.0	104.8	110.0	114.9	118.9	125.1	130.6	114.7
Investment (% GDP)	17.2	23.3	20.9	22.7	25.6	24.3	26.3	23.4
Consumption (% GDP)	62.4	60.5	62.0	62.3	63.8	62.5	62.0	62.2
Export growth	37.1	21.0	23.5	17.1	6.5	25.7	26.4	18.6
Import growth	35.5	25.1	20.6	26.6	21.5	10.0	24.5	20.6
Percentage of capital inflow in form of FDI	26.6	23.9	39.7	42.0	42.6	43.6	n.a.	38.4
Fiscal deficit (% GDP)	–0.3	–0.8	–1.5	–2.2	–1.9	–1.6	n.a.	–1.6
Terms of trade (1986–89 = 100)[b]	100.0	99.8	100.9	95.1	88.2	97.4	109.0	96.3

Source: World Bank (1996a, 1996b); International Monetary Fund (1996a, 1996b).

a. An increase in the index represents an appreciation of the currency.

b. F.O.B./F.O.B.

n.a. = Not available.

exchange rate went from the strong to the weak edge of the band). In addition, average real growth was 3.0 percent, and inflation fell from 26.6 percent in 1990 to 6.9 percent in 1994. In terms of the main policy objectives, growth was half that of Chile, whereas inflation fell much more markedly, by 76 percent rather than a mere 56 percent as in Chile. Those who agree with the Chilean rather than the Mexican authorities in regarding the current account as a third objective will also note that Chile's deficit was on average one-third that of Mexico's, without an increasing trend.

I ascribe these differences in outcomes primarily to the differences in the macroeconomic policies pursued in the two countries since the late 1980s. Both of them had undertaken profound liberalization programs in the preceding years, which one would have expected to raise the supply-side growth rate. The Chilean liberalization started much sooner than that of Mexico, and it may well be that more of its impact had come on stream, so that one should not necessarily have expected Mexico to be capable of sustaining a growth rate of more than 5 percent. But 3 percent was anemic by the standard of Mexico's own historical experience before the debt crisis. Even omitting the years of oil-driven supergrowth in 1978–81, Mexico grew by an average 6.1 percent per year from 1952 to 1978. The investment ratio had actually edged up since the 1970s, from an average 19.8 percent in 1970–77 to 20.3 percent in 1990–94, so that cannot explain the growth shortfall.

What cannot be explained by the supply side must have been due to a deficiency of demand.[1] In this post-Keynesian age it would be suspect to argue that this might have been a result of the virtuous fiscal policies pursued by Mexico. In any event, the point is moot, since Chilean fiscal policies were even more virtuous—an average fiscal surplus of 1.6 percent of GDP as against a marginal deficit of 0.4 percent of GDP in Mexico.[2] There likewise seems little reason to point to investment. Although the average level of investment was higher in Chile than in Mexico, it actually increased in Chile by only 1 percentage point of GDP between 1990 and 1994, as against an increase of 1.7 percentage points over the same period in Mexico.[3] The consumption share of GDP rose by 2 percentage points in

1. This is also argued by Blecker (1996).
2. One could argue that correct accounting would require deducting a quasi-fiscal deficit of around 1 percent of GDP from this, but that would still have left Chile more "contractionary" than Mexico. Changes in the terms of trade were similar between the two countries, unless one goes back before the oil price decline in 1986, so this does not help explain the difference.
3. Admittedly those end dates underestimate the trend increase in investment as a share of GDP: see table 3-2.

Chile and stayed flat in Mexico. In fact, the main reason for the less buoyant demand growth in Mexico was the external sector. The current account deficit increased by 4.6 percent of GDP in Mexico, whereas it fell marginally (by 0.7 percent of GDP) in Chile. Given a multiplier of 2, a discrepancy of 5 percentage points of GDP in the growth of external demand could explain 10 percentage points less growth (that is, lower growth of about 2 percent per year). Without the deterioration of its current account balance, Mexico might thus have been expected to grow by at least 4 percent and perhaps as much as 5 percent per year, instead of 3 percent.

Why did the current account deteriorate? It can hardly be explained by a high growth rate that led to demand pressing against capacity. Two other obvious explanations are the appreciation of the real exchange rate and the import liberalization that started in the mid-1980s and continued into the 1990s, culminating in the inauguration of NAFTA at the beginning of 1994.

The usual response to a complaint that the exchange rate had become overvalued has been that exports were growing rapidly. This is perfectly true, as table 3-1 confirms. An average rate of export growth of 14.8 percent per year from 1990–94 is much higher than world markets were growing at over that period and much higher than Mexico's own previous history.[4] However, a country that has just undertaken a substantial trade liberalization should expect its trade to grow unusually rapidly; the sad fact is that the impressive growth of Mexico's exports did not keep up with the frenzied growth of its imports (an average of 22.5 percent per year). A rapid trade liberalization generally needs to be accompanied by a real depreciation, precisely to generate the superfast growth of exports that will both prevent an undue deterioration of the current account and maintain an adequate level of domestic demand. Instead, Mexico allowed a real appreciation and financed the resulting current account deficit with the funds that were flowing in so bountifully on the capital account.

This is the critical point where policy was so different in Chile. Rather than use the exchange rate as a nominal anchor (that is, to maintain a predetermined rate of devaluation regardless of the evolution of the real exchange rate, out of conviction that this would force the domestic rate of inflation down), Chile's basic policy was to devalue in line with the inflation differential to maintain its target for the real exchange rate. This prevents the exchange rate from playing a role as a nominal anchor. It has been argued that such a policy necessarily implies increasing inflation, but

4. Excluding oil, the increase was even faster, an average of 16.4 percent per year.

Chilean experience shows that this is false.[5] What one can legitimately argue is that it is a more inflationary policy than the Mexican one of nonaccommodation. Indeed, the data confirm that inflation decelerated less rapidly in Chile than in Mexico (starting from a similar level in 1990, it fell by 20 percentage points in Mexico and only 15 points in Chile). But the proposition that inflation is closely pinned down by the exchange rate is simply wrong, as this comparison confirms once again. Instead, the inertial element in inflation results in countries that persist in using the exchange rate as a nominal anchor ending up with an overvalued exchange rate by the time that inflation is brought down to the world level.

The Chilean decision to make maintenance of a competitive exchange rate a central feature of its macroeconomic policy stance stemmed from its experience in 1982. Previous years had witnessed policies similar to those pursued in Mexico in the first half of the 1990s—a fixed exchange rate from 1979 on that was supposed to act as a nominal anchor and quickly slow inflation in accord with the doctrines of international monetarism, but which instead slowed inflation only gradually in response to an increasing overvaluation. In conjunction with a credit boom intermediated by a newly liberalized and largely unregulated banking system and fed by a gullible international capital market that liked the ideological story it was sold, the overvaluation resulted in a vast current account deficit (some 14 percent of GDP at its peak in 1981) that was initially financed willingly by capital inflows.

Since the fiscal accounts were in surplus, the government reassured the markets (with what subsequently became known as the Lawson Doctrine) that there could not be any problem of sustainability. But the bubble collapsed in 1982 nonetheless, with a vengeance that makes Mexico's tribulations of 1995 look modest by comparison. Chilean GDP fell 14 percent in 1982, unemployment rose to over 30 percent, the real wage fell by 35 percent, bankruptcies tripled (which led to a financial crash that needed a bailout that cost 26 percent of GDP), imports halved, consumption fell some 24 percent, and investment fell by 50 percent.[6] The total adjustment cost peaked at about 35 percent of GDP, half of which was secondary (that is, avoidable).[7]

5. Adams and Gros (1986).
6. However, a part of this has been recovered in subsequent years.
7. All figures are taken from Meller (1990).

The new economic team that took over after the crisis appears to have agreed with the academic diagnoses that pointed to three principal failings in the preceding model.[8] First, financial liberalization was not accompanied by an adequate system of prudential supervision. The exchange rate was pegged in 1979, although inflation was still running at some 35 percent per year. In addition, any chance of inflation decelerating promptly—as was promised by the international monetarist model that was the basis for the decision to freeze the exchange rate—was eliminated by the retention of backward-looking wage indexation.[9] The new economic team that was brought in after the crisis sought to remedy these three defects. In particular, they achieved and subsequently sought to maintain a competitive exchange rate, to ensure that when growth revived it would be export led rather than debt led. To that end, a crawling peg was reinstated after a period of floating and several discrete devaluations.

The achievement of a highly competitive exchange rate was undoubtedly aided by the ruthless nature of the dictatorship of Augusto Pinochet, which was still running the country at that time, which was able to cut real wages in a way that would have been difficult for a more democratic government. It has remained a central objective of Chilean macroeconomic policy ever since to maintain a competitive exchange rate and limit the current account deficit to a level that implies progress in reducing the debt indicators.

Confidence began to revive in the mid-1980s, and with it voluntary capital inflows resumed. After a temporary lull in 1989–90, associated with the referendum on the return of democracy, the attempt of Pinochet's team to buy the election, and the fears that a new democratic government would revert to populist policies, the new administration of Patricio Aylwin was faced by the full force of capital inflows. The most interesting part of the Chilean story is of the measures taken to prevent these inflows from blowing the country off course.

Chile experienced a (net) capital inflow that vastly exceeded its cumulative current account deficit, with the difference being added to its reserves. Chilean reserves grew from $3.6 billion at the end of 1989 to $13.1 billion at the end of 1994, from six to thirteen months of imports. Although it is difficult to get figures that measure the extent of sterilization from the

8. Corbo, de Melo, and Tybout (1986); Ffrench-Davis (1983).

9. Ffrench-Davis does not include wage indexation in his list; on the contrary, he argues that this cannot have been the crucial factor since real wages were still lower than in 1970. However, one of the consequences of the economic reforms instituted in the 1970s had been a massive redistribution of income away from labor; given that fact, wage indexation can perfectly well have been an important part of the problem.

published data, it appears that the bulk of the capital inflow was sterilized. The Chilean authorities estimate the cost of their sterililization efforts at about 0.5 percent of GDP.[10]

However, Chile did not just buy up reserves and sterilize them. It also implemented a whole range of supporting measures. The first, undertaken in June 1991, was to reduce its uniform import tariff from 15 to 11 percent. Such a liberalization of import restrictions results in an increase in the current account deficit—that is, in effecting the transfer—but it does this in a way that does not threaten the growth of exports. This is a policy reaction that is highly appropriate in an economy that is threatening to overheat, as Chile's was in 1991.

Exchange rate policy can also help. A scheduled crawling depreciation, such as that which Chile maintained, helps to disabuse the markets of excessively optimistic expectations regarding the feasibility of maintaining a fixed exchange rate for ever, expectations that magnify the expected return from moving funds in and thus accentuate the inflow problem. An important step can be to increase the band for exchange rate fluctuations. If the band is credible, this has two important advantages. If the exchange rate appreciates to the strong edge of the band, then market participants will expect that it will in due course revert to the middle. This means that they will deduct the expected depreciation back to the middle of the band from the domestic currency return to compare with foreign yields before deciding whether to shift funds in. So if the band is ±10 percent, and market participants expect that the rate will revert to parity after five years, then the domestic interest rate can be 2 percent per year higher during the intervening five years without there being any incentive to arbitrage funds in. Another advantage is that investors in the tradable sector will tend to look at the parity when estimating the profitability of a potential investment project, rather than at the current market rate. Chile widened the band for exchange rate fluctuations in a series of steps—most recently in 1992, when the band went from ±5 percent to ±10 percent.

The other way of making it less profitable to arbitrage funds into the money market is to decrease domestic interest rates. The constraint on that is normally provided by the need to keep a rein on demand, to maintain inflation on a downward path. But there is of course a way to reconcile lower interest rates with continued demand restraint, and that is to tighten fiscal policy. Chile has maintained a taut fiscal stance, although the surplus has not grown further from the 1.8 percent of GDP recorded in 1989, except

10. See Ffrench-Davis and others (1995, p. 10) for further discussion of this topic.

marginally and apparently temporarily in 1992–93. Although most economists are enthusiastic advocates of fiscal tightening as an antidote to excessive capital inflows, they tend to overlook the difficulty of persuading the political system to raise taxes or cut expenditures, because foreigners want to lend so much money.[11]

The fiscal surplus matters in this context because it is a form of saving. However, any other saving is just as good in relieving the pressure of demand, thus permitting interest rates to be lowered without aggravating inflation. What is special about government saving is that it is closer to being a policy variable. But government does also have some levers through which it may be able to increase private saving. The switch to private provision of pensions in Chile (which dates from 1981) certainly helped to give the country a healthy savings rate in recent years.

Governments under balance of payments pressure sometimes give special subsidies of one form or another to encourage inward investment, as Chile did, through its program of debt-equity swaps, during the debt crisis. At the very least, these should be promptly phased out when a country starts to experience excessive capital inflows, as Chile phased out its debt-equity program in the late 1980s. The controversial issue is whether a country should go beyond this and discourage capital inflows, as Chile has also done. It retains a minimum holding period of a year for all foreign equity-type investments, both foreign direct investment (FDI) and portfolio equity investment. It also imposed a reserve requirement against foreign holdings of bank deposits and other interest-bearing claims of 20 percent in 1991, and increased this to 30 percent in 1992. A small tax of 1.2 percent was also imposed on short-term external credits in 1991.

The final possible policy response to an excessive capital inflow is to liberalize capital outflows. This has to be handled carefully; one of the things that can deter investors from bringing their money in is the fear that they may have trouble getting it out again should conditions deteriorate. As a result, a liberalization of outflow controls can actually prompt a net inflow. There is empirical evidence that this perverse effect has actually materialized on occasion.[12] But it is possible to liberalize selectively those

11. It is also sometimes argued that further fiscal consolidation could so strengthen confidence as to increase the inflow, analogously to the anti-Keynesian demand stimulation that most now accept can occur when fiscal policy is tightened in a situation where government finances are felt to be out of control. My presumption would be that this effect would already have been exhausted by the time that excess capital inflows became a problem, so that I would not further qualify the case for fiscal tightening on this ground.

12. Labán and Larraín (1993).

sectors where this risk is minimal, which is what Chile did in liberalizing outward FDI and allowing pension and mutual funds to place a part of their portfolios abroad.

These measures have helped to contain the pressure from capital inflows, but this has nonetheless been so strong that the authorities have been forced to concede on two occasions. A discrete revaluation of the band of 5 percent occurred in January 1992 and another of 10 percent in November 1994. Cumulative real appreciation from 1990 to the end of 1994 averaged nearly 5 percent per year, or 4 percent per year if other Latin American countries are excluded (on the ground that their exchange rates tend to be too unstable to provide a meaningful measure of trends). The two discrete revaluations were very much forced responses to strong market pressures. The speculators "won." In fact, however, a part of these revaluations simply offset what was clearly (at least with the benefit of hindsight) an overshooting of real depreciation at the end of the 1980s. The Chilean authorities have now also accepted that they should expect a secular real appreciation because of Balassa/Samuelson productivity bias. Since December 1995 they have deducted 2 percent a year from the rate of crawling depreciation to allow for this up front, in the hope of preempting periodic speculative crises that end up with forced revaluations.

No single one of these policies could have been expected to keep the real exchange rate competitive in the face of the massive capital inflows Chile faced. But together they sufficed to keep the situation under control. There were costs to this policy, notably the slower deceleration of inflation and the cost of sterilization. But the benefits, in terms of faster growth and avoidance of the risks that result from excessive foreign indebtedness, surely outweighed the costs several times over.

Colombia

Chile is not alone in having pursued such a macroeconomic strategy in recent years. Indeed, Chile is a relatively recent convert to the attempt to even out the business cycle; the traditional champion of this strategy in Latin America has been Colombia. Like Mexico, Colombia experienced an export boom in the late 1970s, also based on the high price of its principal export product, which in the case of Colombia is (or at least was) coffee. Unlike Mexico, which used the high oil prices as collateral to increase its absorption by more than its permanent income had risen, Colombia made a conscious effort (as it had done in previous cyclical upswings) to run a budget surplus, to build up reserves, to avoid foreign borrowing, and to prevent a real appreciation that would threaten its nontraditional export industries.[13] (Admittedly its resolve began to weaken toward the end.) In short, it tried to follow Keynesian precepts of stabilizing the economy in the face of cyclical shocks; or one could say it sought to follow the Friedmanian precept of keeping absorption in line with permanent income. Colombia reaped its rewards in the 1980s, when it was the only country in Latin America that avoided debt rescheduling and maintained positive per capita growth throughout the decade.

In recent years Colombia has also been faced by large capital inflows (almost certainly larger than those recorded in the official statistics shown in table 3-3, because capital inflows were disguised by misinvoicing, especially before liberalization in 1992). It has also placed a high priority on maintaining a competitive exchange rate, although it also overshot in devaluing too much in the late 1980s. To that end it modified its long-standing crawling peg by surrounding it by a wide band, first de facto in 1991 and then de jure in early 1994. After a substantial liberalization of its capital account, Colombia reintroduced capital inflow controls in 1993 with a view to limiting inflows of short-term capital and pressures for appreciation of the peso.[14] Despite these controls, the band was revalued under strong market pressure in late 1994, when the central bank perceived that it was confronted by a choice between defending the exchange rate band and the monetary target and chose to give the latter priority.

Colombian economic growth averaged 4.0 percent per year over the 1990–94 period while inflation remained a high 26 percent on average, with only modest deceleration from 32 percent in 1990 to 23 percent in 1994. The current account moved from a recorded surplus in the early years of the decade to a deficit of 4.5 percent of GDP in 1994 and even more since. A surplus was generally regarded as inappropriate, so some adjustment was welcomed. Because much of the capital inflow is financing the develop-

---

13. This was much to the chagrin of the bankers, who lobbied the International Monetary Fund and the U.S. Treasury Department to lean on Colombia to change its hostility to the bounty they were offering.

14. Colombians can only borrow abroad with a license. Although these are granted freely, they carry an obligation to make a deposit, currently of up to 140 percent of the value of the loan (but progressively less as the maturity of the loan increases), with the central bank. The cost is in fact prohibitive (as is intended) for short-term loans. Initially loans with a maturity greater than eighteen months were exempted, but this was progressively extended to three years and then to five years. Although the reserve requirement is higher than in Chile, the base is narrower. It does not apply to inflows of portfolio investment, or to loans that are used to buy capital goods from abroad, or to foreign direct investment (FDI), or to short-term import credits.

Table 3-3. The Colombian Economy, 1990–95
Percent (unless otherwise specified)

	Average 1986–89	1990	1991	1992	1993	1994	1995	Average 1990–94
Real GDP growth	4.6	4.3	2.0	4.0	5.2	5.7	5.3	4.0
CPI inflation	24.8	32.4	26.8	25.1	22.6	22.6	21.5	25.9
Capital inflow (% GNP)	2.7	0.9	0.6	–0.1	1.4	2.6	n.a.	1.1
Current account deficit (% GDP)	–0.1	–1.3	–5.7	–2.1	4.2	4.5	n.a.	–0.1
Real effective exchange rate (1968–89 = 100)[a]	n.a.	100.0	103.4	112.8	118.5	132.6	134.0	113.5
Investment (% GDP)	21.6	18.6	16.0	17.2	19.9	19.8	22.5	25.3
Consumption (% GDP)	66.0	65.4	65.2	70.2	70.5	70.2	68.2	39.2
Export growth	41.2	52.8	33.9	6.5	21.5	16.4	35.3	25.3
Import growth	35.4	43.3	21.1	45.5	55.9	32.5	28.6	39.2
Percentage of capital inflow in form of FDI	67.0	140.0	199.0	n.a.	127.0	62.6	n.a.	105.7
Fiscal deficit (% GDP)	1.2	–3.9	–2.6	1.9	0.5	n.a.	n.a.	–0.8
Terms of trade (1986–89 = 100)[b]	100.0	90.2	85.8	80.3	89.1	101.2	112.2	89.3

Source: World Bank (1996a, 1996b); International Monetary Fund (1996a, 1996b).
a. An increase in the index represents an appreciation of the currency.
b. F.O.B./F.O.B.
n.a. = Not available.

ment of the Cusiana oil field, and the current account will benefit to the tune of about 2 percent of GDP when this comes on stream, the deficit is regarded as only marginally too large for comfort.

Apart from demonstrating that Chile is not an aberration, the Colombian story is interesting because of the crisis that did not happen. In mid-1995 the president who had been elected the previous year was accused of having knowingly financed his election campaign with narcomoney. Had Colombia been experiencing a current account deficit of Mexican proportions, and had it had substantial outstanding short-term, dollar-denominated debt, it is easy to believe that the resulting political crisis might have undermined confidence in the economy, much as the Colosio assassination did in Mexico.[15] But in fact Colombia's position was strong enough to enable it (at least so far) to absorb the shock, with no financial repercussions more serious than having the exchange rate migrate to the weak edge of the band.

A Target for Mexico

If Mexico were to decide to emulate the macroeconomic policy stance of Chile and Colombia, it would need to make a conscious decision regarding the current account deficit that would be desirable. What principles should govern the choice of such a target?

First, it should be feasible—that is, within the level of what the market will be willing to provide in an average year. This is unlikely to be a serious constraint once the crisis is definitively over. All the evidence is that the market wants to lend emerging markets more than it is good for them to accept. (I leave to others to come up with an intellectually satisfying explanation of this paradoxical fact, but I agree with McKinnon and Pill that it now has to be treated as fact.[16])

Second, it should be sustainable. In particular, the increase in net external debt should be sufficiently modest to avoid a progressive buildup of debt relative to the ability to generate debt service payments. Indeed, where a country starts with a high level of debt, prudence suggests the desirability of an even slower increase in debt until the debt indicators have been brought in line with reasonable levels. The ability to generate debt service payments is sometimes measured by exports and sometimes by GDP. In the case of Mexico, where exports are almost sure to grow more rapidly than GDP in the coming years, the more conservative criterion will be provided

15. Most foreign debt is now of an initial maturity of five years.
16. Labán and Larraín (1993).

by the debt/GDP ratio. If one accepts the conventional rule of thumb that the maximum safe debt/GDP (D/Y) ratio is 40 percent, then the steady-state current account deficit (d/Y) would be

$$d/Y = (d/D)(D/Y) = y (D/Y) = 0.4y \tag{1}$$

where y is the steady-state growth rate of nominal income, equal to that of the debt. So if nominal income (measured, like the debt, in dollars) grows at a dollar inflation rate of 3 percent plus 5 percent real growth in Mexico, or 8 percent (0.08) in total, the safe steady-state current account deficit would be 3.2 percent of GDP. This calculation confirms that deficits of the size witnessed in 1992–94, which were in the range of 6 to 8 percent of GDP when growth was nowhere near 5 percent, were reckless in the extreme.

Presumably none of us feel comfortable appealing to rules of thumb with neither secure theoretical foundations nor compelling empirical evidence to buttress them. The only defense is that the alternatives are even less appealing. One alternative would be to frown on any capital mobility and hold up a balanced current account as a policy objective. This is patently stupid. Capital mobility offers clear welfare gains: the opportunity of redistributing world savings to the areas of highest return, the intertemporal smoothing of consumption, risk diversification, the ability to draw on the intellectual property of foreign corporations, and enhancement of competition in the financial sector. It is quite clear that some countries (for example, South Korea and Singapore) have benefited enormously from the chance to grow faster as a result of borrowing abroad; thus increasing investment above what could have been afforded from domestic saving. Countries should be able to exploit these gains. Mexico, being a relatively low-income country with large unmet investment needs and abundant opportunities to expand its industrial sector to supply the NAFTA market, is a natural capital importer for the next several decades.

The other alternative is for the government to disavow any concern for the balance of payments. Let it balance its budget and follow a monetary policy that either allows the exchange rate to float freely and targets some appropriate nominal magnitude (like the inflation rate, according to the latest fad, which seems a lot more sensible than most of its predecessors), or else peg the nominal exchange rate by following the classical monetary rules. Let the balance of payments emerge from the free play of market forces, disregarding the current account outcome entirely.[17]

17. See Corden (1994) for explicit advocacy of such an approach.

If the capital markets behaved as they are supposed to according to the rational expectations textbooks, it would be difficult to fault this approach. But in fact the markets seem too susceptible to herd behavior to make this sensible. They do overlend, and then try to withdraw their money in a panic when they realize that they have done so. Given that there are severe costs to being the subject of an attack, it is only prudent for a government to minimize the chance of overexposure.

An attempt to quantify what is meant by prudence leads one to the sort of formula offered by equation (1) above. Even in the absence of a compelling theoretical basis for this type of approach, it seems legitimate to modify the formula to recognize a number of factors.[18]

A HIGH OR LOW LEVEL OF DEBT. If a country starts with debt that is above or below the benchmark chosen as safe in steady state, then in the short run it will need to run a lower (or be able to run a higher) current account deficit than suggested by the formula. Mexico's debt/export ratio was 228 percent in 1994, somewhat above the traditional 200 percent threshold, while its debt-to-GDP ratio was 35 percent, somewhat below the 40 percent threshold. Its debt/export ratio has presumably come down since then, as exports have maintained their strong growth while debt nearly stabilized with the correction of the current account deficit. However, the debt-to-GDP ratio must have soared because of the collapse of Mexico's GDP as measured in dollars. I therefore cannot see that this factor provides a case for targeting a current account deficit greater than suggested by the formula.

THE COMPOSITION OF BORROWING. It has usually been assumed that some forms of foreign borrowing are notably more stable than others. In particular, it has been taken for granted that FDI is more stable than foreign acquisition of short-term claims. This presumption was questioned on statistical grounds in a paper by Claessens and others.[19] However, Guillermo Calvo argued in his discussion of that paper that the standard measures of volatility presented in it did not address the real issue, which is the fear of occasional large changes rather than of frequent small ones. For this one needs measures of volatility that place a larger weight on "spikes" and "outliers" than the standard measures (based on the variance) do. Frankel and Rose seem to have provided some econometric confirmation of Calvo's hunch that the conventional wisdom is probably correct.[20] Accord-

18. See Milesi-Ferretti and Razin (1996).
19. Claessens, Dooley, and Warner (1994).
20. Frankel and Rose (1995).

ingly, I regard a current account deficit as less worrying when it is largely financed by an inflow of FDI than when the counterpart is an inflow of short-term capital. I would not disregard FDI entirely, because it too needs to be serviced; but a 50 percent weight might be the right order of magnitude. Although the flow of FDI into Mexico has built up substantially in recent years, it is still a small part of the inflow, and a 50 percent weight would still leave Mexico's adjusted current account deficit at 6.5 percent of GDP in 1994. On a forward-looking basis, this factor might raise the safely sustainable deficit to 4 percent of GDP.

THE CONSUMPTION/INVESTMENT MIX. If a capital inflow is used to build up productive capacity, then the borrower will find it easier (other things being equal) to service the debt than if it is used to expand consumption, even though there may be respectable reasons in terms of intertemporal smoothing for the increased consumption.[21] A purist might argue that one can never know whether the antimonde without foreign borrowing would have been one of less consumption or of less investment. However, most of us are content to use intertemporal comparisons to deduce that if the 4.6 percent of GDP increase in Mexico's current account deficit between 1990 and 1994 was accompanied by a rise in the investment share of only 1.7 points, then 63 percent of the capital inflow went into consumption (actually public consumption and inventory accumulation). That is not reassuring.

THE CONSTRAINT ON OUTPUT. In an earlier section I argued that output in Mexico had been demand constrained during the 1990–94 period. In that circumstance it made no sense at all to maintain high interest rates to attract capital. Mexico would have been better off with lower interest rates, a smaller capital inflow, a more competitive exchange rate, a lower current account deficit, and faster output growth.[22] There would of course have been a price to pay, in the form of a slower deceleration of inflation— although, if the policy change had been big enough to avert the subsequent collapse, then the inflation rate today would have been much lower than it currently is. Note that this factor impacts on the exchange rate through a

21. Note that it would be incorrect to look at the *level* of investment and argue that (for example) Thailand could justify a higher level of foreign borrowing than that suggested by equation (1) on the basis of its high share of investment in GDP, because the impact of that high investment level is already allowed for in (1) through its effect on the expected future growth rate.

22. It could be counterargued that Mexico was already suffering from an asset price boom that would have been accentuated by easier monetary policy. This might have called for measures like higher margin requirements and mortgage downpayments to prevent lower interest rates to business borrowers spilling over into further increases in asset prices.

different mechanism than the preceding ones in a crawling band system. They all influence the target current account deficit that underlies the calculation of the parity, whereas this factor should influence where the exchange rate lies within the band. Specifically, weak demand should induce a monetary easing that would drive the exchange rate toward the weak edge of the band.

One factor that should not be presumed to alter the safe level of foreign borrowing is membership in NAFTA. For better or worse, NAFTA did not contain any monetary provisions analogous to the European Monetary System that would give fellow members of NAFTA either special responsibilities in monitoring each other's policies or special privileges in drawing on each other's resources. It is true that in the 1994–95 crisis the United States provided help of a magnitude unlikely to be given to any other country, but the cost of the crisis to Mexico was nonetheless horrendous. Moreover, it is fairly clear that it would be politically impossible to repeat such an exercise were Mexico to encounter similar difficulties again. The only prudent policy is to avoid getting into a similar situation again.

Conclusions

Ever since it gained its independence in 1821, Mexico has been an enthusiastic borrower from the international capital market whenever the opportunity has presented itself. For much of the time, however, the opportunity was closed off by the failure to service outstanding debt. In a historical context, the new boom-bust cycle of recent years is remarkable mainly for its accelerated timetable. Lending revived a mere seven years after the debt crisis of 1982, as compared with a sixty-one–year gap after the crisis of 1827, a seventeen-year interval after the crisis of 1911, and a hiatus of about forty years after the default of 1932.[23] The fact that the lending boom of the early 1990s lasted less than five years before its rude interruption in 1994 is more in keeping with Mexico's normal historical experience!

It seems that creditworthiness has been reestablished even more quickly since the 1994–95 crisis than it was in the 1980s, in a matter of a year or so. This lends urgency to the policy question as to how Mexico can ensure that the past pattern of instability (with its highly disruptive consequences for the real economy) can be changed. I have argued that the key need is for a change in macroeconomic strategy. Because this argument is so often

23. Aggarwal (1989).

contradicted by an assertion that any attempt to resist transfer of the inflow dictated by the all-powerful capital markets is doomed to failure, I have gone into considerable detail in describing how an alternative strategy has been used by two other Latin American countries, with rather satisfactory results. There are trade-offs, but I doubt whether many people would not judge that the price, in terms of a somewhat less rapid deceleration of inflation and the cost of sterilizing excess reserve inflows, was not well worth paying.

Implementation of this alternative strategy requires deliberate contemplation of what size of capital inflow it would be sensible to plan for in the medium term. The presumption is not that bigger inflows are automatically better (even though Mexico is a natural capital importer at the present stage of its development) but that the markets are likely to offer more than it is prudent to accept. The medium-term target should be geared largely to avoiding any increase in Mexico's burden of debt relative to either exports or GDP. That guideline is, I think, state of the art. Although I acknowledge that the state of the art is woefully inadequate, there are no grounds for supposing that Mexico can expect to avoid the constraints that apply to other countries because of its membership in NAFTA. The target will need to be pursued by the deployment of a wide battery of policy tools, similar to those used by Chile and Colombia—perhaps including measures aimed directly at discouraging short-term capital inflows. One must avoid unrealistic expectations of how much capital controls can accomplish. But it is precisely because such controls are largely ineffective in limiting outflows when crises occur that it is important to limit inflows when times are good, thus (one hopes) preempting a crisis in the first place.

In addition, I have argued that the exchange rate should be allowed to move within the band to promote domestic objectives. In particular, if Mexico should again get into a state such as it was in during the early 1990s, where growth was constrained by weak demand and inflation was on a declining trend, then it should be prepared to loosen monetary policy so as to push the exchange rate toward the weak edge of the band by discouraging capital imports. Similarly, if world interest rates again become so low that there is a temporary flood of capital into regions like Latin America, then recipient countries like Mexico should aim to match the interest rate cuts, as long as this will not create an inflationary pressure of demand, rather than allowing their exchange rates to go to the strong edge of the band.

Comment by Enrique G. Mendoza

In this chapter John Williamson argues that the Mexican crisis was caused by the conventional mechanism of trade flows that links a currency peg to real overvaluation of the currency, a gradual loss of competitiveness in external trade, and a ballooning current account deficit that eventually becomes unsustainable. This view of balance-of-payments crises dates back to the classic models of Dornbusch and Rodriguez, which Dornbusch and Werner proposed as an interpretation of the Mexican case.[24] The chapter makes a substantial contribution in that it derives much richer policy conclusions than those that follow from the Dornbusch-Rodriguez model. Rather than simply arguing for devaluation and dismantling of indexation practices, Williamson argues for targeting of the real exchange rate, tight fiscal policy, careful management of capital inflows, and strict bank supervision. Moreover, he presents a basic rule to judge the sustainability of the current account, qualifying it by noting that global capital markets are highly imperfect; hence, policies should aim at optimizing the mix of foreign borrowing and mitigating the effects of herding and overlending waves. The chapter's comparative analysis of the experiences of Chile, Colombia, and Mexico provides strong empirical evidence in favor of these policies.

In this commentary I would like to question Williamson's diagnosis of the Mexican crisis, although most of his policy recommendations are consistent with the predictions of alternative theories of Mexico's crisis that seem more plausible. I also have a few comments on both the analysis of the Chilean experience and the analysis of current account sustainability.

About the Diagnosis

The fact that Mexico's large current account deficit and real appreciation were signs of trouble is indisputable. What is controversial is why these are signs of trouble. How do the dynamics of the current account and the real exchange rate enter into the picture of Mexico's crisis? As noted, the chapter follows Dornbusch and Werner in arguing that the mix of a currency peg with price inertia induced real appreciation and loss of competitiveness, which enlarged the current account deficit and ended up undermining the peg itself.[25] The logical consistency of this view is not an issue;

24. Dornbusch (1982); Rodriguez (1982); Dornbusch and Werner (1994).
25. Dornbusch and Werner (1994).

neither is the fact that it may be the best way to explain several episodes of currency crises. However, as an explanation of Mexico circa 1988–95, it is a misleading approach for the following reasons:

—As I and others have argued, Mexico's crisis was mainly a crisis of the capital account (the country was unable to fulfill its *financial* obligations).[26] The large current account deficit and real appreciation were symptoms of a disease, but what killed Mexico were first the runs on peso-denominated, short-term public debt (Cetes) in March and November, triggered in part by attempts to prop up the banking system during a liquidity squeeze, and finally the run on dollar-denominated Tesobonos and the refusal to roll them over, in a situation in which Tesobonos of less than 90 days' maturity had grown much larger than foreign reserves (see figure 3-1). The liquidity squeeze in turn was in part the result of adverse foreign shocks to the quantity of money, in an environment in which the dollar value of M2 had also grown much larger than reserves. Econometric analysis of M2 suggests that the predictable effect of rising U.S. interest rates accounts for roughly half of the reserve losses observed in 1994 (see figure 3-2). Thus, Mexico's crisis was a crisis of financial *stocks,* not a crisis of trade *flows.*

—In the flows theory, whether the policy is to target the real exchange rate period-by-period or try a big devaluation at some point makes little difference. In practice, though, it is often the case that devaluations do not happen without some difficulties in the aftermath. The aftermath in the case of Mexico's devaluation, however, was a cataclysmic real and financial crisis that the flows approach cannot explain. Dornbusch and Werner called for about a 20 percent real depreciation early in 1994, about half of which had been accomplished before the devaluation.[27] A relatively modest 10 percent devaluation should have completed the adjustment. Yet the devaluation—far from helping, and though highly effective to close the current account gap and adjust the real exchange rate—was only the first stage of the worse Mexican crisis since the Great Depression. The depth of the crisis, the run on Tesobonos, and the propagation of the stock market collapse to emerging markets worldwide (the Tequila effect) surprised policymakers and academic experts alike. Models of herd behavior or self-fulfilling crises, fundamentally different from the Dornbusch-Rodriguez flow models, seem better suited to explain these phenomena.[28]

26. Calvo and Mendoza (1996, forthcoming).
27. Dornbusch and Werner (1994).
28. Cole and Kehoe (1996); Chari and Kehoe (1996); Sachs, Tornell and Velasco (1996); Calvo and Mendoza (1996, forthcoming).

Figure 3-1. Mexican Foreign Reserves and Short-Term Public Debt

End-of-month stocks in millions of U.S. dollars

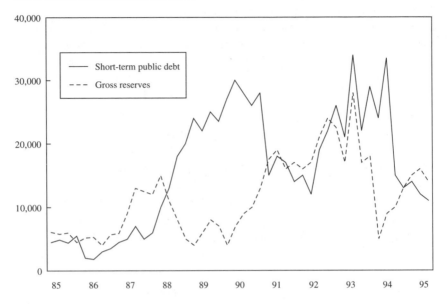

Source: Data provided by Banco de México.

—The processes of real appreciation and widening external deficit may both be endogenous to an ultimate cause that may be lack of credibility on the duration of currency pegs and stabilization plans, or equilibrium dynamics of structural reforms. The latter produce the desired answer qualitatively. However, quantitative studies suggest that it is unlikely that the sharp real appreciations typically associated with exchange-rate–based stabilizations can result from the equilibrium transition process triggered by far-reaching reforms like NAFTA.[29] In contrast, elsewhere we have shown that a stochastic "credibility" model in which the probability of devaluation takes the J-shaped form consistent with empirical evidence, and with the view that reputation is painfully gained in the early stages of peg and then gradually lost as imbalances build up, comes close to reproducing the Mexican real appreciation and current account deficit.[30]

—Several stylized facts also seem inconsistent with the flows view based on price and wage inertia. Mexico's real exchange rate was not too out of line from a historical postwar perspective (see figure 3-3). Real

29. Rebelo and Végh (1995); Mendoza (1995).
30. Mendoza and Uribe (1996).

Figure 3-2. Mexican Actual and Predicted Real M2 Money Balances

Millions of 1988 pesos

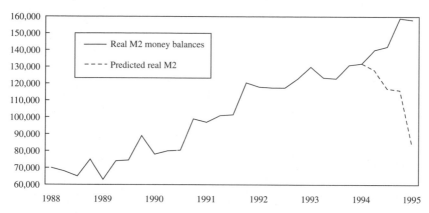

Source: Author's estimates using data provided by Banco de México.

appreciation based on the consumer price index did not reflect that prices of tradables in Mexico were rising faster than in the United States, but that Mexican nontradables inflation was slow to converge (see figure 3-4). In addition, rather than observing across-the-board real wage increases, there was wide dispersion in the behavior of real wages, with several sectors experiencing substantial real wage declines while others reported large real wage increases.[31]

About Chile

Chilean policymakers have been more conservative and gradualist than their Mexican counterparts in many respects. Still, the experiences of Chile and Mexico have differed in more than the aim of the Chilean authorities to target the real exchange rate, and their profound fear to let the current account deficit become larger than 3 or 4 percent of GDP. Three differences are worth noting:

—Mexico's reforms were implemented against the background of a 70 to 80 percent persistent decline in the terms of trade, at a time when Chile was experiencing a persistent *300* percent increase (see figure 3-5). Thus, the strength of Chile's current account may have a lot to do to with policies (and here the chapter should add the remarkable management of the Copper

31. See Calvo and Mendoza (1996) for details.

Figure 3-3. Mexican Real and Nominal Exchange Rates

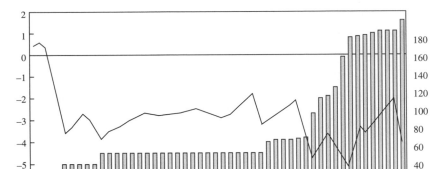

Note: The real exchange rate index is P/EP*, where P is the Mexican consumer price index (CPI), E is the nominal exchange rate in nuevos pesos per U.S. dollar, and P* is the U.S. CPI. The base of the index is 1970 = 100.
Source: Author's calculations; International Monetary Fund (1996a).

Stabilization Fund), but also it may reflect good luck. Evidence from empirical growth analysis points clearly to the key role that the terms of trade play in explaining growth persistence and cross-country growth experiences.[32]

—In assessing Chile's fiscal stance, one must consider the quasi-fiscal losses incurred by the central bank because of the "nonperforming" assets it was forced to acquire as part of the package to rescue the financial system in 1983, and to some extent because of sterilized intervention operations. Central bank figures estimate that this quasi-fiscal deficit was about 1 to 2 percent of GDP per year still in 1994–95. Chile's fiscal position is thus less impressive than table 3-2 suggests; hence, not surprisingly the Central Bank president resigned rather than continue to agree to subsidize commercial banks at this hefty rate. Moreover, Chile's fiscal stance varied little during the period in question, while Mexico's overall public sector financial position shifted from a deficit of 12 percent of GDP to a surplus of 1½ percent of GDP. Perhaps Mexico's modest growth performance is less of a puzzle in light of the sharp and persistent fall in the terms of trade and the tremendous fiscal contraction that took place.

32. Inter-American Development Bank (1995); Easterly, Pritchett, and Summers (1993); Barro and Sala-i-Martin (1995); Mendoza (forthcoming).

Figure 3-4. Mexican Twelve-Month Inflation Rates

Percent

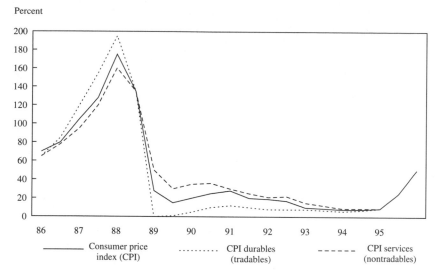

Source: Data provided by Banco de México.

—The monetary transmission of central bank policy is poorly under-
stood in the context of near-full indexation of the Chilean economy. In
Chile, virtually all financial assets, except those of short maturity, are
formally indexed to the CPI with a delay of about a month and a week,
through a unit of account known as the UF (identical to the UDIS recently
introduced in Mexico). So are the prices of durable goods and several
contractual services, such as school fees. The central bank conducts policy
by managing the indexed interest rate in short-term central bank paper, but
every study of the connection between this rate and the true real interest rate
of the economy (or between the behavior of interest rates, monetary aggre-
gates, and economic activity measures) has provided poor results.[33] Most
notably, the imperfections of the indexation mechanism imply that the key
UF interest rate has no resemblance to actual ex post and ex ante real
interest rates, as shown in figure 3-6. If, as I conjecture, this also implies
that prices in Chilean pesos may have little meaning, then the Chilean
peso–based CPI may also have little meaning, and so does the CPI-based
measure of Chile's real exchange rate.

33. Rosende and Herrera (1991); Rojas (1993); Mendoza (1992); Fernandez and
Mendoza (1994).

Figure 3-5. Terms of Trade between Chile and Mexico

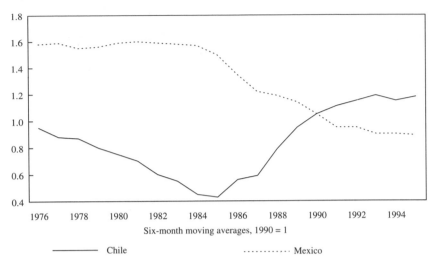

Six-month moving averages, 1990 = 1

——— Chile   ·········· Mexico

Source: World Bank (1996a).

About Sustainable Current Accounts

The rule of thumb that an upper bound for the current account deficit as a share of GDP (CA/Y) is determined by an "optimal" debt to GDP ratio (B/Y) of 40 percent multiplied by the "natural" rate of output growth (y) is highly appealing for its simplicity. Yet it only makes sense in the long run. At any other time frequency, particularly over the short run at which policymakers and the IMF worry about the effects of structural changes and exogenous shocks on the current account, it is a less than optimal rule.

The rule is formally correct when the economy has converged to the long-run, balanced growth path. At that point, CA/Y must be by necessity constant, and hence by definition CA/Y = y (B/Y). The key is to understand what determines y and B/Y in the long-run, balanced growth path, and how short-run debt accumulation relates to its long-run equilibrium. In this regard, recent empirical and theoretical work on transitional dynamics suggests that the date in which balanced-growth results hold can be in the distant future. It is not unusual to observe periods of transition of more than twenty-five years.[34] Consider Mexico as starting off as a "new country" when NAFTA was confirmed in late 1993. Clearly, expecting the rule of

34. King and Rebelo (1990); Cooley and Hansen (1992); Mendoza and Tesar (1995); Rebelo and Vegh (1995).

Figure 3-6. Chilean Interest Rates

Quarterly returns on 90- to 365-day loans, monthly financial system averages

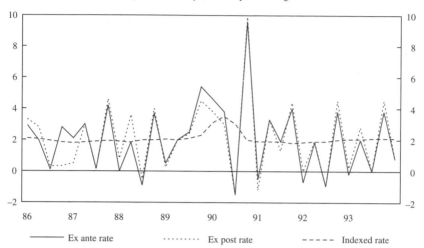

Ex ante rate ·········· Ex post rate – – – – Indexed rate

Note: Indexed rate is the quoted UF interest rate, the ex post rate is computed using the consumer price index, and the ex ante rate is based on the seasonally adjusted model of inflation estimated by Fernandez and Mendoza (1994).
Source: Data supplied by Banco Central de Chile.

thumb to hold any time "soon" after that would make little sense. We have shown that radical policy reforms produce current account deficits in excess of 6 percent of GDP even for large industrial countries where reforms are almost fully credible.[35]

One must also question the view in this chapter that we do not have secure theoretical foundations to analyze current account sustainability, in the sense of determining B/Y and its short-run dynamics. The principles of solvency and optimality of foreign borrowing at a basic level are no different from those of private or corporate borrowing, which date back to Irving Fisher's *Theory of Interest* and were recently examined in the context of current-account sustainability.[36] These principles define what is a sustainable current account path.

Solvency dictates that the present discounted value of the resources to be borrowed or lent (net of interest) must not exceed initial debt—that is, the present value of the trade balance must not exceed a country's current foreign debt. Optimality indicates that, although several current account paths are consistent with solvency, in most cases only one may satisfy the condition that the marginal costs and benefits of sacrificing a unit of current

35. Mendoza and Tesar (1995).
36. Milesi-Ferretti and Razin (1996).

consumption are equalized. The classic textbook example is the case of a small open economy without uncertainty in which investment faces adjustment costs and foreign borrowing can be undertaken at a constant real interest rate equal to the rate of time preference.[37] In such a case, detrended consumption is constant over time, whereas net output gradually rises towards the long-run, balanced-growth path. Large initial current account deficits are sustainable, in exchange for relatively small surpluses later on and a perpetual trade surplus sufficient to service the long-run foreign debt (figure 3-7). Clearly, in the short run forcing a country to keep its current account deficit no larger than implied by the long-run condition would be harmful for social welfare, particularly if the short run and the long run are a quarter century apart.

The problem is not that the theory is undeveloped but that its use in practice involves the familiar complications associated with uncertainty in financial markets (compounded by the special nature of the risks involved in international capital markets). That is, it could be that, as of 1993, assessments of Mexico's net worth hinted that a huge current account deficit was sustainable, but the news of 1994's political instability showed that Mexico's country credit rating was not that good. Similarly, a bad and persistent terms-of-trade shock could severely limit the repayment capacity of a country and force financial markets to reassess its creditworthiness.

There are recent advances in quantitative applications of the basic model just described that consider uncertainty, taxes and capital controls, and full-blown supply-side features that seem promising in providing the means to assess the sustainability of a large current account deficit in the short run.[38] As with the Dornbusch model, however, these models would still be hard pressed to explain the events that followed the December 1994 devaluation, but they do shed some light on what analyzing sustainability involves.

Variations of this sustainability model that introduce uncertainty with regard to the duration of stabilization policies and structural reforms can explain large external deficits and real appreciations as an endogenous outcome, resulting from the adverse effects of lack of credibility on the rewards for saving. In this class of models, a large foreign deficit is sustainable in the sense that at every point in time the intertemporal budget constraints hold and savings decisions are optimal. This is so even though

37. Blanchard and Fischer (1989).
38. See Mendoza (1991a , 1991b) and the survey by Baxter (1995).

Figure 3-7. Equilibrium Dynamics of the Small Open Economy

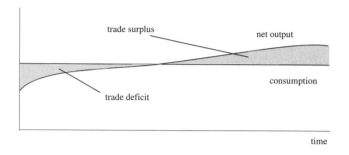

there is in fact a currency collapse at the end and agents know that with the collapse the foreign deficits will undertake an abrupt reversal. Economic agents do not dislike this outcome. In fact, estimates obtained show that for Mexico the experience was welfare improving relative to not having stabilized at all back in 1988, although much less so than if a fully credible plan could have been implemented.[39]

The qualifications to the rule of thumb that Williamson notes—dealing with problems of herd behavior, capital markets imperfections, and exogenous shocks (positive and negative) to capital flows—are additional examples of the factors that make current account sustainability hard to analyze from the perspective that I mentioned. These sort of issues are not "buts and ifs" that qualify the flows approach to explain payments crises, but are in fact the building blocks of a new theory. This new theory seeks to put together elements to explain how financial vulnerability emerges, how currency collapses arrive, and how collapses can be followed by deep and potentially protracted crisis in the real and financial sectors of the economy that can propagate through global equity markets. I have argued here, for example, that in Mexico's case credibility may explain the gradual emergence of vulnerability, that anticipation of banking-system problems may explain the currency collapse, and that herd behavior and self-fulfilling debt crises may explain why devaluation rather than the quick fix was the big problem. It is encouraging to see that recently several authors have focused on these issues. Consensus seems to be emerging that the next generation of payments crises will be crises of stocks and not crises of flows.

---

39. Mendoza and Uribe (1996).

General Discussion

Robert Blecker mentioned that since 1982 the Mexican economic growth rate was not only disappointing but dismal, especially in comparison with the previous twenty years. His main question was why there were reasons to be optimistic this time; did Mexico learn the lesson, and would it become another Chile? A similar concern was echoed by Sidney Weintraub. Although he acknowledged that the recovery was much quicker this time in terms of access to capital markets and exports were booming, the domestic economy was still doing poorly. Weintraub questioned whether the recovery could continue when it was so dependent on the performance of the export sector.

Several participants also questioned aspects of Williamson's analysis of the causes behind the deterioration of the current account deficit and lackluster growth in Mexico in the period before the crisis. Williamson argued that there were demand constraints associated to the exchange rate policy—that is, domestic tradeables became noncompetitive. However, Zia Qureshi argued that supply-side variables, such as slow productivity growth in the period after the structural reforms, accounted for much of the deterioration in the current account. Also, both Barry Bosworth and Sidney Weintraub argued that it was difficult to analyze the evolution of the current account deficit without focusing on the domestic saving and investment balance, which showed a rising gap caused primarily by the decline in domestic saving. Bosworth also suggested that a more relevant exercise could be to compare Mexico in the early 1990s with Chile in the 1979–83 period, when it was following policies similar to Mexico's before the crisis.

References

Adams, Charles, and Daniel Gros. 1986. "The Consequences of Real Exchange Rate Rules for Macroeconomic Stability: Some Illustrative Examples." IMF *Staff Papers* 33 (September): 439–76.
Aggarwal, Vinod K. 1989. "Interpreting the History of Mexico's External Crises." In *The International Debt Crisis in Historical Perspective*, edited by Barry Eichengreen and Peter H. Lindert, 140–88. MIT Press.
Banco de México. 1996. *The Mexican Economy*. Mexico City.
Barro, Robert J., and Xavier Sala-i-Martin. 1995. *Economic Growth*. McGraw-Hill.
Baxter, Marianne. 1995. "International Trade and Business Cycles." In *Handbook of International Economics* ,vol. III, edited by Gregory Grossman and Kenneth Rogoff, 1801–1864. North-Holland.

Blanchard, Olivier, and Stanley Fischer. 1989. *Lectures on Macroeconomics*. MIT Press.

Blecker, Robert A. 1996. "NAFTA, the Peso Crisis, and the Contradictions in the Mexican Economic Growth Strategy." Mimeo, American University.

Calvo, Guillermo A., and Mendoza, Enrique G. 1996. "Petty Crime and Cruel Punishment: Lessons from the Mexican Debacle." *American Economic Review* 86 (May, *Papers and Proceedings, 1996*): 170–75.

Calvo, Guillermo A., and Mendoza, Enrique G. Forthcoming. "Mexico's Balance of Payments Crisis: A Chronicle of a Death Foretold." *Journal of International Economics*.

Chari, V. V., and Patrick J. Kehoe. 1996. "Hot Money." Federal Reserve Bank of Minneapolis.

Claessens, Stijn, Michael P. Dooley, and Andrew Warner. 1994. "Portfolio Capital Flows: Hot or Cool?" *World Bank Economics Review* 9 (1): 153–74.

Cole, Harold L., and Timothy Kehoe. Forthcoming. "Self-Fulfilling Debt Crisis." *Journal of International Economics*.

Cooley, Thomas F., and Gary D. Hansen. 1992. "Tax Distortions in a Neoclassical Monetary Economy." *Journal of Economic Theory* 58 (December): 290–316.

Corbo, Vittorio, Jaime de Melo, and James Tybout. 1986. "What Went Wrong with the Recent Reforms in the Southern Cone." *Economic Development and Cultural Change* 34 (3): 607–40.

Corden, W. Max. 1994. *Economic Policy, Exchange Rates, and the International System*. University of Chicago Press.

Dornbusch, Rudiger. 1982. "Stabilization Policies in Developing Countries: What Have We Learned?" *World Development* 10 (September): 701–708.

Dornbusch, Rudiger, and Alejandro Werner. 1994. "Mexico: Stabilization, Reform, and No Growth." *Brookings Papers on Economic Activity* 1: 253–315.

Easterly, William K., Lant M. Pritchett, and Lawrence Summers. 1993. "Good Policy or Good Luck? Country Growth Performance and Temporary Shocks." *Journal of Monetary Economics* 32: 459–84.

Fernandez, Fernando, and Enrique G. Mendoza. 1994. "Monetary Transmission and Financial Indexation: Evidence from the Chilean Economy." PPAA No. 94/17. Washington: International Monetary Fund.

Ffrench-Davis, Ricardo. 1983. "The Monetarist Experiment in Chile: A Critical Survey." *World Development* 11 (November): 905–926.

Ffrench-Davis, Ricardo, Manuel Agosin, and Andras Uthoff. 1995. "Capital Movements, Export Strategy, and Macroeconomic Stability in Chile." In *Coping with Capital Surges*, edited by Ricardo Ffrench-Davis and Stephany Griffith-Jones, 99–144. Boulder, Colo.: Lynne Reiner.

Frankel, Jeffrey A., and Andrew K. Rose. 1995. "Exchange Rate Crashes in Emerging Markets: An Empirical Treatment." University of California at Berkeley, Department of Economics.

Inter-American Development Bank. 1995. "Macroeconomic Volatility in Latin America: Causes, Consequences and Policies to Assure Stability." Washington: Office of the Chief Economist.

International Monetary Fund. 1996a. *International Financial Statistics*. Washington.

_____. 1996b. *Government Financial Statistics*. Washington.

King, Robert G., and Sergio T. Rebelo. 1990. "Public Policy and Economics Growth: Developing Neoclassical Implications." *Journal of Political Economy* 98 (October, part 2): S126–S150.

Labán, Raúl, and Felipe Larraín. 1993. "Can a Liberalization of Capital Outflows Increase Net Capital Inflows?" Documento de Trabajo 155. Santiago, Chile: Catholic University.

McKinnon, Ronald I., and Huw Pill. 1995. "Credible Liberalizations and International Capital Flows: The Over-borrowing Syndrome." Stanford University, Department of Economics.

Meller, Patricio. 1990. "Three Policy Experiments: Chile." In *Latin American Adjustment: How Much Has Happened?*, edited by John Williamson, 54–85. Washington: Institute for International Economics.

Mendoza, Enrique G. 1991a. "Real Business Cycles in a Small Open Economy." *American Economic Review* 81 (4, *Papers and Proceedings, 1991*): 797–818.

_____. 1991b. "Capital Controls and the Gains from Trade in a Business Cycle Model of a Small Open Economy." *IMF Staff Papers* 38: 480–505.

_____. 1992. "Fisherian Transmission and Efficient Arbitrage under Partial Financial Indexation: The Case of Chile." *IMF Staff Papers* 39 (1): 121–47.

_____. 1995. "The Terms of Trade, the Real Exchange Rate and Economic Fluctuations." *International Economic Review* 36: 101–137.

_____. Forthcoming. "Terms-of-Trade Uncertainty and Economic Growth: Are Risk Indicators Significant in Growth Regressions?" *Journal of Development Economics*.

Mendoza, Enrique G., and Linda L. Tesar. 1995. "Supply-Side Economics in a Global Economy." Working Paper 5086. Cambridge, Mass: National Bureau of Economic Research (April).

Mendoza, Enrique G., and Martin Uribe. 1996. "The Syndrome of Exchange-Rate-Based Stabilizations and the Uncertain Duration of Currency Pegs." IFDP No. 548. Washington: Board of Governors of the Federal Reserve System.

Milesi-Ferretti, Gian Maria, and Assaf Razin. 1996. "Sustainability of Persistent Current Account Deficits." Working Paper 5467. Cambridge, Mass.: National Bureau of Economic Research (February).

Milesi-Ferretti, Gian Maria, and Assaf Razin. Forthcoming. *Current Account Sustainability*. Princeton Essays in International Economics.

Rebelo, Sergio T., and Carlos A. Végh. 1995. "Real Effects of Exchange-Rate-Based Stabilization: An Analysis of Competing Theories." *NBER Macro Annual*. Cambridge, Mass.: National Bureau of Economic Research.

Rodriguez, Carlos A. 1982. "The Argentine Stabilization Plan of December 20th." *World Development* 10: 801–811.

Rojas, Patricio. 1993. "El Dinero como un Objetivo Intermedio de la Politica Monetaria en Chile." *Cuadernos de Economia* 30 (90): 139–78.

Rosende, Francisco, and Luis O. Herrera. 1991. "Teoria y Politica Monetaria: Elementos para el Analisis." *Cuadernos de Economia* 83: 55–93.

Sachs, Jeffrey, Aaron Tornell, and Andres Velasco. Forthcoming. "Mexico's Crisis: Sudden Death or Death Foretold?" *Journal of International Economics*.

World Bank. 1996a. *World Tables, 1995*. Washington.

_____. 1996b. *World Debt Tables, 1996*. Washington.

4 United States–Mexico Relations: Environmental Issues

Juan Carlos Belausteguigoitia and Luis F. Guadarrama

THE history of United States relations with Mexico has always been complex. From territorial feuds to economic interdependence, the relationship has reflected a wide range of strategies, varying from open confrontation to fruitful cooperation. Furthermore, the binational agenda has gained complexity since January 1, 1994, when Canada, the United States, and Mexico formed a subhemispheric free trade region, the North American Free Trade Agreement (NAFTA). Although environmental issues were a controversial aspect of that agreement, they actually have a much longer history in U.S.–Mexico relations; and, notwithstanding their complexity, this part of the relationship has evolved mostly along a path of cooperation. For instance, the environment has often been the subject (sometimes the only one) on which any agreements are reached in the yearly meetings between the presidents of the United States and Mexico.[1] This chapter is an effort to analyze the history of this relationship, the NAFTA challenges and opportunities, and the way the relationship should develop in the future.

In the first part of this chapter, we outline the major issues that dominate the environmental agenda and provide a brief description of the existing forums in which they are addressed. We then analyze in greater detail the context in which some of these issues and their respective instruments arise, explaining why we believe that cooperation will be more effective than confrontation and how it can yield better results. Finally, we sum up the main findings and perspectives on the environmental agenda shared by Mexico and the United States. As support for this discussion, we provide additional information in six appendixes on the specific cooperation efforts and instruments in the binational environmental agenda, as well as a history

---

1. See Sánchez (1988). The author points out that during the most difficult times in the U.S.–Mexico relationship recently—that is, between 1983 and 1986—the environment was the only issue on which any agreement was reached.

91

of the Mexican institutional framework for evaluating and implementing environmental policies.

The Issues

Four broad issues dominate the bilateral environmental agenda: border pollution, pollution havens, common environmental standards, and the impact of trade liberalization on the environment.

Border Pollution

Border pollution has long been an important element of the common environmental agenda between the United States and Mexico. There is also a long history of cooperation between the two countries on the most important specifics of this issue. The problem of access to common water sources and the definition of international boundaries prompted the creation of International Border and Water Commissions (IBWC and Comisión Internacional de Límites y Aguas [CILA] in Mexico) in each country.[2] Since 1944, the commissions have had a strong environmental aspect because of problems like the increased salinity of the Colorado River. More recently, in 1983, the Border Environmental Cooperation Agreement (known as the La Paz Agreement) was created to address, in five annexes (presented in appendix B to this chapter), the most important environmental issues facing the border:

—Sewage flows from Tijuana to some parts of San Diego;

—Hazardous waste spills on the land segment of the border;

—Transportation of hazardous wastes between Mexico and the United States;

—Trans-boundary air pollution caused by copper smelters located along the border, in what is known as the "Gray Triangle" in southern Arizona and northern Sonora; and

—Urban air pollution in twin border cities.[3]

In the process of establishing NAFTA, three new organizations were created to address border issues. The Integrated Border Environmental Program (IBEP) and its successor, the Border XXI Program, provide the

2. A complete description of the IBWC is found in appendix A.

3. A complete description of each of the annexes of the La Paz Agreement, and their performance in addressing the specific problem, is provided in appendix B.

guidelines for binational cooperation along the border.[4] This cooperation is mainly directed toward small investment and study projects. The Border Ecological Cooperation Commission (BECC) and the North American Development Bank (NADBank) were created to address the lack of an environmental infrastructure (water, sanitary, and waste facilities) in the border area.[5] The BECC helps in the design of projects that may then be financed in part by NADBank and in part by private investors.

Pollution Havens

There is widespread concern regarding the effects that different environmental regulatory frameworks might have on the incentives firms have to locate in one country or another, and on the level of competitiveness of existing firms operating in different countries. This issue and its potential effects on financial flows within North America were important to the NAFTA negotiations. Specific concerns included the perception that Mexico had weaker environmental laws and enforcement that might promote business relocation. In addition, by promoting relocation of "dirty" industries rather than compliance with the stronger standards, there would be a negative overall effect on the environment. (Later we argue that these concerns are overstated and should not be regarded as pressing issues in the environmental agenda.)

In any case, one provision of NAFTA explicitly states that each country has the right to establish its own environmental controls on any investment made in its own territory. NAFTA also prohibits the lowering of environmental standards to attract and maintain investment. Furthermore, the North American Agreement on Environmental Cooperation (NAAEC) and the Commission on Environmental Cooperation (CEC) were designed to supplement the environmental provisions and objectives of NAFTA, further ensuring that trade liberalization will not come at the expense of environmental protection.[6] The NAAEC establishes a framework for trilateral cooperation on environmental matters and commits the parties to effective enforcement of their respective environmental laws. The CEC was

4. A more complete description of both these programs, their objectives, their means, and their performance is found in appendix C.

5. A further description of these instruments is found in appendix D.

6. A further description of the objectives and instruments of the CEC is found in appendix E.

created as an operating body to carry out the objectives of the NAAEC and the environmental provisions within NAFTA.

Standards

The push for freer trade under NAFTA heightened concerns about its potentially adverse impact on broad social goals, raising questions about the need for common standards on health, safety, and environmental quality that would extend across national borders. The concerns are concentrated in two areas. First, high product standards in the United States could be challenged as protectionist measures, leading to pressures to lower the standards as part of a move toward greater harmonization. In addition, although product standards have long played a major role in international trade agreements, process and production methods (PPM) standards (which are critical to many environmental concerns) are not as prominently specified. One example is provided by the dispute over dolphins caught in tuna nets. The main reason for the U.S. embargo on tuna imports from Mexico was that in the production process, Mexican tuna catchers killed large numbers of dolphins. Mexico challenged this embargo for (among many reasons) its reliance on process standards, and a General Agreement on Tariffs and Trade (GATT) panel ruled in Mexico's favor.

Inside NAFTA, these issues were addressed with provisions that ensure that the United States, Mexico, and Canada can maintain and enforce their existing federal and state health, safety, and environmental standards, as well as all international treaty obligations.

Impact of Trade Liberalization on the Environment

Controversy arises from the idea that liberalized trade, by increasing economic activity, may have negative effects on the environment on a global scale. Yet others argue that trade, by allocating the resources more efficiently, may have a positive environmental effect. Environmentalists on both sides of the border are still debating these issues. But all NAFTA partners accept that although free trade might improve the environment though better allocation of resources and an overall increase in income levels among the three partners, free trade is not a surrogate for well-designed, tightly enforced environmental policy.

In Mexico there is some concern about the effects free trade may have on the sectoral composition of output. Mexico's lower effective standards may raise growth in the more pollution-intensive sectors. A heavy reliance on comparative advantages may produce an excessive concentration of production in a few goods, mainly in the agricultural sector.

Some of these concerns are addressed through the Commission on Environmental Cooperation, which is charged with assessing the environmental impacts of NAFTA and assuring that each country's own environmental regulations are enforced. The NAFTA provisions also emphasize that in any conflict between NAFTA and environmental agreements in which any of the parties is a participant, the latter will prevail. This applies to agreements such as the Montreal Protocol, the Basel Convention, and the Convention on International Trade in Endangered Species (CITES).

The Context

In this section we provide a more detailed discussion of the issues, including a summary of the socioeconomic and environmental situation in the border area. For the other three issues (pollution havens, standards, and the effects of trade on the environment), we present some findings on how they relate on the binational and global levels.

The Border Area

The border between Mexico and the United States extends almost 3,200 kilometers from the Pacific Ocean to the Gulf of Mexico. The border region, as defined in 1983 in the Border Environmental Cooperation Agreement (the La Paz Agreement), is the area within one hundred kilometers of the border. It includes parts of the Mexican states of Baja California, Sonora, Chihuahua, Coahuila, Nuevo León, and Tamaulipas, and of the U.S. states of California, Arizona, New Mexico, and Texas. About 10,574,000 people live in this region, 51 percent in Mexico and 49 percent in the United States.

Almost 90 percent of the population in the border region lives in urban zones, and often in "Twin Cities" formed by the pairing of one Mexican city with one American city. There are fourteen Twin Cities representing the main industrial and commercial centers of the border region. The population is highly concentrated in San Diego and Imperial counties in California, in the municipalities of Tijuana, Tecate, and Mexicali in Mexico, and in the Ciudad Juárez–El Paso zone. Around 60 percent of the border population lives in these zones. In the rest of the region the population density is less than four people per square kilometer.

Population growth in both sides of the border region is higher than the rate of general population growth in each country. Between 1950 and 1980 the population tripled on the Mexican side and doubled on the U.S. side. It is estimated that population in the Mexican side will double within the next twenty years (table 4-1).

Despite the differences in population growth, the levels of poverty on the Mexican side of the border region remain lower than the national average. Specifically, indicators of water access, private home ownership, access to a sewage system, and access to electric energy (as proxies to poverty indicators) show that the border region ranks above the national average (table 4-2).

Income levels in the U.S. border region income levels are more than double those of the Mexican side, reaching even a greater differential in the San Diego–Tijuana region, where the income level on the U.S. side is 6.5 times the Mexican level.[7]

Economic growth on the Mexican side of the border has been based mainly in the maquiladora industry, a type of production unit devised in the 1960s under the National Border Plan (Programa Nacional Fronterizo). These plants can import raw materials, components, and capital goods free of import duties, then take advantage of low labor costs and assemble the finished goods. These goods must then be exported, and the wastes generated by the imported materials must be returned to the plant's country of origin (annex 3 of the La Paz Agreement [see appendix B to this chapter]).

Most maquiladora plants are owned by U.S. firms. This program grew substantially in the 1980s, when most other productive sectors faced serious stagnation. Currently, there are more than 2,000 maquiladora plants employing more than 500,000 people. About 12 percent of the national manufacturing sector jobs are located in the border municipalities. The most important maquiladora industry sectors are electronics components and transport equipment.

State of the Environment[8]

Unfortunately, in recent decades the rapid economic and population growth in the border region has exceeded the growth in the capacity to control and prevent pollution as well as to preserve and manage natural resources. The region faces a multitude of environmental problems: deteri-

---

7. Secretaría de Desarollo Social (SEDESOL) (1995).
8. Secretaría de Medio Ambiente, Recursos Naturales y Pesca (SEMARNAP) (1996).

Table 4-1. Population of the Border Region

Country	Population (thousands)		Annual growth rate, 1990–95 (percent)	
	1990	1995	Border region	National
United States	4,412	5,230	3.4	1.0
Mexico	3,889	5,344	5.4	1.9

Source: Instituto Nacional de Estadística, Geografía e Informática de Mexico (INEGI) (1990).

oration of ecosystems, depletion of water resources, water pollution, air pollution, and management of solid and hazardous wastes.

DETERIORATION OF ECOSYSTEMS AND BIODIVERSITY EXHAUSTION. Mexico and the United States share abundant natural resources in their border region. Although desert-type habitat predominates, the climate and the topographic diversity observed in the mountain and coastal areas creates a variety of habitats, including forests, pastures, wetlands, deserts, marine ecosystems, and mangroves. The biological diversity is enormous, including 400 endemic species, 700 neotropical migratory species, and 85 endangered species. Both governments have established protected natural areas to promote the conservation of the region's biodiversity. But this biodiversity has been affected by deforestation, urban growth, tourism, cattle raising, illegal hunting, illegal trade of endemic and threatened species, and the introduction of exotic species.

DEPLETION OF WATER RESOURCES. The border region includes two important watersheds: the Bravo/Grande River and the Colorado River. Other water bodies in the region include the Tijuana, Nuevo, Alamo, Gila, Santa Cruz, San Pedro, Yaqui, Casas Grandes, Conchos, Pecos, Salado, and San Juan rivers, as well as twenty-five underground watersheds feeding wet zones with important natural biological systems. However, water is scarce in almost the entire border region because of the booming population and the growing economy. Soil erosion and water salinity are also increasingly significant problems.

WATER POLLUTION. Water pollution is one of the most important issues facing the border region. Municipal and agricultural waste waters are discharged into several waterways without adequate treatment. Although industrial wastes are better controlled than before, some are still discharged into waterways. One major concern (and one where substantial effort is being directed) is to install additional water treatment plants along the border region. The existing capacity of treatment plants is only 34 percent of demand. Annex 1 of the La Paz Agreement created a procedure to finance and construct a treatment plant to reduce contamination along parts of the San Diego shore caused by Tijuana's wastewater. The treatment plant

Table 4-2. Comparative Poverty Indicators for the Border Region, 1990

| | Percentage of population with | | | Ratio of private home ownership to total population |
	Direct access to drinkable water	Access to sewage system	Access to electric energy	
Mexico	79.4	63.6	87.5	19.7
Mexican border region	85.5	68.1	89.3	21.6

Source: INEGI (1990).

is under construction and is projected to start service in 1997 (see annex 2 in appendix B). In addition, BECC and NADBank are currently involved in the financing of a series of treatment plants in several cities along the border (see annex 4 in appendix B for a description and assessment of their efforts).

AIR POLLUTION.   The air pollutants of greatest concern in the border region's urban zones are particulate matter (specifically PM10), carbon monoxide (CO), ozone (O_3) and sulfur dioxide (SO_2). On the U.S. side, several border cities such as El Paso, Doña Ana County, Imperial County, San Diego, Douglas, Nogales, and Yuma on the U.S. side do not comply with the air quality standards set by the U.S. Environmental Protection Agency. Similarly, the Mexican cities of Tijuana, Mexicali, San Luis Río Colorado, Nogales, Agua Prieta, and Ciudad Juárez do not comply with domestic air quality standards set by Mexico's National Institute of Ecology (INE).

Annex 5 of the La Paz Agreement introduced an innovative approach to the problem of air pollution in the Twin Cities of El Paso–Ciudad Juárez (see appendix B). It created an international resource management basin in which the two cities cooperate in monitoring pollution levels. This also raises the potential for future harmonization of air quality standards within a binational air quality control district (see appendix B at the end of this chapter for a more detailed explanation).

SOLID AND HAZARDOUS WASTES.   A major matter of concern is the lack of infrastructure for solid and hazardous waste management: treatment plants, landfill sites, and burning plants. This induces inadequate waste disposal and imposes severe threats to the environment and human health. In one survey, 1,673 firms were identified as generating sources for the estimated 80,000 tons of hazardous wastes in the Mexican border region.[9] About 90 percent of these firms were maquiladoras. It was estimated that in 1990 only 21 percent of the generating firms that are supposed

9. SEDESOL (1994).

to return their hazardous wastes to the United States actually did so. Of the generating firms, 5.4 percent correctly disposed of their wastes in Mexico, and the rest did not declare where their waste disposal sites were. The General Attorney for the Environment (PROFEPA) has reported some major improvements in the enforcement of annex 3 of the La Paz Agreement (see appendix B for the most recent data on compliance). Finally, the BECC and NADBank have been studying ways to provide financing of waste treatment plants; but they are not currently financing any project (see appendix D for further details).

Pollution Havens and Standards

Despite the common recognition that international trade is one of the foremost contributors to higher levels of economic activity and income, many believe that freer trade can be harmful to the environment. For example, there is a perception that weak environmental laws and low health and safety standards are a source of competitive gain. As there are less compliance costs in a regime with low standards, industries will migrate to those "pollution havens," contributing to more environmental damage. There may also be jobs and investment losses in the countries or regions with more strict environmental standards. Alternatively, the competitive losses and arguments that high standards are a form of disguised protectionism may create strong pressures to lower the higher standards to the level of those that are less stringent so that they may more readily find a minimum common denominator.

Competitiveness

National industries and firms gain or lose competitive advantages over time as a result of a variety of factors, among which environmental requirements are only one small element. (For example, environmental control costs represent only about 1.1 percent of the total value added of U.S. industry). Furthermore, protection and subsidies—one interpretation of weak environmental requirements—are generally viewed to breed inefficiency on the long run. An example is provided by noting that the proportion of "dirty" industries is higher in closed economies than in those economies open to trade.[10] High levels of environmental protection can have positive effects on the competitiveness of domestic producers and

10. See Lucas, Wheeler, and Hettige (1992).

countries. Properly crafted environmental regulation and adequately designed standards can promote continuous technological change, cleaner production methods, and greater efficiency.[11] They can also promote development of new industrial sectors to provide environmental equipment and services. Finally, countries with high environmental standards are likely to enjoy a comparative advantage in the growing international market for environmentally friendly products and services.

Standards

This discussion suggests that competitive pressures to reduce product standards to a minimal common denominator are of minor importance. However, increased reliance on PPM standards (which control the way products are manufactured and processed and natural resources extracted) are often seen as protectionist and not useful in achieving global or regional environmental protection. This is because most PPMs have local effects and only infrequently have an impact across national boundaries. When PPM standards are set by national regulation, they are established according to their effects on the domestic economy and environment; normally, their impact is not felt across a national boundary. This is in contrast with product standards, which do have an impact when the product is exported. When PPM standards are set at the international level, nonenvironmental objectives (such as trade protection) have predominated, leaving little role for environmental objectives.[12] When there are effects of PPMs across national boundaries, they are best addressed through international cooperation, as the U.S.–Mexico Border Area experience has shown, and not by incorporating PPM standards into trade agreements. The Montreal Protocol is a positive example of this type of international cooperation, whereas the tuna harvesting dispute is an example of the difficulties that arise with a confrontational approach.

It is important to stress that variations in national environmental regulations reflect differing environmental and development conditions as well as preferences, priorities, and values. These differences must be recognized when designing different strategies and instruments for achieving environmental objectives. It is especially true for the comparison of U.S. and Mexican environmental regulations.

11. See Porter and van der Linde (1995).
12. See Organization for Economic Cooperation and Development (OECD) (1995).

The U.S. Environmental Protection Agency undertook a comparison of U.S. and Mexican environmental laws covering water, air, hazardous waste, pesticides, and industrial chemicals.[13] The report concluded that, overall, the U.S. and Mexican regulatory regimes aimed at comparable levels of environmental protection. Thus, although Mexico and the United States appear to have different priorities and preferences, their regulatory regimes cannot have major effects on competitiveness.[14] "Mexico's environmental laws, regulations and standards are in many respects similar to those of the United States. The 1988 General Law of Ecological Balance and Environmental Protection embodies many principles and approaches similar to ours. The regulations and technical standards implementing the Mexican law are generally comparable to their counterparts in the United States, although each regime includes provisions that the other lack. To the extent that differences in scope are due to the early stage of development of Mexico's program, it would be too early to draw conclusions about overall stringency or comparability."[15]

The environmental authorities in Mexico have taken strong steps toward better resource management. They have acknowledged the potential benefits of a well-designed regulatory system in promoting competitiveness and in capturing the intrinsic benefits of free trade on a sustainable basis.

Industrial Migration

According to the hypothesis regarding the existence of "pollution havens," "dirty" industries could have incentives to establish themselves in those countries or regions with the least stringent environmental requirements. Although it seems plausible, up to now there has been little evidence on the issue.[16] Some studies point out that the differential costs of environmental compliance have played a minor role in decisions on plant locations. A study made by the United States Trade Representative in 1992 concluded that on the state level (within the United States) as well as internationally,

13. See Office of the President of the United States (1993).
14. The OECD stresses that "high levels of environmental protection can have positive effects on competitiveness," although it also recognizes that there are "concerns over the potential loss of competitiveness—whether real or perceived" from different levels of environmental protection.
15. OECD (1995, p. 25).
16. See Jaffe and others (1995); Lucas, Wheeler, and Hettige (1992), where the authors argue that any displacement of toxic intensity toward developing countries may have been the result of restrictive trade policies rather than regulatory cost differences; and Birdsall and Wheeler (1992).

investment patterns have not been significantly affected by differences in environmental control costs.[17] This study suggested that the conditions that should exist to make migration attractive to an industry include the following:

—Environmental costs should constitute a great share of total operating costs;

—Existing trade barriers should be considerable;

—Costs associated with relocation should not be high; and

—Differences in environmental control costs should be large and expected to remain so. Evidence suggests that these conditions rarely exist in the U.S.–Mexico trade relationship.

According to the same study, environmental control costs represent about 1.1 percent of the total value added of U.S. industry. Furthermore, 86 percent of U.S. industry has a pollution abatement cost of less than 2 percent. Most of the industries with higher control costs already have low trade barriers relative to their Mexican competitors. Only eleven of 442 industrial sectors had both high trade barriers and high control costs. These eleven sectors are highly intensive in the use of capital. Finally, Mexican environmental requirements are significantly more strict than only a few years ago and will become more stringent in the future.[18]

Effects of Trade Liberalization on the Environment

An open, equitable, secure, nondiscriminatory, and predictable multilateral trading system supported with sustainable policies benefits all trading partners.[19] In general terms, trade liberalization will have a positive impact on the environment by improving allocation of resources, promoting economic growth, and increasing welfare, provided effective environmental policies are implemented. A recent report from the Organization for Economic Cooperation and Development (OECD) identified five categories of trade-related effects on the environment:

Scale: freer trade increases the amount of resources available for environmental protection as well as promoting investment in environmental technologies;

17. See United States Trade Representative (1992).
18. For a description on the evolution of the institutional framework governing Mexican environmental policy, see appendix F.
19. United Nations Conference on Environment and Development (1992).

Structural: freer trade improves allocative efficiency among, and within, countries;

Product: freer trade facilitates the sale and transfer of environmentally-friendly goods and services;

Technology: freer trade can facilitate the transfer of environmentally-friendly technologies and improve environmental management capacity;

Regulatory: freer trade can help in establishing rules that may affect the design and implementation of environmental policies.[20]

However, all of these potential gains require an integration of trade and environmental policies. That is, the beneficial effects of liberalizing trade require internalization of the relevant environmental costs, removal of distortions, and promotion of cooperative efforts.

As economies develop, the economic sectors in which they have a comparative advantage shifts because of modifications in factor endowments, improvements in human capital, and technological change.[21] It is possible that the changes in the sectoral composition of output could lead to an increase in the pollution intensive industries. However, on the one hand the available evidence suggests that pollution intensity (the amount of emissions per unit of output) has grown most rapidly in developing countries that were relatively closed to trade and had high rates of growth. On the other hand, shifts toward less pollution-intensive sectoral composition have been observed in relatively open economies with relatively high income levels. At low income levels, the growth in gross domestic product (GDP) leads to an even greater growth in emission levels. But as income levels continue to rise, the growth of emissions tends to slow and overall pollution intensity tends to decrease. As trade increases income and the openness of the economy broadens, we should therefore expect a shift in sectoral composition toward less pollution-intensive commodities.[22]

One way to examine the extent to which Mexican experience corresponds to this model is to look at the evolution of its exports to the United States. We classify an industry's pollution intensity with a damage index that varies from 1 to 10, with 10 being a high level of damage. The most important export sectors according to their growth and share of exports to the United States from 1991 to 1995 are the following:

20. See OECD (1995).
21. See Lucas, Wheeler, and Hettige (1992).
22. Lucas, Wheeler, and Hettige (1992).

—Metal Goods and Machinery   Damage index : 5
—Textiles, Apparel, and Footwear   Damage index : 3
—Food, Beverages, and Tobacco   Damage index : 2
—Basic Metal Products   Damage index : 4
—Paper and Printed Goods   Damage index : 4

The most important import sectors according to their growth and share of imports from the United States from 1991 to 1995 are the following:

—Chemical, Rubber and Plastics   Damage index : 7
—Metal Goods and Machinery   Damage index : 5
—Textiles, Apparel, and Footwear   Damage index : 3
—Other Manufactures[23]   Damage index : —
—Food, Beverages and Tobacco   Damage index : 2

As a point of reference, the oil refining sector has an overall damage index of 9, and its share of Mexico's exports has been declining since the mid-1980s.

A preliminary assessment of these data shows that the sectorial composition of Mexican exports to the United States is not tilted toward heavily polluting products, at least not relative to the sectoral composition of U.S. exports to Mexico. Further analysis is needed to accurately assess this issue.

Benefits of Cooperation

The solution to the environmental concerns of Mexico and the United States requires a collective effort and not just unilateral action. Achievement of environmental objectives will require a mix of positive inducements, ranging from constructive diplomacy to financial inputs. In general, economic sanctions are poor instruments for advancing the implementation of border environmental agreements. Moreover, the threat of sanctions can be a deterrent to reaching cooperative environmental agreements.[24] Although cooperation between the United States and Mexico on environmental aspects has been the norm and has brought positive results, there is room for improvement. Episodes such as the tuna harvesting dispute, in which the environmental gains came at a high cost, could be settled in a more cost-effective way.

Environmental agreements at the international level represent one of the most complex kinds of negotiations. The list of environmental problems

23. No specific index has been assigned to this sector; it may range from light to medium impact.
24. See Mumme (1993).

requiring attention grows longer every day: trans-boundary air pollution, deforestation, desertification and drought, conservation of biological diversity, protection of the oceans and seas, traffic in toxic and dangerous products and wastes, and so on. Yet international agreements on these issues have produced little improvement because it takes so long to achieve international cooperation. Moreover, environmental protection strategies that seemed appropriate when they were negotiated may no longer be relevant when the agreement is in place.[25]

In addition to the usual barriers to expeditious policymaking posed by bureaucracies and interest groups, international agreements face additional obstacles. These include conflicts between developed and developing countries, the persistence of national sovereignty as a goal unto itself, and the lack of sufficient incentives to bring countries to the negotiating table. These three problems are related to the international legal system, and they are part of the reason for pessimism regarding future cooperation to manage shared resources such as the oceans, space, the atmosphere, or the diversity of species. In addition, our incomplete knowledge of environmental problems serves as a deterrent to quick action.

NORTH-SOUTH CONFLICTS.   The disagreements are not simply over money or making new technologies available on favorable terms to developing countries. Although the North wants a focus on equal effort at the margin to reduce environmental damage, the South points to the cumulative effect on the environment over time and the income in the North and seeks some redistribution of the available resources. That is, the United States would find it relatively easy to meet a target for pollution output that is marginally below the current level, whereas Mexico is favored by a standard of equal per capital effluents.

SOVEREIGNTY.   The conflicts over sovereignty refer to the efforts nations make not only to maintain control over all actions within their geopolitical borders but also to have autonomy over actions that affect common areas and resources. As a consequence, many international agreements incorporate weak monitoring and enforcement provisions.

INCENTIVES FOR COOPERATION.   Some countries perceive little or no benefit to participating in international agreement. They are potential free riders that benefit from an environmentally safer world without sharing any of the attendant responsibility or cost. Furthermore, the benefits of pollution control efforts often accrue long after the costs are incurred, yielding weak political incentives. A significant portion of the funds pro-

25. See Susskind (1994).

vided through international organizations and development banks for pollution abatement projects are not being used.

SCIENTIFIC UNCERTAINTY.   Environmental issues often involve a high degree of scientific uncertainty, which complicates decisionmaking. For example, if a country wants to delay implementation of costly pollution abatement measures, it can always call for further study before long-term commitments are made.

In view of these difficulties, international agreements need to focus on creating positive ways in which countries will gain if they cooperate. Agreement should be kept flexible, with established procedures (such as annexes or appendices) for revisions as more information becomes available. This would make it possible to avoid a new round of ratification every time the terms of a treaty need to be refined in light of new developments.

Finally, in the process of international environmental negotiation, there is an expanded role for social organizations and the international community. Nongovernmental interests play an increasingly important role in crafting environmental treaties, offering new points of view and helping to achieve more balanced, fairer agreements. It is greatly advisable to include the opinions of nongovernmental organizations during the negotiations.[26] But things should not end there; facilitating their role in subsequent stages of the relationship is also essential. As an example, these organizations are an invaluable help in postnegotiation monitoring: they can hold countries accountable for the promises they make in a treaty.

Conclusions

Environmental issues in the Mexico–U.S. relationship have evolved from a focus on trans-boundary pollution issues to an emphasis on the link between environmental concerns and trade, including the effect environmental standards have on competitiveness. Because of the confrontational way in which these last issues have been dealt with, not only bilaterally but globally, many would think that conflict is a common and unavoidable feature of environmental policymaking. Such is the pattern as the trade and environment issue arises in forums such as the World Trade Organization, the Organization for Economic Cooperation and Development, and the United Nations.

In contrast, with respect to their common border, Mexico and the United States have shown that environmental challenges can be met through cooperation. Examples are provided by the El Paso–Ciudad Juárez common air

26. See Susskind and Ozawa (1992).

quality management basin, and the La Paz Agreement. There may be an element of conflict, but the focus has been on cooperation for a wide range of environmental issues: border, competitiveness, and trade. Significant differences exist between the two countries in their stages of economic development, their preferences, their priorities, and their institutional and financial capacity. These relative conditions cannot be expected to change dramatically even in the medium to long term, but a cooperative approach to common problems cannot be ruled out.

Appendix A
The International Border and Water Commissions (IBWC and CILA)

In 1889, the governments of Mexico and the United States signed a treaty creating the International Border and Water Commissions (IBWC) with the intent of solving border disputes between the two countries caused by the changing course of both Colorado and Grande (Bravo) rivers. The IBWC remains in operation to this day.

The commission's mandate was modified in 1944 with the signing of the Treaty on Water Use from the Colorado, Tijuana, and Grande rivers (known as the Water Treaty). Essentially the first dealing with joint U.S. and Mexican environmental issues, the key issues of this agreement were the salinization of the Colorado river, the poor quality of the water that reached Mexico, and water pollution in the Bravo/Grande river. Besides dispute settlement provisions, the IBWC acquired new functions dealing with the quality, conservation, and use of water resources along the entire length of the U.S.–Mexican border.

The IBWC is the oldest and most established environmental agreement between Mexico and the United States. It provides the institutional basis for the management of surface water quality, sewage, and sanitation problems and establishes a partial regime for managing floods and droughts on the Grande/Bravo and Colorado rivers. It fosters binational solutions to common environmental problems as they emerge and provoke public concern along the border. It does not, however, identify specific and emerging environmental problems, prioritize them, or create additional consultative bodies to advise either government on these issues.

The IBWC is made up of one U.S. chapter (IBWC proper) and one Mexican chapter (CILA—Comisión Internacional de Límites y Aguas). These commissions are part of the Department of State of the United States and of the Ministry of External Relations (Secretaría de Relaciones Exteriores) of Mexico, respectively.

Appendix B
Border Environmental Cooperation Agreement
(La Paz Agreement)

Signed in August 1983 in the city of La Paz in the Mexican state of Baja
California Sur, the La Paz Agreement established a framework for cooperation on the prevention, reduction and elimination of air, water, and soil
pollution along the border. As opposed to the IBWC, the La Paz Agreement
allowed for the identification of the most important environmental issues
and the creation of consultative bodies to deal with them. The agreement's
stated objective is to "establish a cooperative mechanism to preserve and
foster the environment along the common border, based on principles of
equality, reciprocity, and mutual benefit." The general goals are reduction,
prevention, and elimination of any common pollution problem according to
the legislation of each country. It is important to note that the La Paz
Agreement is the basis on which all the border cooperation on environmental issues is built. Subsequent agreements rely heavily on the definitions and
framework of this accord, such as the geographical definition of the border
area (100 kilometers on each side of the border).

Actual cooperation schemes and operative procedures are incorporated
in annexes to the agreement; five currently exist:

—*Annex 1*: Signed in July 1985, this annex deals with the construction
and operation of water treatment plants in the Tijuana/San Diego zone.
Designed to find a solution to the problem of sewage flows in some parts of
San Diego, the annex originally outlined a plan to build two secondary
treatment plants in Mexico to deal with Tijuana's sewage. However, geological and financial obstacles complicated the implementation of this proposal. In 1988 and 1989, additional discussions based on the La Paz
Agreement led to an alternative scheme consisting of the construction of a
single facility in the United States (San Ysidro, California) that better dealt
with the geological obstacles encountered by the first plan. Financing costs
were distributed based on the notion of "appointing costs according to the
benefits" of the treatment facility. Using this formula, Mexico was to
contribute $41 million—about 21 percent of the total cost of $192 million.
The treatment plan is now scheduled to begin operation in 1997.

—*Annex 2*: Also signed in July 1985, annex 2 was subsequently complemented by an emergency plan on hazardous waste spills in the border area
in 1988. This annex specifically deals with the establishment of a joint
response team to handle any emergency hazardous waste spills in the
border area.

—*Annex 3*: The intent of this annex, signed in November 1986, was to establish procedures and regulations for the transportation and trade of trans-boundary hazardous wastes between Mexico and the United States. In general, these restrictions require prior notification and approval before waste can be transported from one country to the other. It also provides for any readmission of wastes to the country where the waste originated. Under this agreement, the exporting nation must provide 45 days' notice of its intention to ship hazardous substances to the importing nation, during which that country will choose whether or not it will accept the shipment of waste. The exporting country must readmit any shipment that the importing country, for whatever reason, decides to reject.

The main concern of this annex continues to be the monitoring of hazardous substances used in the maquiladora industry. As has been shown, the maquiladora industry is the principal source of hazardous waste in the northern border of Mexico. Specifically, the maquiladora industry uses a temporarily imported raw material; if this substance or input evolves into hazardous waste, it must be returned to its place of origin.

Though systematic data are lacking, the level of compliance with this annex appears to be low. In 1988, an Environmental Protection Agency study on Sonora and Baja California's maquiladora industry showed that only 1 percent of companies shipped their waste back to the United States, which is the principal place of origin for the maquiladora plants. But with increased collaboration between the U.S. Customs Service and the Mexican Aduanas and with the production and consolidation of more systematic data by the Attorney General for Environmental Protection (PROFEPA), compliance levels have risen. The following table shows the percentage of regulated sources of hazardous waste and the percentage of wastes generated by the maquiladora industry which were returned to the country of origin.

COMPLIANCE LEVELS OF HAZARDOUS WASTE CONTROL AND ANNEX III REQUIREMENTS (PERCENT)

	1992	1996
Generating sources of hazardous waste under control	45	82
Hazardous wastes generated by maquiladoras and returned to their country of origin	21	86

Source: Authors' calculations made with data from the Attorney General for Environmental Protection (PROFEPA).

—*Annex 4:* Signed in January 1987, this annex was devised to deal with trans-boundary air pollution caused by copper smelters located along the border, but mainly in the border area comprised of southern Arizona and northern Sonora, known as the "Gray Triangle." It targets three smelters in particular (one in Douglas, Arizona, another in Nacozari, Sonora, and the last one in Cananea, Sonora) by obliging them to meet common and specific environmental standards and by fostering information exchange between the two countries. Under the terms of this agreement, the United States promised to close the smelter in Douglas, due to its deteriorating conditions, while Mexico agreed to install acid plants to control SO_2 emissions on both Mexican smelters. On the one hand, a key feature of this annex as well as of annex 5 is the extremely specific method employed to address an environmental problem. The first three annexes, on the other hand, simply establish a framework through which actions are to be taken. Annex 4 also establishes specific SO_2 standards for the remaining Mexican plans and has functioned well overall, even throughout the privatization process of the Mexican plants.

—*Annex 5:* With the aim of analyzing and determining possible solutions to the difficulties of urban air pollution, annex 5, signed in October 1989, targets pairs of border cities, designated as "study areas." The first one is the metropolitan area of El Paso, Texas, and Ciudad Juárez, Chihuahua. The agreement obliges each city to install monitoring devices and meteorological stations to collect and analyze data and explores the possibility of harmonizing air pollution and air quality standards in the study area. Eventually, the possibility exists that the governments of the United States and Mexico will propose a binational air quality control district that would initially focus on joint pollution, control measures, and voluntary compliance, and perhaps acquire additional goals as well.

Initially, there were four working groups created by the accord with experts from both countries:
—Water Resources Working Group
—Hazardous Waste Working Group
—Air Working Group
—Emergency Response and Prevention Working Group
In 1991, two more Working Groups were added:
—Law Enforcement Working Group
—Pollution Prevention Working Group
On May 7, 1996, the governments of United States and Mexico further extended annex 5 by signing an agreement designating an international air quality management basin for the Twin Cities of El Paso and Cuidad Juárez, thus establishing a joint committee to develop trans-boundary man-

agement strategies for air pollution control. This allows the extension of Texas air quality regulations on the common air basin.[27]

Appendix C
Integrated Border Environmental Plan (IBEP)
and Border XXI

The Integrated Border Environmental Plan (IBEP) was established by an initiative put forward by the presidents of Mexico and the United States in November 1990. When considering the feasibility of the free trade agreement, both recognized that any economic benefits derived from increased trade along the border could result in severe environmental damage. The IBEP, which began operations in 1992 and finished its first stage in 1994, was designed to promote sustainable economic growth by protecting the environment and preserving the ecological equilibrium. Specifically, its main objectives included the following:

—Enforcement of the existing laws and regulations;

—Reduction of pollution through the implementation of new technology;

—Promotion of a wider cooperation in areas such as urban and regional planning, education, and increased environmental awareness; and

—Fostering a better understanding of the environmental situation in the border area.

Available evidence suggests that the development and conclusion of many projects proved successful. In general, however, the objectives and the reach of the plan were not fully achieved.

Building on the accomplishments of the IBEP, Border XXI is to be based on more community level participation and a restructured operation mechanism. The program has designated more working groups and will have more bilateral agencies involved. At this time, Border XXI has nine working groups:

—Working group on air;

—Contingency planning and emergency response;

—Enforcement;

—Environmental health;

—Hazardous and solid wastes;

27. We would like to thank Peter M. Emerson for pointing out the most recent achievements in the implementation of annex 5 of the La Paz Agreement.

—Information resources management;

—Natural resources;

—Pollution prevention; and

—Water resources.

The objective of expanded public involvement is to be fostered through public meetings, public comment periods, and other targeted outreach efforts to encourage information exchange and dialogue between governments and the public. The program also aims to support state and local efforts to develop more effective regional approachs to environmental management. Interagency cooperation will be reflected in increased involvement of natural resource management and health authorities in addition to the normal focus on environmental agencies.

Appendix D
The U.S.–Mexico Environmental Cooperation Agreement

This agreement, growing out of the NAFTA negotiations, created the North American Development Bank (NADBank) and the Border Environmental Cooperation Commission (BECC).

The North American Development Bank (NADBank)

NADBank helps finance environmental infrastructure projects along both sides of the Mexico–U.S. border. It functions basically as the lead bank, in conjunction with an investment bank, to organize the financial agents investing in the projects. The bank mainly assists possible investors and complements funds available; it does not finance a project entirely.

The projects on which the NADBank works include the following:

—Wastewater-related projects (mainly treatment plants);

—Potable water projects; and

—Municipal solid waste projects.

Mexico and the United States are equal partners in NADBank's effort; the bank's board of directors includes three members from each country:

—United States: Secretary of the Treasury, Secretary of State, Environmental Protection Agency Administrator

—Mexico: Secretario de Hacienda (Secretary of the Treasury), Secretario de Comercio (Secretary of Commerce), and Secretario de Medio Ambiente, Recursos Naturales y Pesca (Secretary of Environment, Natural Resources and Fisheries)

Mexico and the United States also share equal responsibility for NADBank's capitalization—each must contribute $225 million in paid-in capital and $1,275 million in callable capital. This total of $3 billion will be used over NADBank's first four years. Both countries have already paid the first half of their commitments.

Border Environmental Cooperation Commission (BECC)

The principal objectives of the BECC are to assess the technical, financial, and social feasibility of the projects to be financed with NADBank help. Every project to be handled by the bank must pass through the BECC certification process. Thus far, BECC has received fifty-nine projects, with a value in excess of $800 million, to be certified since its creation in 1993. Three projects were certified in 1995 and another five in 1996:

—Water Treatment Plant in Ensenada, Baja California ($8 million);

—Water Treatment Plant in Brawley, California ($17 million);

—Water Reuse Plant in El Paso, Texas ($11.7 million);

—Water Supply and Distribution Project in Nogales, Sonora ($21.6 million);

—Upgrading of Water Treatment Facilities in Douglas, Arizona ($2 million);

—Water Treatment Plant for the FINSA Industrial Park in Matamoros, Tamaulipas ($1 million);

—Water Supply and Treatment of Waste Water in Naco, Sonora ($750,000); and

—Water Treatment Project for 250 homes in marginal areas of El Paso, Texas ($110,000).

Of these eight projects, NADBank's Executive Committee has authorized and recommended four totaling approximately $40 million:

—Brawley, California;

—Matamoros, Tamaulipas;

—Nogales, Sonora; and

—Naco, Sonora.

These projects are in the last stage to close the loan.

Appendix E
Environmental Provisions inside NAFTA

The existing provisions within NAFTA on environmental issues ensure that the United States can maintain and enforce its own federal and state health, safety, and environmental standards, as well as satisfy all international treaty obligations. Mexico is in a similar position with limitations in controlled products, such as endangered species. Additionally, NAFTA endorses the principle of sustainable development and incorporates environmental provisions on investment and dispute settlement, making it a remarkably environmentally concerned trade agreement. NAFTA's specific environmental provisions include the following:

—If there is ever any incompatibility between NAFTA and any other environmental agreements in which any party to NAFTA is taking part, the latter would prevail. This applies to agreements such as the Montreal Protocol, the Basel Convention, and CITES.

—Each country has the right to establish its own level of protection according to its own objectives and circumstances.

—Each country has the right to establish its own measures to assess the environmental impact of any investment made in its own territory. To this end, NAFTA explicitly prohibits any country from lowering its standards to attract and maintain investment.

—NAFTA allows any of the parties to adopt any measure not consistent with free trade, when the objective is to protect the environment.

Although most analysts believe that NAFTA's provisions alone would suffice to guarantee satisfactory environmental performance in a free trade context, the United States also proposed the creation of a side agreement that would deal specifically with environmental issues: the North American Agreement on Environmental Cooperation. (A side agreement for labor issues was also signed.) This agreement supplements the environmental provisions and objectives of NAFTA, further ensuring that trade liberalization will not be achieved at the expense of environmental protection. It establishes a framework for trilateral cooperation on environmental matters and commits all parties to the effective enforcement of their respective environmental laws, with these objectives:

—To promote conservation and enhance environmental well-being in North America in order to enhance the population's quality of life;

—To promote sustainable development;

—To foster trilateral cooperation;

—To bolster the environmental protections in NAFTA;

—To assure that environmental measures do not become unnecessary barriers to trade, do not promote trade distortions, and do not become hidden protectionism;

—To advance cooperation in law enforcement.

The obligations include the following:

—Environmental law and regulation are to be established by each country according to its preferences and priorities. Nevertheless, each country has the obligation to provide, in this regulative framework, high levels of environmental protection.

—The side agreement prohibits the enforcement of any law or regulation outside of its country of origin.

—Each party commits to an active enforcement of its regulation. The side agreement does not allow for any authority of any one party to take actions to enforce the regulation of another party.

—Each country commits to do the following:

• To provide information regarding the state of the environment in its territory;

• To develop plans to deal with environmental emergencies;

• To promote education, research, and development in environmental issue areas;

• To assess environmental impacts; and

• To promote the use of economic instruments in environmental policy.

—Each country will inform others of any decision concerning the ban or restriction of the use of certain types of pesticides or other chemical substances and will study the possibility of prohibiting the export of such products.

—Each country will guarantee that the administrative and legal procedures in the application of the law are fair, open, and transparent.

Perhaps the most significant elements of this agreement are the provisions creating the trinational Commission for Environmental Cooperation (CEC). The CEC provides the parties of NAFTA with a structure to study issues, create working groups, and solve problems of common concern. As the operating body of the agreement, the CEC is comprised of a Council, a Secretariat, and a Joint Public Advisory Committee, and it includes the environmental ministers of Mexico and Canada and the administrator of the Environmental Protection Agency of the United States. It will serve as a forum for discussing and making recommendations on all issues and in settling actual or potential disputes. The Secretariat is headed by an executive director who will be chosen for a renewable three-year term. The executive director's nationality will be rotated among the parties; the Secretariat is currently headed by a Mexican.

Among the main functions of the Secretariat are the authoring of an annual public report covering the commission's activities during the previous year and the creation of an analytical framework with which to assess the environmental impacts of NAFTA. The Joint Public Advisory Committee includes five representative members from each country. It will advise the council and provide technical, scientific, and other information to the Secretariat, as well as provide input to the annual program and budget of the council.

The CEC will interact with NAFTA institutions by supporting the environmental goals already detailed within the main agreement. Specifically, CEC will cooperate with the Free Trade Commission, which deals with the enforcement issues of NAFTA through the following means:

—The CEC will provide a space for public inquiry and for the reception of public comments concerning NAFTA's environmental goals;

—The CEC will provide expert assistance when one of the parties believes another is not in compliance with any environmental measure for the purpose of attracting investment; and

—The CEC will work to prevent or resolve environment-related disputes by making recommendations to the Free Trade Commission.

As for the promotion of effective enforcement, the commission will encourage the sharing of environmental enforcement technologies and information between the parties and will report on their environmental enforcement activities. The Secretariat will prepare factual records on enforcement matters based on submissions from the public in the three countries. The council will address complaints between parties regarding compliance, with attention being paid to the effective enforcement of environmental laws, and will resolve them through consultations or the establishment of dispute settlement panels.

The CEC is currently working on the following:

—A methodology for assessing the environmental impacts of NAFTA;

—Discussing the project for eradication of four dangerous chemical substances in North America (each country is still in the deciding process of which four substances to ban—according to their own priorities—resources, preferences, and overall socioeconomic conditions);

—A Memo of Understanding for Cooperation on the Promotion of Environmental Management Systems, to be signed by the Chambers of Commerce in the United States and Canada and by the Confederation of Industrial Chambers of Mexico.

Appendix F
Environmental Institutional Framework in Mexico

Mexico has a long tradition of laws and institutions relating to environmental protection and natural resources conservation. Though the first legislation on forest conservation was established in 1838, the Mexican government's recognition of the importance of environmental problems has taken place largely since 1970. In the interim, Mexico developed an institutional framework on which environmental policy is currently based.

In 1972, the Undersecretariat for Environmental Improvement was created as part of the Health and Assistance Secretariat (SSA), with the objective of including environmental considerations in public health policy. In 1982 the Secretariat of Urban Development and Ecology (SEDUE) was created and was put in charge of environmental policy through the Undersecretary of Ecology. In 1992 most of the functions of SEDUE were transferred to the Secretariat of Social Development (SEDESOL), with the objective of integrating and consolidating national social policy—that is, urban and regional development, housing, and environmental policies. Along with SEDESOL, two additional agencies were created to assist with this task: the National Institute of Ecology (INE) and the General Attorney for Environmental Protection (PROFEPA).

Since 1992, INE has been responsible for the normative aspects of the environmental policy. It is also in charge of design and evaluation of the environmental policies and laws, evaluation of environmental impacts, and implementation of programs. PROFEPA is responsible for the environmental policy enforcement. INE and PROFEPA together are the means by which SEDESOL's environmental duties are carried out.

There were other agencies, besides SEDESOL, with environmental duties. For instance, the Secretariat of Agriculture and Water Resources (SARH) was in charge of the management of natural protected areas and forests; the National Water Commission (CNA), an autonomous body under SARH, was in charge of water resources management; the Secretariat of Fisheries (SP) was in charge of the management of Mexico's fisheries; and the National Commission for the Knowledge and Use of Biodiversity (CONABIO), an independent federal entity, was responsible for promoting biodiversity conservation.

In 1994, all the environmental and natural resource policy was transferred to the newly created Secretariat of Environment, Natural Resources and Fisheries (SEMARNAP). INE, PROFEPA, and CNA are currently autonomous agencies of SEMARNAP. By providing federal treatment of these environmental concerns, this new structure illustrates the importance of such issues to the Mexican government. With respect to federal spending on environmental policy, from 1989 to 1995 the total grew more than twentyfold, from almost 9 million pesos to 181.5 million pesos.

Comment by Peter M. Emerson

I am pleased to have this opportunity to review chapter 4 by Belausteguigoitia and Guadarrama on U.S.–Mexico environmental issues. It provides an interesting framework for thinking about how we might strengthen
the institutions and public support for environmental problem-solving in
both countries.

Under the best circumstances, the environment can be a divisive issue.
Conflict is a common feature of environmental policy. It has the potential to
strain relationships and push neighbors apart.

Environmental issues are often fraught with emotion, social preferences
differ, and the relevant science may be complex or even vigorously contested. For certain, environmental quality gets shortchanged because people
(businesses and governments) do not want to be responsible for the costs
they impose on others. Nor do people quickly step forward to reveal the
benefits of many environmental services they consume. Governments inter-
vene to correct these "failures," but sometimes heavy-handedly and by
making political concessions that alienate.

With respect to joint U.S.–Mexico environmental issues, a huge economic asymmetry and national sovereignty considerations add even more
tension to the task of reaching agreement on environmental goals and ways
to achieve them.

Despite these difficulties, the authors make the case that the relationship
between the United States and Mexico on natural resources and the environment has evolved—for the most part—in a cooperative fashion. Although there are many unsolved environmental problems, I agree with this
observation. Each nation in this dyad has already accepted the principle that
it has a responsibility to ensure that its activities do not cause significant
environmental harm in the other country. The 1983 La Paz Agreement, the
1992 Rio Declaration, and NAFTA's environmental side accord are all
built on this principle of extraterritorial responsibility. Now both countries
need to take the next step forward by adopting specific mechanisms to
implement the principle and enable their citizens to act together to reduce
environmental damages.

The authors discuss selected environmental issues, binational agreements and institutions both pre- and post-NAFTA, international trade and
pollution havens, and the benefits of cooperation. Much of their emphasis
is directed to the U.S.–Mexico border region because of truly pressing
pollution problems that involve both countries.

Without diminishing the importance of the border region, I believe that it would be valuable to expand the range of environmental issues discussed in the first part of chapter 4. The text tends to understate the historical agenda and does not adequately prepare the reader for the future. For example, two important trade and environment issues—the tuna-dolphin dispute between Mexico and the United States, and the enforcement of health, safety, and environmental standards—could merit more prominence. Discussion of North American efforts to manage dangerous chemicals (such as polychlorinated biphenyls [PCBs] and DDT), to report comparable data on toxic releases, and to encourage public participation in setting priorities might better reflect future environmental interdependencies. Some controversial topics such as long-range transport of sulfur dioxide emissions, extension of the Gulf of Mexico's Intracoastal Waterway, and the siting of hazardous waste facilities could be added.

With respect to the discussion of the opportunities for cooperation, institution-building, and stronger linkages on environmental protection, I would like to offer three suggestions. First, the federal governments could be urged to use their authority under the La Paz Agreement to create new governance institutions in the border region that would support decentralized, trans-boundary resource management.

Take the case of El Paso, Texas, and Ciudad Juárez, Chihuahua—"sister cities" that share a single air basin and a serious air pollution problem. Health-based air quality standards are regularly violated in both cities, and the problem can be expected to get worse with rapid population and industrial growth. Furthermore, although both countries have sophisticated national clean air statutes, independent administration of their statutes will not solve the cross-border problem.

On May 7, 1996, the U.S. and Mexican governments signed a pioneering agreement designating an international air quality management basin for the two cities and establishing a joint committee to develop trans-boundary management strategies for the control of air pollution.[28] Among other things, the new agreement creates the possibility of extending air quality regulations that are already on the books in Texas to allow polluters to make pollution reduction investments throughout the common air basin.

---

28. U.S.–Mexico Binational Commission. 1996. "Appendix 1 to Annex V of the Agreement Between The United Mexican States And The United States Of America On The Cooperation For The Protection and Improvement Of The Environment In The Border Area." Mexico City, Mexico (May 7).

A practical consequence of trans-boundary management is that U.S. businesses in higher-income El Paso, where many pollution abatement investments have already been made, will have an incentive to invest in lower-income Ciudad Juárez, where fewer pollution abatement investments have been made and larger reductions in pollution are possible. In addition, suppliers of clean technology and alternative fuels may enter the market to help finance these cross-border investments in exchange for a share of the pollution reduction credits generated.

The May 7th agreement is an example of federal government efforts to create incentives and mechanisms that make it easier for local authorities and polluters in both cities to take responsibility for efficient cleanup, without getting bogged down in conflicts that arise because of the international border and their differing stages of economic development. Furthermore, the May 7th agreement complements efforts to decentralize air quality regulation in both countries and can probably be extended to the management of other resources, such as cross-border aquifers.

Another way to build stronger linkages on environmental protection is to help both countries follow through on their NAFTA-related environmental commitments. These commitments include provisions in the trade agreement, the trilateral Commission for Environmental Cooperation, and a binational planning process and institutions to provide infrastructure investments in the U.S.–Mexico border region. They reflect a practical strategy for dealing with conflicts between trade liberalization and environmental protection without dictating uniformity of standards or otherwise impinging on a nation's sovereign control over environmental matters within its own borders.

In the United States, the annual appropriation to support our NAFTA-related environmental commitments is about $280 million (table 4-3). Similar appropriations are being made in Mexico. Although it is too early to measure the full impact of this spending, we need to begin the process of seeking answers to important questions:

—Is there evidence of a new capacity to solve environmental problems before they become obstacles to trade?

—Are the new institutions successfully designing and financing wastewater treatment facilities in the border region?

—Do local communities support these projects?

—Are the governments promoting creative strategies, such as a deposit-refund system to recover hazardous chemicals or a "block grant program" to implement comprehensive U.S.–Mexico border environmental plans?

Table 4-3. Federal Government Spending on NAFTA's Environmental Institutions and U.S.–Mexico Border Environmental Plans, 1994, 1995, 1996, and 1997

Millions of U.S. dollars

Agency	Enacted			Requested 1997	1997 Appropriations	
	1994	1995	1996	1997	House	Senate
Environmental Protection Agency						
Wastewater treatment plants	58.0	100.0	100.0	100.0	100.0	100.0
Grants to colonias, wastewater treatment	60.0	50.0	50.0	50.0	50.0	50.0
U.S.–Mexico Border Plan	14.1	19.0	25.0	25.0	25.0[a]	25.0
Commission on Environmental Cooperation	2.0	5.0	5.0	3.5	3.5[a]	3.5
U.S. Department of Agriculture						
Grants to colonias, drinking water	25.7	25.0	18.7	25.0	18.7	18.7
U.S. Department of the Interior						
Natural resource management	0.9	3.8	3.7	3.8	3.8	3.8
U.S. Department of State						
International Boundary and Water Commission	25.6	19.5	18.7	25.8	25.0	26.0
Border Environmental Cooperation Commission	—	1.3	1.8	1.8	1.7	1.8
Conservation Fund	20.0	0	0	0	0	0
U.S. Department of the Treasury						
North American Development Bank	—	56.0	56.0	56.0	50.6	56.0
U.S. Department of Health and Human Services						
Food and Drug Administration	1.6	0	0	0	0	0
	207.9	279.8	279.2	290.9	278.3	284.8

Sources: *Budget of the United States Government, Fiscal Years 1995, 1996, and 1997*. Additional information supplied by Robert Tuccillo, Office of Management and Budget analyst. Prepared by Peter Emerson, Environmental Defense Fund.

a. May be subject to a $5.0 million reduction for international programs and $1.0 million reduction for NAFTA programs.

To maintain the support of legislators who appropriate these government funds, those responsible for implementing NAFTA's environmental strategy will soon need to show that they are solving environmental problems relating to trade and the U.S.–Mexico border region.

Finally, there may be ways to more fully engage private sector firms that operate in both countries in building stronger linkages on environmental protection. Perhaps the Commission for Environmental Cooperation is leading the way by helping Canadian, U.S., and Mexican business associations and their members develop internationally accepted benchmarks for environmental management systems, auditing, labeling, and performance evaluation. These benchmarks and other environmental management initiatives backed by multinational firms may help solve problems caused by differing standards that regulate product characteristics and methods of production. These efforts could contribute favorably to better self-regulation and to environmental performance that exceeds minimum standards, as a number of large firms are now promising.

Building on the principle that good environmental management is good business management, the managers of companies and industrial parks have found cost-saving actions that improve their environmental performance. In many cases, information and appropriate technology can help save energy, keep waste streams segregated, and make use of residual materials that would otherwise be headed to the landfill. To help design eco-friendly industrial parks, one multinational firm has developed a computer planning model to match industries by linking by-products and wastes with feedstock requirements to achieve the right mix of target companies. Chaparral Steel, a member of the Business Council for Sustainable Development for the Gulf of Mexico, has taken advantage of by-product synergies in linking a steel mill, an automobile shredding operation, and a cement manufacturing plant.

With respect to U.S.–Mexico environmental relations, Belausteguigoitia and Guadarrama provide convincing evidence that the countries recognize their joint interests and responsibilities. The authors could do more, however, to show that the two nations are not necessarily good at acting together to solve environmental problems. Evidence of this can be found in the border region, where environmental damage and threats to human health cause tension within and between countries.

To improve their performance, the United States and Mexico can implement appropriate trans-boundary governance institutions, follow through on their NAFTA environmental commitments, and more fully engage the private sector on environmental matters. Other things being equal, these actions will create new conditions favorable to both environmental improvement and income growth.

General Discussion

Barry Bosworth suggested that too little attention was being paid to the issue of who is going to pay. Many Americans would suggest that Mexico simply adopt the U.S. environmental, health, and safety standards; but they would also believe that Mexico should pay all of the costs, despite its much lower level of income. Peter Emerson pointed out that, at least in the border region, Americans were willing to pay a portion of the costs of reducing pollutants on the Mexican side. Juan Belausteguigoitia argued that Mexico should pay. However, at least initially, the standards should not be the same in the two countries because of different levels of income, resource endowments, and preferences. Nora Lustig questioned the value of the side agreements to NAFTA. According to chapter 4, most of the progress in resolving environmental issues was the result of prior agreements or institutions.

References

Birdsall, Nancy, and David Wheeler. 1992. "Trade Policy and Industrial Pollution in Latin America: Where are the Pollution Havens?" In *International Trade and the Environment,* edited by Patrick Low, 159–67. Discussion Paper 159. Washington: World Bank.

Instituto Nacional de Estadística, Geografía e Informática de México (INEGI). 1990. *Censo General de Población y Vivienda.* Mexico City.

Jaffe, Adam B., and others. 1995. "Environmental Regulation and the Competitiveness of U.S. Manufacturing: What does the Evidence Tell Us?" *Journal of Economic Literature.* 33(1): 132–63.

Lucas, Robert E. B., David Wheeler, and Hemamala Hettige. 1992. "Economic Development, Environmental Regulation, and the International Migration of Toxic Industrial Pollution, 1960–1988." In *International Trade and the Environment,* edited by Patrick Low, 67–82. Discussion Paper 159. Washington: World Bank.

Mumme, Stephen. 1994. "Enforcing International Environmental Agreements: Lessons from the U.S.–Mexico Border." *Journal of Environment and Development* 3 (1): 40–73.

Office of the President of the United States. 1993. "The NAFTA: Expanding U.S. Exports, Jobs, and Growth: Report on Environmental Issues." Govenment Printing Office (November).

Organization for Economic Cooperation and Development. 1995. *Report on Trade and Environment to the OECD Council at the Ministerial Level.* Paris.

Porter, Michael, and Claas van der Linde. 1995. "Toward a New Conception of the Environment-Competitiveness Relationship." *Journal of Economic Perspectives* 9(4): 97–118.

Sanchez, Roberto. 1988. *Conflictos ambientales y Negociaci en Binacional entre Mexico y Los Estados Unidos, El medio ambiente como de conflicto en la ralaci en binacional Mexico Estados Unidos.* Mexico City.

Secretaría de Desarollo Social (SEDESOL). 1995. *Informe de la Situación General en Materia de Equilibrio Ecológico y Protección al Ambiente 1993–1994.* Mexico City.

Secretaría de Medio Ambiente, Recursos Naturales y Pesca (SEMARNAP). *Program Frontera XXI.* Mexico City.

Susskind, Lawrence E. 1994. *Environmental Diplomacy: Negotiating more Effective Global Agreements.* Oxford University Press.

Susskind, Lawrence, and Connie Ozawa. 1992. "Negotiating More Effective International Environmental Agreements." In *The International Politics of the Environment,* edited by Andrew Hurrell and Benedict Kinsbury, 142–65. Oxford, England: Clarendon Press.

United Nations Conference on Environment and Development (UNCED). 1992. *Agenda 21.* Rio de Janeiro, Brazil.

United States Trade Representative. 1992. *Review of U.S.–Mexico Environmental Issues.* Washington: Department of Commerce.

5 Drug Trafficking in Mexico

Peter H. Smith

HARSH realities of drugs and drug trafficking contradict the current upbeat mood of U.S.–Mexican relations. Within official circles, negotiation and implementation of the North American Free Trade Agreement (NAFTA) have marked a new beginning in the bilateral relationship. Now that the cold war has passed, according to conventional wisdom, the two countries are free to pursue a natural harmony of interests. Washington's prompt and positive response to the Mexican peso crisis offers apt illustration of this new understanding, from this perspective, as does Mexico City's cooperation on foreign policy. Against this backdrop, however, the problem of illicit drugs evokes apprehension and concern. According to the U.S. State Department, "no country in the world poses a more immediate narcotics threat to the United States than Mexico." And as President Ernesto Zedillo Ponce de León has remarked on more than one occasion, drug trafficking has become "Mexico's number one security threat."[1] What underlies this shared sense of alarm?

To examine this question, I here explore three interrelated themes:

—The transformation of *narcotráfico* in Mexico from the late 1970s to the mid-1990s;

—Domestic political implications of drug trafficking within Mexico; and

—The current and potential impact of the drug issue on U.S.–Mexican relations.

1. U.S. Department of State (1996, pp. 140, 142).

The author thanks Gabriela Lemus, Peter Lupska, and María Celia Toro for helpful comments on a previous draft of this chapter.

Transformation of the Industry

Drug trafficking in Mexico has undergone fundamental change in recent years. From the 1930s through the 1970s, Mexico occupied a straightforward role in the international market, supplying some of the heroin and most of the marijuana imported by the United States. Both crops were raised by small-scale farmers in specific regions. Opium poppies were cultivated in the north-central states of Sinaloa, Durango, and Chihuahua, and to a lesser extent in Sonora; cannabis (for marijuana) was grown throughout the country, not only throughout the northwest but also with notable concentrations in Michoacán, Jalisco, and Nayarit. During the 1950s and 1960s Mexico supplied as much as 75 percent of the U.S. market for marijuana and 10 to 15 percent of the demand for heroin. By the mid-1970s, after the rupture of the infamous "French connection" from Turkey through Marseilles to the United States in 1972, Mexico managed to supply 80 percent of the U.S. market for heroin.[2]

Throughout this period much of the processing and transportation of final products rested in the hands of less than a dozen large and illegal organizations, although the marijuana industry was less centralized than the opium and heroin business. During the 1970s key organizations were identified with family names: Herrera, Aviles Pérez, Valenzuela, Araujo, Sicilia-Falcón. As a rule, these groups maintained close relations with local farmers, from whom they regularly purchased crops; they kept their headquarters in key production areas (Culiacán being one well-known site); and though they earned substantial profits, they did not expand their operations to reach new markets with new goods. They resorted to bribery and intimidation, of course, but mostly on the local and regional level, and they maintained relatively low political profiles.[3] Although they exercised effective control over the Mexican narcotics trade, in other words, they did not constitute "cartels" in the same way as their Colombian counterparts.[4] They were local organizations dealing in locally grown products.

In time, Mexican marijuana and opium became the targets of aggressive antidrug policies. In September 1969 the Nixon administration launched Operation Intercept, subjecting border crossings to intensive scrutiny and time-consuming harassment for nearly three weeks; after much frustration

2. Ruiz-Cabañas (1989, pp. 48–50).
3. See Trueba Lara (1995, pp. 54–56); Lupsha (1991, pp. 41–58 [especially pp. 44–48]).
4. Lupsha (1981, pp. 95–115 [especially pp. 100–102]).

and scant seizures, the effort gave way to a face-saving Operation Cooperation the following month. It was in 1975 that, once again under pressure from the United States, the Mexican government initiated its *Campaña Permanente* against illicit drugs. Spearheaded by Operation Condor, the *Campaña* launched a coordinated attack that focused on eradication of crops, interdiction of shipments, and disruption of commercial organizations. One particularly conspicuous element was collaboration with U.S. government agencies. Another was deployment of the Mexican army, which eventually devoted up to one-quarter of its personnel and resources to the antidrug campaign.[5]

The *Campaña* had remarkable results. Apparently as a consequence, Mexico's share of the U.S. marijuana market plunged from more than 75 percent in 1976 to 11 percent in 1979, 8 percent in 1980, and as low as 4 percent in 1981. Similarly, the Mexican share of the heroin market dropped from 67 percent in 1976 to 25 percent in 1980. (This did not mean, of course, that American consumers were using less drugs. Instead, the vacuum in the marijuana market was quickly filled by growers in Jamaica and Colombia and within the United States, and stepped-up quantities of heroin came from Afghanistan, Iran, and Pakistan.) Eventually, Mexican entrepreneurs managed to recuperate a sizable portion of market share: by the mid-1980s Mexico was supplying around 30 percent of the marijuana consumed in the United States and about 40 percent of the heroin.

An unintended outcome of this policy initiative was intensified cartelization of the Mexican drug industry. Although Operation Condor pushed some prominent traffickers out of the business—such as Pedro Aviles Pérez of Sinaloa—it also tended to strengthen the relative position of those who could survive. This led to increased concentration. The *Campaña* also encouraged the leaders of survivor cartels to reorganize their enterprises, relying heavily on their comparative advantages: bribery and violence. (Probably the most notorious kingpin of this era was Miguel Angel Félix Gallardo, leader of the Guadalajara gang.[6]) As a result of law enforcement efforts, in other words, the Mexican drug industry came under the control of entrepreneurial organizations that were fewer in number, stronger in resources, and more dangerous to society and government.

Since the mid-1980s Mexico has held fairly steady positions in the international markets for marijuana and heroin. Quantitative measures of

---

5. Craig (1980, pp. 345–63).
6. See Toro (1995, pp. 79–80, note 78); Trueba Lara (1995, pp. 56–60).

PETER H. SMITH

Figure 5-1. Marijuana Production in Mexico, 1985–95

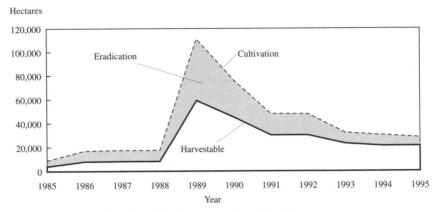

Source: U.S. Department of State (1989, p. 113); U.S. Department of State (1996, p. 149).

production are notoriously unreliable, but they can sketch broad outlines of the situation.[7] According to the estimates in figure 5-1, the area of "harvestable" marijuana plantings in Mexico (after eradication) increased from around 5,000 hectares in the late 1980s to more than 15,000 hectares in the early 1990s, then falling back to 7,000 hectares by mid-decade; despite such fluctuations the effective yield for 1995, approximately 5,500 metric tons, was about the same amount as in 1988. (The inflated production estimates for 1989–90 are highly suspect and should probably be disregarded altogether.[8]) Part of the decline in the 1990s may result from the expansion of domestic U.S. marijuana production, which may claim as much as one-half of the national market. Even so, Mexico was thought to produce 80 percent of marijuana imported by the United States as of the mid-1990s.

And as the U.S. market for heroin has strengthened, Mexican growers have placed increased emphasis on opium. According to figure 5-2, estimated cultivation practically doubled between 1986–87 and 1995, climbing from 6,000 or 7,000 hectares to 13,500 hectares. Notwithstanding intensified eradication efforts, therefore, the harvestable crop was more than 5,000

7. The source of these data, the U.S. Department of State, stipulates that the numbers represent a "best effort" to capture dimensions of the drug trade, but concedes: "The picture is not as precise as we would like it to be. The numbers range from cultivation figures, relatively hard data derived by proven means, to crop production and drug yield estimates, softer figures where many more variables come into play. *We publish these numbers with an important caveat: the yield figures are potential, not actual numbers. Although they are useful for examining trends, they are only approximations. They should not be treated as hard data.*" (Emphasis in original.) U.S. Department of State (1996, p. 19).

8. See Reuter (1996, pp. 63–80 [especially pp. 66–69]).

Figure 5-2. Opium Production in Mexico, 1985–95

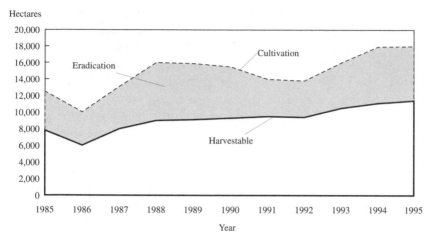

Source: U.S. Department of State (1989, p. 113); U.S. Department of State (1996, p. 149).

hectares (which could yield 50 to 60 metric tons of final product). By the mid-1990s Mexico was producing approximately 20 to 30 percent of the heroin consumed in the United States. With regard to both marijuana and opium, in other words, Mexico was maintaining its traditional market position.

But there also was a major change, which came about when *narcotraficantes* from Colombia began seeking new routes for shipping cocaine into the United States. As U.S. law enforcement agencies cracked down on shipments through the Caribbean and South Florida in the early to mid-1980s, Colombian entrepreneurs—especially leaders of the sophisticated Cali cartel—turned their attention toward Mexico. Initially, they ferried relatively modest shipments of cocaine in Cessnas or other small planes from Colombia to Mexico and then, with the aid of Mexican collaborators, sent them overland to the United States. In the early 1990s, as operations matured, Colombians began flying their merchandise to central and southern Mexico in converted Boeing 727s and Caravelles capable of handling multiton loads; Mexican carriers would then take them north in trucks, small planes, and trains across the border into the United States— where operatives under the Colombians would break down the shipments for wholesale and retail distribution. Within the cocaine trade, Mexicans became classic middlemen.

These joint ventures with Colombians had far-reaching consequences. First, Mexico became the primary transit route for cocaine entering the

United States. As of 1989, the U.S. State Department estimated that 30 percent of U.S.-bound cocaine passed through Mexico; by 1992, the estimate surpassed 50 percent; for other years, the estimate has been as high as 75 to 80 percent.[9] Along parallel lines, figure 5-3 reveals that seizures of cocaine in Mexico began a steep upward climb in 1985; they more than tripled between 1988 and 1990, and they remained at very high levels until 1993.[10] No matter what the indicator, one fact was inescapably clear: Mexico had become a major player in the international market for cocaine.

As is emphasized below, this development would have profound implications for Mexico. The turn toward cocaine would magnify the economic stakes in illicit drugs. It would reduce the traditional emphasis on marijuana. It would redefine the relationship between politics and *traficantes*. Most fundamentally, perhaps, it would lead to the formation of brutal and world-class cartels.

The Consolidation of Cartels

Mexico's entry into the cocaine trade reshaped both the structure and the power of trafficking organizations. As indicated above, traditional marketing groups maintained close ties with producers, operated at local levels, and maintained low political profiles. The increase in cocaine traffic changed this picture in far-reaching ways. Where the Colombians forged joint partnerships with existing groups, as in Guadalajara, it expanded and strengthened their economic base; and where the Colombians enticed other criminal organizations into the cocaine trade, as in the state of Tamaulipas, it led to the emergence of new contenders. The profitability of the cocaine business also greatly augmented the economic resources of trafficking groups. According to Thomas Constantine, current head of the Drug Enforcement Administration (DEA), annual profits for Mexican *traficantes* now approach $7 billion per year; the Mexican attorney general's office has placed the figure as high as $30 billion per year. In addition, the emphasis on cocaine has severed the long-standing relationship between farmers and distributors. Mexican traffickers therefore have less allegiance to local areas, and less reason to concentrate their attention on the local scene; they all compete against each other for the same goods and the same market. In

9. See U.S. Department of State (1989, p. 92; 1992, p. 167; 1996, p. 141).
10. For slightly different data revealing the same basic trend see Toro (1995, pp. 33–34).

Figure 5-3. Seizures of Cocaine in Mexico, 1985–95

Metric tons

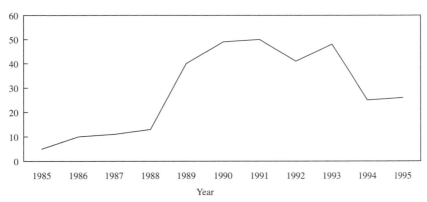

Source: U.S. Department of State (1989, p. 114); U.S. Department of State (1996, p. 149).

view of their power and reach, they have formed international "cartels" in the colloquial sense of the term.[11]

As revealed in table 5-1, Mexico currently has at least five drug cartels of international stature and scope: the Guadalajara cartel, strengthened and refurbished by recent alliances with Colombian suppliers; the Tijuana cartel, which handles most northward shipments into the lucrative California market; the Sinaloa cartel, a traditional grouping fortified by leaders who broke off from the Tijuana group; the Ciudad Juárez (or Chihuahua) cartel, which dominates traffic from east of Tijuana to Ciudad Juárez–El Paso; and the Gulf cartel, based in the state of Tamaulipas, which has controlled trafficking along the U.S. border from Matamoros to Brownsville down the eastern coast of Mexico and around the Yucatán peninsula. There are a half dozen or more additional groups that play significant roles in the drug trade, and many other minor participants; but it is the Big Five cartels that dominate the market, cultivate connections with the upper echelons of Mexican politics, and maintain key links to South America.[12] These are

11. In reference to illicit drugs, the term "cartel" commonly applies to participation in an effective oligopsony/oligopoly. Unlike trusts or classic cartels, drug organizations do not normally engage in collusion to establish market prices, though they sometimes reach tacit agreement on market boundaries.

12. Lupsha (1994a, p. 10). Partly because conditions change so rapidly, there is inconsistency and uncertainty in the designation of Mexico's leading cartels. Lupsha does not mention the Guadalajara group in this 1994 publication, for instance, though it is frequently discussed in other sources.

Table 5-1. Mexican Drug Cartels

Location	Current leadership[a]	Comments
Gulf	Oscar Malherbe de León	Key product: cocaine, in close collaboration with Colombian partners. Section of U.S.–Mexican border: formerly from east of El Paso to Brownsville, now diminishing. Weakened by arrests of ex-kingpins Juan García Abrego and Humberto García Abrego.
Juárez	Amado Carrillo Fuentes	Products: marijuana, heroin, cocaine. Section of U.S. border: central area from west of Nogales to east of El Paso, now expanding. Replacing Gulf cartel as key interlocutor with Colombians.
Tijuana	Benjamín Arellano Félix	Traditional products: marijuana and heroin, recently moving into cocaine and now methamphetamines. Section of U.S. border: western end, with access to San Diego and Los Angeles. Recently involved in rivalry with Sinaloa group. Run by Benjamín Arellano Félix together with brothers Javier and Ramón, related by family to legendary boss Miguel Angel Félix Gallardo.
Sinaloa	"Mayo" Zambada	Key products: marijuana, heroin, cocaine. Section of U.S. border: western coast. Weakened by arrests of Héctor ("El Guero") Palma and Joaquín ("El Chapo") Guzmán, renegade ex-members of Tijuana cartel, and by dispute with Arellano brothers over cocaine market share.
Guadalajara	Miguel Caro Quintero	Key products: marijuana and heroin, more recently cocaine. Section of U.S. border: strip from San Luis to east of Nogales (in northern state of Sonora). Recuperating from arrests in the 1980s of Rafael Caro Quintero (brother of Miguel) and of Miguel Angel Félix Gallardo. A traditional, long-standing cartel, with capacity to referee disputes within Mexican drug federation.

Sources: Lupsha (1991, 1994a, 1994b, 1996); Trueba Lara (1995, pp. 60–73); Fineman and Rotella (1995); Rotella (1995).
a. As of June 1996.

major operations, with vast funds at their disposal and paramilitary forces for their own protection.

With the arrival of the cocaine trade, the Ciudad Juárez and Gulf cartels—virtually unknown in drug circles before the late 1980s—assumed unprecedented importance. Around 1994 it was estimated that the Gulf cartel (then under Juan García Abrego) handled as much as one-third of all cocaine shipments to the United States for the Cali cartel. When Mexican prosecutors then turned their attention to the Gulf cartel (largely because of its alleged involvement in the September 1994 assassination of political leader José Francisco Ruiz Massieu), the crackdown created new opportunities for the Ciudad Juárez group under Amado Carrillo Fuentes. By early 1995, in fact, García Abrego was captured and deported to the United States, and the Chihuahua group quickly moved to take advantage of the situation. In short order, it was rumored that Carrillo Fuentes had become the "prime intermediary" along the market route from Colombia to the United States.[13]

Relationships among these cartels are competitive and tense. Although Peter Lupsha has spoken of a Mexican "federation" of drug lords, there appears to be more rivalry than coordination among the factions.[14] This sometimes leads to violent conflict between members (or hit men) of the different gangs. On other occasions, kingpins entice (or wait for) Mexican and/or U.S. law enforcement agents to weaken other rivals. For example, when Mexican police finally managed to track down Joaquín Guzmán (El Chapo) of the Sinaloa cartel, then locked in a bitter struggle with the Tijuana cartel, the arrest "in effect turned the government into an enforcer for the Arellanos."[15] In the meantime, connections with Colombians appear to be highly opportunistic. The dismantling of the Cali cartel during 1995 led to fragmentation of Colombian gangs, as second- and third-tier lieutenants took over from the former capos, a pattern that made cocaine delivery less reliable and punctual than before. (As part of this development, according to Lupsha, the new Colombian leaders have started to restore old transit routes through the Caribbean and south Florida, with the result that Mexico now accounts for only 55 to 60 percent of total cocaine shipments to the United States.) In response, Mexican cartels have begun to establish their own links with coca and coca paste suppliers in Peru and Bolivia—in effect, bypassing the Colombian pipeline altogether and moving toward vertical integration of their operations.[16]

Ever the opportunists, Mexican cartel leaders have also turned toward the manufacture and distribution of methamphetamines, one of the fastest-growing markets in the United States. In the form of crystal or "speed," methamphetamines have gained notable popularity among U.S. middle-class, white-collar workers in their twenties and thirties. Once again, the

13. Reding (1995b, p. C4).
14. Lupsha (1996).
15. Reding (1995a, p. 2).
16. Lupsha (1996).

cartels have seized an opportunity: with the crackdown on methamphet-amine laboratories in the United States, especially in southern California, Mexicans have taken up the slack. As a result of increasing production and availability, the average price for the drug has dropped by 20 percent (from $50 per gram to $40 per gram). As Drug Enforcement Administration (DEA) head Constantine has put it: "The Mexican traffickers who flooded the U.S. with marijuana and heroin in the 1970s and 1980s and cocaine in the 1990s threaten to overwhelm us with methamphetamine now." With regard to this class of drugs, Constantine added: "We believe that the major drug gangs operating out of Mexico pose the largest threat currently."[17]

Political Implications

Transformation of the *narcotráfico* business in Mexico has coincided with long-term changes in the country's political system. From the late 1920s to the 1980s, an authoritarian regime marked by a close alliance between technocrats, politicians, and leaders of key groups—especially labor and the peasantry—successfully imposed social and political stability. These coalitions were frequently sealed in explicit compacts, or *pactos*, that achieved and implemented consensus on economic policy. Key decisions were made at the top, behind closed doors, as an official party (the Partido Revolucionario Institucional, or PRI) routinely and regularly triumphed in elections that were not highly contested. Opposition voices were muted, the media conspired openly with the ruling establishment, and there were few instances of rebellion and protest. From the 1940s on, even the armed forces accepted a civilian monopoly on the presidential office. Turbulent Mexico, land of the first major social revolution in the twentieth century, thus succumbed to forces of political domination. With traces of envy and admiration, the Peruvian novelist-politician Mario Vargas Llosa once chris-tened Mexico's system as "the perfect dictatorship."

As far back as the 1970s, however, the dominant-party system in Mexico began to undergo fundamental rearrangements in its power structure. The historic coalition started to weaken. The peasantry no longer represented a significant resource; organized labor lost authority; and although small- and medium-size business remained a fragile sector, large-scale business was accumulating power and independence from the government. In addition, the party system shifted. Though still strong, the PRI came to stand at the center of a three-party system, with the Partido Revolucionario

17. Dillon (1995).

Democrático (PRD) on the left and the Partido de Acción Nacional (PAN) on the right—both of the latter attracting considerable support from the urban middle class. At the same time, traditional fiefdoms reemerged: old-time politicians (so-called *dinosaurios*) found refuge in state governorships, for instance, and in niches within the party apparatus of the PRI.

In summary, Mexico has been undergoing a significant erosion of institutional authority. There is less power at the center, even in the presidency, than there used to be. To be sure, Carlos Salinas de Gortari was able to exert authority in an exceptional way, partly through personal guile and partly through his lifelong immersion in the system; but Ernesto Zedillo has neither the resources nor the opportunity to demonstrate such strength. Power is no longer as concentrated or extensive as it was for many years.[18]

Adding to this dissipation of institutional authority is what might be called a "familial" crisis—the emergence of profound schisms within Mexico's political elite, once regarded as the "revolutionary family." For decades, the coherence (and internal discipline) of this ruling elite comprised a central foundation for the persistence of political stability. Although there had been stresses and strains from the 1940s through the 1980s, and occasional cracks in the edifice of power (including the splitoff of the *corriente democrática* against the PRI in 1986), there was nothing to compare with the fissures of the 1990s. Overt symptoms of these new tensions did not appear until 1994, but they pointed clearly to subterranean pressures and trends that were unfolding throughout the Salinas *sexenio*.

A central and spectacular scene in this drama revolves around two pairs of brothers: Carlos Salinas de Gortari and his older brother, Raúl; and José Francisco Ruiz Massieu and his younger brother, Mario. Both families have long been pillars of the Mexican establishment. José Francisco had also married (and divorced) a sister of the Salinas brothers and was serving as secretary general of the PRI in late 1994. There was said to be affection, rivalry, and tension among all four men.

Drugs and drug trafficking soon entered this picture. As he left a political gathering in September 1994, José Francisco Ruiz Massieu was assassinated in downtown Mexico City. His brother Mario, then assistant attorney general, was placed in charge of the investigation. Within a month Mario issued a statement suggesting that drug bosses might have ordered the murder, and that high-level politicians were in league with *narcotraficantes*. In late November, about a week before Carlos Salinas was to step down from the presidency, Mario publicly resigned from both his

18. Dresser (1995); Zaid (1995); González Sandoval and González Graf (1995).

position and the PRI, accusing party leaders (but not Salinas) of conspiring to cover up the assassination.

On February 28, 1995, governmental authorities (presumably with Zedillo's permission) arrested Raúl Salinas de Gortari in connection with the Ruiz Massieu assassination. Rumors immediately began to circulate that Carlos Salinas must have been involved in the plot, on the ground that Raúl would never have undertaken such a brazen scheme without his brother's approval. On March 1 the deputy attorney general, Pablo Chapa Bezanilla, accused Mario Ruiz Massieu of obstructing justice during the investigation of his brother's assassination. The next day, Carlos Salinas de Gortari began a hunger strike to clear his reputation. Mario Ruiz Massieu left Mexico for the United States, where he was soon arrested (for carrying large amounts of undisclosed cash) while boarding a plane for Madrid. Carlos Salinas ended his hunger strike on March 4, after the Zedillo government released a mollifying statement, but he soon left the country in disgrace.

The Salinas–Ruiz Massieu intrigues evoke images of Renaissance Italy under the Borgias, rather than a modernizing country of the late twentieth century, but they are also fraught with profound political significance. They reveal a split within the ruling elite that has become more public and irreversible than at any time since the mid-1930s. They also indicate a breakdown in rules of civility that long prevailed within the national elite. Even at the highest levels of the political establishment, violence and murder came to replace the once-prized arts of bargaining, negotiation, and co-optation.

In effect, Mexico has been witnessing political disintegration at two distinct levels—among its uppermost institutions, and within the political class. These developments intersect and multiply their mutual effects. In this fashion, they set the scene for the ascendancy of the country's new-age drug barons. Furthermore, the deterioration of Mexico's long-standing system tends to magnify the political significance of drug traffickers, who face relatively few constraints on their action.

Impacts of Drug Trafficking

The restructuring of the Mexican drug trade in the late 1980s and early 1990s has exerted profound impacts on the country's political regime and its transformation. One has entailed an escalation of corruption. To be sure, Mexico has a long history of political corruption, often tacitly accepted as a necessary evil, but the windfall of cocaine profits brought this practice to unprecedented levels. With estimated annual gross revenues of $27 billion or $30 billion and about $7 billion in annual profits, according to some calculations, Mexico's nouveaux riches cartels can afford to spend as much as $500 million per year on bribery—more than twice the total annual budget of the attorney general's office.[19] They have disbursed these funds shrewdly (and characteristically) as follows:

—Top-level *políticos* who could provide protection;

—Heads of agencies engaged in antidrug activities; and

—Rank-and-file foot soldiers in Mexico's antidrug units.

In keeping with this strategy, one key target has been the federal judicial police force.[20] A prime example of such subornation occurred in August 1994, when a planeload of Colombian cocaine was captured by federal transportation police after a crash landing in the state of Zacatecas. Shortly thereafter, a rival group of enforcement agents—from the federal *judicial* police—actually hijacked the shipment from the transportation police and delivered it to *traficantes* for delivery to the U.S. market, where the goods showed up within a few days. The street value of this multiton shipment was estimated at $200 million.[21]

Instances of corruption are difficult to prove, especially as individual cases remain under investigation at the time of this writing. According to preliminary evidence and widespread rumor, however, several prominent figures appear to have enriched themselves through their complicity with *traficantes*. As a result, according to one outspoken analyst, there existed "a web of collusion between high-ranking government officials and kingpins of the country's booming drug cartels."[22]

Broadly speaking, as Miguel Ruiz-Cabañas has pointed out, deployment of the federal police (and enlistment of the national army) in Mexico's *Campaña Permanente* has merely exposed rank-and-file officers and soldiers to risks of corruption: "To the degree that drug traffic tends to generate corruption and violence wherever it operates . . . the Mexican police corps has been constantly exposed to situations that encourage corruption. Some of these cases involve middle- to high-ranking officials. In my estimation, one of the most negative consequences brought on by the drug-trafficking problem has been to delay and hinder the much-needed professionalization of the Mexican police corps."[23]

19. Fineman and Rotella (1995).
20. Lupsha (1991, especially pp. 48–53).
21. Fineman and Rotella (1995).
22. Reding (1995a).
23. Ruiz-Cabañas (1992, p. 158).

In this sense, corruption tends to be systemic. From the standpoint of the traffickers, agencies and units engaged in the fight against drugs are highly attractive targets for payoffs: bribing the sheriff (and, if necessary, the entire posse) is likely to yield instant and substantial benefits.[24]

A second consequence of the expansion of drug trafficking, especially the movement of cocaine, has been the escalation of violence. Some of this reflects tension and rivalry between opposing gangs: throughout the mid-1990s, for instance, the Tijuana and Sinaloa cartels have been locked in a bitter struggle for control of the Pacific corridor. This might result from expansion in the economic stakes involved, as the dollar volume of Mexico's drug trade swelled rapidly in the late 1980s and early 1990s. The increase in violence may also demonstrate the influence of Colombians, especially former associates of the rough-and-tumble Medellín cartel, which unleashed a civil war in their own country for several excruciating years. Further, the rise in violence may represent a response by traffickers to heightened law enforcement, which has multiplied the number of clashes and raids (Mexico's antidrug budget tripled between 1987 and 1989). But whatever the cause, the effect has been to produce a string of high-level assassinations, morbidly known within the trade as "excellent cadavers":

—a former state attorney general of Sinaloa, murdered while jogging in a Mexico City park;

—the head of the Sinaloa human rights commission, apparently slain on the orders of a federal police commander;

—a Roman Catholic cardinal, Juan Jesús Posadas Ocampo, assassinated (either on purpose or as a result of mistaken identity) at the Guadalajara airport in May 1993;[25]

—a federal police commander, allegedly killed by fellow officers;

—the police chief of Tijuana, ambushed on a highway;

—a former state attorney general of the state of Jalisco, shot on his way to teach a class in law; and

—a new federal chief of police, appointed by Zedillo, poisoned in his sleep and temporarily paralyzed as a result.

In addition, there is widespread conjecture that the assassinations of Luís Donaldo Colosio and of José Francisco Ruiz Massieu were related to drug trafficking in one way or another.

Once again, this mounting wave of violence has helped destroy the long-standing codes of gentility that for generations settled intra-elite dis-

---

24. On corruption of the military see Lupsha (1991, pp. 53–55).
25. Reding (1995a, pp. 2–3).

putation within the political system. Drugs and drug trafficking have thus undercut a fundamental pillar of Mexico's ancien régime.

There have been other costs associated with drug trafficking and, especially, with antidrug policy. One has been the frequent (some would way systematic) violation of human rights. Particularly in the early 1990s, sweeps and crackdowns resulted in injury, death, and torture of hundreds of *campesinos*. Another has been the delegation of political power to Mexican armed forces: as part and parcel of the antidrug campaign, the military has become "the supreme authority" in such states as Sinaloa, Jalisco, Oaxaca, and, more recently, Chihuahua.[26] Empowerment of the armed forces occurs at the direct expense of civilian authority.

In combination, corruption and violence have contributed to the broadest and most far-reaching challenge to Mexican politics: maintenance of law and order and, more generally, the capacity to govern. Soon after taking office, in fact, President Zedillo received an official report warning: "The power of the drug-trafficking organizations could lead to situations of ungovernability, using whatever political or economic space in which institutions show weakness or inattention; the advance of drug-trafficking promotes impunity and uncertainty in the institutions, justifies violence and increases intimidation of the authorities."[27]

This threat to legal authority takes multiple forms. One is open defiance of the government, most spectacularly through assassination. Another comes from the replacement of de jure constitutional rule by de facto informal authority, especially in poppy-growing regions and in host cities for the top cartels; in such areas, drug kingpins wield supreme power. They rule their fiefdoms without regard to centralized government, much in the manner of traditional *caciques* in eras past. A third kind of threat, perhaps the most effective and sinister of all, results from the entanglement of political leaders within the drug-trafficking network itself. The logic of the traffickers is disarmingly straightforward: if top-level politicians stand to benefit from *narcotráfico,* they will not take serious action against it.

All these challenges serve to underscore Eduardo Valle Espinosa's observation about the *traficantes*: "They have been able to create a state within a state."[28] It is in this fundamental sense, of course, that the drug trade has come to represent a genuine threat to Mexico's national security.

---

26. Doyle (1993, pp. 83–88).
27. Fineman and Rotella (1995).
28. See also Valle (1995).

Taken together, these consequences for the political system—violence, corruption, abuse of power—have helped generate widespread skepticism within civil society about the Mexican regime and its leaders. As a result of these developments (plus other disappointments, such as the devastating peso crisis of late 1994), Mexican citizens have often come to assume the worst about the motivations, integrity, and capability of their political leaders. Such disbelief undercuts support for the country's weakening authoritarian system and may hasten its collapse, but it does not necessarily create civic foundations for political democracy. All in all, the progressive alienation of Mexican society from its leadership represents an unnerving and potentially troublesome trend.

Impacts on U.S.–Mexican Relations

Not surprisingly, drug trafficking has had pernicious effects on U.S.–Mexican relations. Especially during election cycles, U.S. politicians have succumbed to the temptation of charging Mexico with responsibility for drug-related problems in American society. Indeed, "Mexico-bashing" has become a lamentably predictable element in public discussions of narcotics throughout the United States. In contrast, Mexicans tend to focus on the presence of U.S. demand for illicit drugs. More than a decade after the initial proclamation of the "war on drugs," they point out, more than 12 million Americans continue to use illicit drugs of one type or another. As of 1994 about 9.8 million Americans used marijuana regularly (a significant increase from the 1992 level of 9.2 million); about 1.3 million were taking cocaine on a monthly basis, more than half (700,000) of whom qualified as heavy users; and many others were steadily consuming heroin and/or synthetic drugs.[29] Moreover, the use of illicit drugs—especially marijuana—among U.S. high-school seniors continued to climb.[30] The fundamental problem, according to this perspective, is not supply from Mexico; it is demand in the United States. The drug issue thus creates conditions and incentives for mutual recrimination.

Adding to this tension is a difference in policy goals. According to official pronouncements, the primary motivation for the U.S. government is "to reduce illegal drug use and its consequences in America." For the United States, drug consumption represents a threat to public health, claiming 20,000 lives per year; it spawns crime, including violent offenses; it encourages delinquency and gang membership in inner-city ghettos; and in

29. Office of the President of the United States (1996a, p. 79).
30. Cimons (1995).

general, it imposes yearly "social costs" of around $67 billion, "mostly from the consequences of drug-related crime." To combat this situation the U.S. government has increased its annual antidrug budget from $4.7 billion in FY 1988 to $13.8 billion in FY 1996 (and a requested $15.0 billion for FY 1997). About one-third of these expenditures go toward demand reduction, including prevention and treatment; fully two-thirds are dedicated to law enforcement, including interdiction and international programs designed to "break foreign and domestic drug sources of supply."[31]

One defining feature of U.S. antidrug policy is its inflexibility. Ever since Ronald Reagan declared a "war on drugs" in the early 1980s, Washington has resolutely attempted to reduce the importation of illicit drugs from foreign countries. Time and again, expert opinion has revealed the unworkability of this approach, calling for emphasis on the reduction of demand, rather than supply (leaving aside the question of legalization, which raises a host of complex issues). Despite mounting expense (and increasing evidence of failure), the U.S. government has stoutly resisted such advice. The explanation for this stubbornness lies not so much in bureaucratic inertia as in the domestic political arena; in this era of public concern, no American president can afford to look "soft" on drug addicts, pushers, or traffickers.[32] Prospects for a major change in U.S. policy are slim indeed.

Mexico faces very different challenges. Although drug use is growing in some areas, especially along routes of transit, the country does not have a major problem of illicit drug consumption. (There is excessive use of inhalants, especially by street children, but that is another story.[33]) As described by María Celia Toro, the most pressing concerns for Mexico are fundamentally political. One has been "to prevent drug traffickers from directly confronting state authority," to obstruct the formation of "states within the state," and to diminish the threat of narcoterrorism. A second, "equally important" goal has been "to prevent U.S. policy and judicial authorities from acting as a surrogate justice system in Mexico."[34] Mexico has thus sought to assert and maintain its sovereignty in the face of Washington's war on drugs. In other words, U.S. policy itself poses a significant danger to Mexican national interests.[35]

31. Office of the President of the United States (1996a, pp. 11–12, 20–21, 35–37; 1996b, especially p. 298).

32. Falco (1996, pp. 120–33).

33. Medina-Mora and Carmen Mariño (1992).

34. Toro (1995, p. 2). See also Toro (1996).

35. "More than any other nation," William O. Walker III has said, "Mexico has been the object of coercive diplomacy by the United States." (Walker, 1992, p. 273.)

This underlying contradiction has been expressed and exacerbated by critical events. One such episode was the torture and murder of DEA agent Enrique Camarena in Guadalajara in 1985, apparently in response to a law-enforcement crackdown the previous year. To avenge Camarena's murder the U.S. government launched Operation Intercept II, partially closing the border for eight days in February 1985 and publicly announcing its displeasure with the slowness of Mexico's investigation. As Toro explains, "Operation Intercept II marked a turning point in terms of Mexico's understanding of the new U.S. policy on drugs . . . and of its consequences for Mexico."[36] As frustration mounted in Washington, the DEA initiated Operation Leyenda, a plan to capture all those (at least nineteen in all) believed to have participated in the Camarena episode. Leyenda involved the capture and kidnapping of two Mexican citizens—René Martín Verdugo-Urquídez (1986) and Humberto Alvarez Machaín (1990)—who were smuggled into the United States to face charges of complicity in the Camarena murder.

These abductions clearly violated long-standing interpretations of international law and represented unilateral high-handedness in the extreme. The U.S. Supreme Court then stepped into the fray, ruling that unlawful searches and seizures in other countries—with or without the participation of U.S. government agents—did not necessarily lead to the loss of jurisdiction for U.S. courts. Foreign nationals were simply not entitled to the constitutional rights enjoyed by U.S. citizens. Eventually, one U.S. judge found that the Verdugo kidnapping violated the U.S.–Mexican Extradition Treaty; another exonerated Alvarez Machaín for lack of evidence in 1993.

Continuing the U.S. turn away from international cooperation toward unilateral action, Congress passed the Anti-Drug Abuse Act of 1986, making it a crime to manufacture or distribute drugs outside the United States "with the intention of exporting them to U.S. territory." The law also conditioned U.S. economic and military aid, votes in multilateral lending institutions, and trade preferences on "full cooperation" with the U.S. campaign against drug trafficking. To fulfill this stipulation, the act established an annual "certification" process by which the U.S. government would assess the antidrug efforts of approximately thirty nations believed to be involved in the international narcotics business. Every year thereafter, the State Department would determine whether these countries "have cooperated fully with the United States, or taken adequate steps on their own, to achieve full compliance with the goals and objectives of the 1988 United

36. Toro (1995, p. 63).

Nations Convention Against Illicit Traffic in Narcotic Drugs and Psy-
chotropic Substances." Governments under review could receive approval
in the form of "certification," disapproval in the form of "decertification,"
or special dispensation because of "vital national interests of the United
States." The statute thus created a situation in which the world's largest
drug-consuming society took it upon itself to pass moral and political
judgment on the effectiveness of antidrug efforts by other nations around
the world.

Mounting pressure from the United States left Mexican governments
with little choice but to accelerate and expand their own efforts against
drugs. In search of an improved bilateral relationship (soon to include
negotiation of NAFTA), Carlos Salinas enlisted Mexico in President
George Bush's militarized war on drugs. He also approved a joint program
between the DEA and the Mexican attorney general's office called the
Northern Border Response Force, which expanded the use of U.S. helicop-
ter and radar along the U.S.–Mexican border; allowed creation of a military
intelligence unit within the U.S. embassy to investigate drug trafficking;
and, most controversially, authorized American-piloted Advanced Warning
Airborne Command System (AWACS) planes to fly over Mexican territory
to monitor drug trafficking activities. According to one reliable report,
Salinas failed to discuss the AWACS flights with his foreign secretary, the
more nationalistically inclined Fernando Solana. When word about the
flyovers became public, weeks into testing and training, there was such
vociferous objection that they had to be canceled.[37]

Similarly, President Zedillo has stepped up action on the antidrug front.
In January 1996 his government authorized the deportation of Juan García
Abrego, reputed leader of the Gulf cartel who (as a U.S. citizen) had
recently made the FBI's Ten Most Wanted list. Although U.S. Attorney
General Janet Reno hailed the decision as "a major victory" in Mexico's
war on drugs, Mexican jurists sharply challenged its constitutionality.
Zedillo has also expanded the role of the military (placing the army in full
control of antidrug efforts in the state of Chihuahua) and has overseen the
arrest of several well-known kingpins. DEA and FBI agents confirm that
cross-border cooperation reached an all-time high during 1995 and 1996.
The Colosio and Ruiz Massieu assassinations were still unsolved, but

37. In attempts to uphold sovereignty and resist U.S. interventionism, the Salinas administration also proposed such agreements as the Mutual Legal Assistance Treaty (1991),
renegotiated the U.S.–Mexican Extradition Treaty, and introduced new guidelines for the
operation of DEA agents in Mexico.

Zedillo and his attorney general have continually vowed that justice will be done.

It was in this context that Mexico faced the annual "certification" process created by the Anti-Drug Abuse Act of 1986. Frustrated by the continuing flow of drugs (especially cocaine) from Mexico to the United States, American politicians—liberal and conservative alike—called for decertification of Mexico. Democratic Senator Dianne Feinstein of California became particularly vocal, joining with archconservative Republican Senator Alfonse d'Amato of New York to issue a pronouncement calling on the Clinton administration to halt further payments to Mexico under the 1995 peso rescue plan unless something were done about drugs. As the moment for the decision approached, Senate Majority Leader (and soon-to-be Republican presidential candidate) Bob Dole sent Clinton a letter calling for decertification: "If we are to be honest," Dole wrote, "we cannot credibly say that the government of Mexico has 'cooperated fully' with the drug enforcement effort."[38]

Amid this swirling controversy, the State Department (in consultation with other government agencies) approached the Mexican issue gingerly. "Entering office in December 1994," the official report began, "President Ernesto Zedillo declared drug trafficking the principal threat to Mexico's national security and promised a major offensive against the drug cartels and drug-related corruption. He and Mexican Attorney General Antonio Lozano recognized that Mexico's law-enforcement efforts were being seriously undercut by narco-corruption and intimidation and by the high-tech capabilities of the trafficking organizations. They intensified the counternarcotics effort, prosecuted corrupt officials, and sought to expand cooperation with U.S. and other governments."

On balance, the State Department concluded, Mexico deserved full certification. The report continued: "Even with positive results and good cooperation with the U.S. and other governments, Mexico has a number of obstacles to overcome. The Zedillo administration has set the stage for action against the major drug cartels in Mexico, and for more effective cooperation with the U.S. and other international partners, but it will need to equip its investigators and prosecutors with the appropriate legal tools to combat modern organized crime and provide adequate material resources. It will need to pass and implement proposed legislation to establish controls on money laundering and chemical diversion. It must move forcefully to

38. Fineman (1996).

dismantle major drug trafficking organizations. Above all, it will have to take serious, system-wide action against endemic corruption."[39]

This was a highly qualified endorsement. In a sense, Mexico had received a "national security" waiver under another name. It was a close call.

NAFTA Effects?

Many analysts interpret the 1996 decision as a consequence of the North American Free Trade Agreement: decertification of Mexico would have amounted to a tacit recognition that NAFTA had been a mistake, and the Clinton administration was unwilling and unprepared to make such a confession. Whatever the truth of this analysis, the link between drug trafficking and free trade has raised a basic question: what is the connection between NAFTA and drugs?

The treaty itself makes no mention of drugs. Silvana Paternostro, among others, implies that this was an error, suggesting that the United States should have been able to extract extensive concessions on antidrug efforts from Mexico in exchange for membership in NAFTA (and from subsequent negotiation of the 1994–95 bailout). With evident approval, she quotes Eduardo Valle: "When it comes to drug trafficking, NAFTA can be a double-edged sword . . . NAFTA, from a commercial perspective, can be the perfect ally for drug trafficking, but politically, it can be the perfect ally to fight drug trafficking."[40] The conclusion is that Washington squandered an opportunity to make major progress against drug trafficking in Mexico and that it should be sure to take advantage of similar chances in the future.

The impact of NAFTA on drug flows, as distinct from antidrug policy, presents a different question. Analyses are still necessarily inconclusive. At one end of the debate are those who argue that freer trade under NAFTA will increase the flow of drugs from Mexico to the United States. As Assistant U.S. Attorney Glenn MacTaggart has said: "If NAFTA provides opportunity for legitimate businesses, it may clearly provide opportunities for illegitimate businessmen." And in a discussion of contradictory tensions in U.S.–Mexican relations, Peter Andreas has observed: "Hiding drug shipments within the growing volume of goods exported from Mexico to the United States has become an increasingly favored method of smuggling cocaine. These trends thrive under the North American Free Trade Agreement." Trans-border trucking, with 2.8 million crossings in 1994 alone,

39. U.S. Department of State (1996, pp. xli–xlii).
40. Paternostro (1995, pp. 41–47, with quote on p. 47).

provides an especially attractive opportunity for smugglers. Andreas notes, therefore, that "trying to close the border to the flow of drugs while opening it to the flow of virtually everything else is a formula for frustration."[41]

Others remain unpersuaded. María Celia Toro, for one, notes that drug smugglers have been hiding illicit goods within legal exports for decades, well before the discussion or implementation of NAFTA. Moreover, she contends, "the implementation of NAFTA will not encourage the practice, which is not a preferred means of smuggling. The practice would involve prohibitive costs and risks that do not make sense for the smuggler, who can more easily operate in other ways. Even if one assumes the so-called ant smuggling—sending small amounts of drugs across the frontier—might increase, it would certainly not be enough to impact the availability of drugs in the United States."[42]

From the standpoint of the traffickers, shipping cocaine or other drugs to the United States in trucks that undergo routine customs examinations by U.S. authorities entails excessive risk. There are other ways to reach the market, and these are totally independent of NAFTA.

A reasonable conclusion is that NAFTA might lead to a modest increase in cross-border transshipment, perhaps as envisioned by Andreas, but that it will not have a large-scale impact, as argued by Toro. What seems more clear, by contrast, is the impact of NAFTA on drug policy and politics. One might imagine first that NAFTA will increase effective pressure on Mexican authorities to comply with U.S. demands for antidrug measures; and second, that NAFTA will increase the likelihood that the U.S. government will continue to grant positive "certification" to Mexican efforts, whatever the true degree of cooperation or effectiveness.

Nine years ago, a blue-ribbon group of prominent citizens known as the Bilateral Commission on the Future of United States–Mexican Relations issued a book-length report on ways of improving relations between the two countries. The chapter on drugs began with the observation: "The narcotics issue presents the United States and Mexico with a bitter paradox. On the one hand, it represents an area of the bilateral relationship where the national interests of both countries are in complete accord: both agree on the need to combat the illegal production, traffic, and use of drugs. On the other hand, the issue of narcotics control has been the source of repeated disagreements between the two countries, disagreements that not only have

41. Andreas (1996b, pp. 51–69, with quotes on pp. 57, 67).
42. Toro (1995, p. 87, n. 168).

hindered joint efforts to combat drug abuse and traffic but also have had negative repercussions on the bilateral relationship as a whole."[43]

This assessment remains as valid today as it was in 1988. In all its nefarious complexity, the drug issue could now erupt in crisis at almost any moment, undermining the relationship between the United States and Mexico and jeopardizing cooperation on a broad array of issues. It is a problem that simply will not go away.

43. Bilateral Commission on the Future of United States–Mexican Relations (1988, p. 113).

Comment by María Celia Toro

Peter Smith explores the reasons that may explain the sense of alarm in both countries regarding drug trafficking. One is the transformation of the Mexican drug trade into a "cartelized" industry, by which he means one under the "control of entrepreneurial organizations . . . fewer in number, stronger in resources, and more dangerous to society and government." Another is the increasingly deleterious political impact of the drug trade in Mexico; the third is the ever-present potential for an international drug-related crisis affecting the overall standing of U.S.–Mexico relations. I would like to comment on these three general arguments.

The Change to a More "Cartelized" Industry as of the Mid-1980s

This change refers to the formation of a powerful, "effective oligopoly" composed of "at least five" groups of "international stature and scope."

There is little doubt that drug traffickers in every single country where such trafficking takes place today are stronger and more dangerous to government and society. But they are, at the same time, less cartelized. That is, there are more groups, not fewer, compared with earlier decades, and these groups are less able to organize themselves for survival as a result of more stringent antidrug law enforcement both in Mexico and in the United States.

Is today's market better organized? One could, with the same data provided by Peter Smith, argue that the drug industry in Mexico is today more disorganized and less oligopolistic than in the early 1980s, when the present conundrum for Mexico began. There is evidence in Peter Smith's discussion that suggests the presence of a highly disorganized market. The increase in cocaine traffic, according to Smith, changed the drug scene in Mexico in far-reaching ways, in particular the "traditional marketing groups" that "maintained close ties with producers, operated at local levels, and maintained low political profiles." Colombian cocaine "led to the emergence of new contenders [who] compete against each other for the same goods and the same market. . . . There appears to be [argues Smith] more rivalry than coordination." In fact, the market may be so disorganized that Colombians and Mexicans are "moving toward vertical integration of their operations," as opppposed to relying on each other for the smuggling of cocaine into the United States.

One can find U.S. official reports and academic writings suggesting the existence of ten or even twenty groups. Reuter and Ronfeldt affirmed that there were about 200 drug trafficking organizations in Mexico toward the end of the 1980s. In fact, I am always amazed by references made three or four times a year in Mexican newspapers alluding to a new group of traffickers believed to be the true drug lords, with names that I had never heard before. To mention just two examples:

—As recently as 1992–93, Rafael Aguilar Guajardo was believed to have one of the strongest links with the Mexican government and the private sector and was said to export up to 60 percent of total U.S. cocaine imports.

—Brothers Pedro and Filiberto Lupercio Serratos were also considered important organizers of the market in Ciudad Juárez, Michoacán, Jalisco, and Chihuahua.

The resilience of the old groups, however, is equally striking. Two of the five groups that Smith identifies are direct heirs of the early 1980s groups (the Arellano Félix brothers) and the Guadalajara group led by the Caro Quinteros.

In other words, the drug industry in Mexico seems to have been more cartelized in the early 1980s than it is today, after fifteen years of sustained antidrug law enforcement, although some of the old groups have managed to survive. Nevertheless, if traffickers do not organize to fix prices and (as I believe) have been unable to strike agreements on market boundaries, and if the market has been booming with more rather than fewer participants, then the term cartel may not be the correct one to describe the Mexican drug market in the 1990s.

Mexican traffickers seem to be desperately fighting to survive enforcement and they, as Smith argues, have plenty of economic resources today to sustain the battle. As of the 1980s, the incentives to become a drug smuggler increased to levels that drug traffickers of past decades would have never dreamed of and that historians will have a hard time believing. The possibility of amassing a fortune practically overnight accounts for the rapid reemergence of old groups that lost their leader and for the appearance of newcomers trying to seize the opportunity. But the risks of participating in this market today (as prices show), imposed by both police and fellow traffickers, are also unprecedented, which accounts for the dramatic increase in violence and in the scope of governmental corruption. More stringent enforcement accounts for both the unprecedented profits and the risks of engaging in drug smuggling today. If this depiction of a highly disorganized market is correct and antidrug policies continue its punitive trend (which is likely), then the "opportunist Mexican traffickers," as Smith aptly describes them, will remain disorganized, powerful, and unbeatable.

The Political Implications

The second reason for alarm is the political implications of the drug trade in Mexico, or what I would call the casualties in the "war" against drugs. I fully share Peter Smith's concern with the serious political consequences of trying to enforce antidrug laws by relying on what are perhaps the weakest of Mexican governmental institutions—namely the police and the judiciary. In addition, we have no way whatsoever to modify the relationship between the Mexican export price and the U.S. import price for drugs, which is what has historically provided the fundamental impulse to drug smuggling.

Smith argues that drug trafficking, especially of cocaine, entered the Mexican political scene in a bad moment. He describes this as a relentless process of "significant erosion of institutional authority" or of political disintegration, which "set the scene for the ascendancy of the country's new-age drug barons."

I am unable to assess Mexico's political troubles, which are real. However, I presume that many of them are only marginally related to drug trafficking, although they are certainly exacerbated by it. What is clear is that, regardless of political trends, the 1980s trafficking boom practically destroyed what were already extremely weak criminal justice systems, as the cases of Bolivia, Colombia, Peru, Ecuador, Panama, and other countries in Latin America show. The erosion of institutional authority—as evidenced in the levels of impunity and of corruption, the use of violence against enforcers and judicial authorities, and the overall incapacity to maintain minimum levels of law and order—is a consequence of heavy-handed enforcement rather than the starting point or the context in which drug smuggling has flourished. Another negative by-product, frequently overlooked and with significant political consequences, has been the creation of an alarming public security problem, as recently fired police agents or disbanded police agencies presumed to be involved in drug trafficking quickly and effectively organize into delinquent groups.

The political impact of all these unintended consequences—which at this point we should be able to anticipate—is of course far from trivial. Trying to enforce ever more stringent antidrug laws in Mexico (tantamount to fighting against the effects of U.S. interdiction efforts) has not only been impossible, but the effort has also truly uncovered the fundamental feebleness of the Mexican police force and the intelligence and judicial systems. The proliferation of drug trafficking activities and groups, the private organization of violence by drug traffickers, and the links between authorities and traffickers represent a major challenge to the state as the ultimate guarantee of law and order. In this sense, drug trafficking has seriously undermined political legitimacy, independently of regime type.

A professional police force and a modern judiciary in the United States or in Europe have been unable to stop the drug traffic for reasons that have been sufficiently analyzed. However, the comparative strength of those institutions accounts for the far fewer casualties in terms of corruption, violence, and respect for the rule of law. Still, even these far more robust law enforcement and criminal justice institutions are currently under severe stress.

Indeed, things were different in the early 1970s, before the launching of major operations against the illicit drug trade in Mexico began. The market was more stable, and the governmental budgets spent in antinarcotic operations both in the United States and in Mexico were considerably smaller. Profits were, in comparison, far lower; and as a consequence, drug-related corruption and violence were of a different order of magnitude. Drug trafficking then was, all in all, less damaging to both government and society.

U.S.–Mexico Relations

Peter Smith has plenty of good reasons to anticipate that drug trafficking in this bilateral relationship will remain a permanent and unpredictable source of conflict. The objectives of both countries regarding the illicit drug trade include goals that go beyond reducing drug smuggling, and they will remain as distant as the wish to interrupt the traffic. Peter Reuter and David Ronfeldt have described U.S. antidrug policy toward Mexico as a "quest for integrity." I would argue that Mexican policy against drugs has had an important outward orientation that could be described as a "quest for autonomy." Both objectives, integrity and autonomy, have become increasingly more difficult to attain. To the extent that antidrug law enforcement budgets remain at an historic high in both countries and antinarcotics operations become ever more sophisticated, the U.S. battle against corruption in Mexico and Mexico's reliance on U.S. intelligence and technical assistance will increase in tandem.

Is there cause for any optimism? What can Mexico realistically shoot for, assuming that a change in U.S. policy or in U.S. levels of drug use is unlikely in the near future? Mexico, with significant and indispensable U.S. support, has been striving since the mid-1980s to prevent cocaine smugglers from establishing a permanent presence in Mexico as a convenient midpoint between the Andean region and the United States. The effort has not been successful so far, and it has taken a heavy toll on Mexican society and institutions. However, according to the last intelligence reports there is a possibility that cocaine smugglers are changing routes yet again, back to the Caribbean and the Florida peninsula. Although the amount of cocaine entering the U.S. market may remain unmodified as a result, Mexico would be better off, at least on that front. But there would still be a serious problem with money-laundering, and Mexico would also face the newly emergent metamphetamine market—both problems, once again, directly linked to more stringent enforcement in the United States.

General Discussion

A number of participants reiterated a point made by both Peter Smith and María Celia Toro: U.S. drug consumption seems unlikely to decline soon, regardless of policies undertaken in Mexico or other countries. In this context, Enrique Mendoza emphasized that fighting drug traffic from one country should be expected to be offset by increased flows from other countries.

Barry Bosworth advanced the view that Smith's discussion implies it is Mexico that should "decertify" the United States, not the other way around. His point was that, because of its position immediately south of the U.S. border, Mexico is paying a heavy price for U.S. drug practices and policies. This price is exacted through the serious adverse effects of the growing drug trade on Mexico's political system and society that Smith describes.

Peter Andreas questioned Smith's discussion of whether NAFTA per se will help or hurt the cross-border drug trade. He argued that this narrow focus may be misleading, advocating instead a broader focus on the relationship between drug traffic, economic restructuring, and the growing economic integration between Mexico and the United States. In particular, NAFTA should be viewed as part of longer-term economic trends, not as an independent event. Peter Reuter agreed with this perspective, arguing that NAFTA itself is likely to have little effect on the bilateral drug trade.

References

Andreas, Peter. 1996a. "U.S.–Mexico: Open Markets, Closed Border." *Foreign Policy* 103 (Summer): 51–69.

_____. 1996b. "Dark Side of NAFTA—A Boom in Mexican Drug Trafficking." *Sacramento Bee,* June 30.

Bilateral Commission on the Future of United States–Mexican Relations. 1988. *The Challenge of Independence: Mexico and the United States.* Lanham, Md.: University Press of America.

Cimons, Marlene. 1995. "Teen-Agers' Marijuana Use Nearly Doubles." *Los Angeles Times*, September 13.

Craig, Richard. 1980. "Operation Condor: Mexico's Anti-Drug Campaign Enters a New Era." *Journal of International Affairs* 22 (August): 345–63.

Dillon, Sam. 1995. "Power in Drug Trade Shifts from Colombia to Mexico." *Sacramento Bee*, December 27.

Doyle, Kate. 1993. "The Militarization of the Drug War in Mexico." *Current History* (February): 83–88.

Dresser, Denise. 1995. "Twilight of the Perfect Dictatorship: The Decline of Dominant-Party Rule in Mexico." Paper prepared for annual meeting of Latin American Studies Association, Washington, September 28–30.

Falco, Mathea. 1996. "U.S. Drug Policy: Addicted to Failure." *Foreign Policy* 102 (Spring): 120–33.

Fineman, Mark. 1996. "Mexico is Edgy As It Awaits U.S. Decision in Progress on Drug War." *Los Angeles Times*, March 1.

Fineman, Mark, and Sebastian Rotella. 1995. "The Drug Web that Entangles Mexico." *Los Angeles Times*, June 15.

González Sandoval, Juan Pablo, and Jaime González Graf, eds. 1995. *Los límites rotos: anuario político*. Mexico City: Oceano.

Lupsha, Peter A. 1981. "Drug Trafficking: Mexico and Colombia in Comparative Perspective." *Journal of International Affairs* 35 (Spring/Summer): 95–115.

_____. 1991. "Drug Lords and Narco-Corruption: The Players Change but the Game Continues." *Crime, Law and Social Change* 16: 41–58.

_____. 1994a. "Mexican Narco-Trafficking: The Dark Side of NAFTA." *Encuentros* 1 (Fall): 9–11.

_____. 1994b. "Nets of Affiliation in the Political Economy of Drug Trafficking and Transnational Crime." In *Economics of the Narcotics Industry* (conference report). Central Intelligence Agency and U.S. Department of State.

_____. 1996. Paper prepared for conference, "The United States and Latin America: Reassessing the Relationship," University of California, San Diego, May 16–18.

Medina-Mora, María Elena, and Maria del Carmen Mariño. 1992. "Drug Abuse in Latin America." In *Drug Policy in the Americas*, edited by Peter H. Smith, 45–56. Boulder, Colo.: Westview Press.

Office of the President of the United States. 1996a. *The National Drug Control Strategy: 1996.*

Office of the President of the United States. 1996b. *The National Drug Control Strategy, 1996: Program, Resources, and Evaluation.*

Paternostro, Silvana. 1995. "Mexico as a Narco-democracy." *World Policy Journal* (Spring): 41–47.

Reding, Andrew. 1995a. "Political Corruption and Drug Trafficking in Mexico: Impunity for High-Level Officials Spurs Lawlessness and Growth of Drug Cartels." Statement before Senate Committee on Foreign Relations Hearing, "The Drug Trade in Mexico and U.S. Policy Implications," 104 Cong. 1 sess., August 8.

_____. 1995b. "The Rise and Fall of the Drug Cartels: With Colombia's Kingpins Nabbed, America Faces More Elusive Targets in Mexico." *Washington Post*, September 17, p. C4.

Reuter, Peter. 1996. "The Mismeasurement of Illegal Drug Markets: The Implication of Its Irrelevance." In *Exploring the Underground Economy*, edited by Susan Pozo, 52–61. Kalamazoo, Mich.: Upjohn Institute.

Rotella, Sebastian. 1995. "Mexico's Cartels Sow Seeds of Corruption, Destruction." *Los Angeles Times,* June 16.

Ruiz-Cabañas, Miguel I. 1989. "Mexico's Changing Illicit Drug Supply Role." In *The Drug Connection in U.S. Mexican Relations,* edited by Guadalupe González and Marta Tienda, 48–50. La Jolla, Calif.: Center for U.S. Mexican Studies, University of California, San Diego.

_____. 1992. "Mexico's Permanent Campaign: Costs, Benefits, Implications." In *Drug Policy in the Americas,* edited by Peter H. Smith, 151–62. Boulder, Colo.: Westview Press.

Toro, María Celia. 1995. *Mexico's "War" on Drugs: Causes and Consequences.* Boulder, Colo: Lynne Rienner.

_____. 1996. "The Internationalization of Police: The Case of the DEA in Mexico." Paper prepared for meeting of the International Studies Association, San Diego, April 16–20.

Trueba Lara, José Luis. 1995. *Política y narcopoder en México.* Mexico City: Editorial Planeta.

U.S. Department of State, Bureau of International Narcotics and Law Enforcement Affairs. 1989. *International Narcotics Strategy Report, March 1989.*

_____. 1992. *International Narcotics Strategy Report, March 1992.*

_____. 1996. *International Narcotics Strategy Report, March 1996.*

Valle, Eduardo. 1995. *El segundo disparo: la narcodemocracia mexicana.* Mexico City: Oceano.

Walker, William O., III. 1992. "International Collaboration in Historical Perspective." In *Drug Policy in the Americas,* edited by Peter H. Smith, 265–81. Boulder, Colo.: Westview Press.

Zaid, Gabriel. 1995. *Adiós al PRI.* Mexico City: Oceano.

6 The Economic Impact of Mexican Immigration

George J. Borjas

THE size and composition by national origin of the immigrant flow entering the United States changed substantially in recent decades. Perhaps the most important aspect of this historic trend is the rapid increase in the number of Mexican-born persons who choose to migrate to the United States. During the 1950s, for example, only about 300,000 *legal* Mexican immigrants entered the United States, or about 12 percent of the immigrant flow. Between 1981 and 1990, nearly 1.7 million Mexicans entered the United States legally, or about 23 percent of the total flow. These immigrants include both the 693,000 Mexicans who entered through "regular" means, as well as the 963,000 who entered illegally but whose status was legalized by the amnesty included in the 1986 Immigration Reform and Control Act (IRCA).[1] Even if we restrict our attention to the Mexican immigrants who did not benefit from the amnesty, the Mexican flow was about 26 percent greater than that of the next largest national origin group (Filipinos). If we take into account both the legal immigrants and the illegal aliens who legalized their status before 1990, the Mexican immigrant flow was nearly three times as large as that of the next largest national origin group.

As a result of the shifts in the size and national origin mix of the immigrant flow, a rapidly growing literature documents the economic impact of immigration on the United States.[2] These studies have already generated a number of results that have influenced the debate over immigration policy. In particular, the literature concludes that the relative skills of successive immigrant cohorts declined during much of the postwar period. There is also less convergence between the earnings of immigrants and natives than was previously believed, making it unlikely that the immigrants who arrived in the 1970s or 1980s will attain wage parity with

1. U.S. Immigration and Naturalization Service (1994).
2. See the survey in Borjas (1994).

U.S. native workers during their working lives. The academic studies have found that much of the relative decline in immigrant skills can be attributed to changes in the national origin mix of immigrant flows. Because immigrants from less-developed countries do not tend to perform well in the U.S. labor market, the rapidly increasing share of the immigrant flow that originates in Mexico, the rest of Latin America, and Asia generates a less "successful" immigrant flow. Finally, the evidence suggests that the large increase in the number of less skilled immigrants may have had an adverse effect on the employment opportunities of less skilled U.S. natives, as well as greatly increased the number of immigrants who receive public assistance in the United States.

This chapter summarizes the current evidence regarding the economic impact of Mexican immigration. Any analysis of this impact must begin with the explicit recognition of what is perhaps the salient characteristic of Mexican immigrants in the United States: The skills of Mexican immigrants, on average, are substantially below those of other immigrant groups and of U.S. natives. This disparity in skills across the various groups has important economic consequences for both the United States and Mexico. In particular, the large-scale migration of less skilled Mexican workers has probably affected adversely the economic opportunities of less skilled U.S. native workers in the United States, while improving the opportunities of those less skilled workers who remain in Mexico. The less skilled nature of the flow of Mexican workers also implies that Mexican immigrants are disproportionately more likely to participate in public assistance programs in the United States. At the same time, the United States has benefited from this migration flow mainly because the goods and services produced by less skilled workers are now cheaper. The available evidence, however, suggests that the net economic gain for the United States is relatively small.

Socioeconomic Profile of Mexican Immigrants in the United States

Before 1965, U.S. immigration policy was guided by the quota system regarding national origins. Under this system, visas allocated to applicants from the Eastern Hemisphere were awarded mainly on the basis of national origin (with two countries, Germany and the United Kingdom, receiving about 60 percent of the available slots). In contrast, those individuals from the Western Hemisphere were exempt from the quotas and faced no numerical restrictions on the number of visas, presumably because of the close economic and political ties between the United States and its geographic neighbors. Visas for Western Hemisphere applicants were awarded on a first-come, first-served basis as long as these individuals satisfied a long list of health, moral, and political requirements.

The 1965 Amendments to the Immigration and Nationality Act (and subsequent amendments) leveled the playing field for all visa applicants, regardless of their country of origin or of its hemispheric location. Family reunification became the central goal of immigration policy, with entry visas being awarded mainly to applicants who have relatives already in the United States.

The economic impact of immigration from Mexico, of course, is determined not only by the immigration statutes but also by the large number of Mexicans who illegally choose to enter the United States. The latest wave of illegal immigration from Mexico began in the late 1960s, after the discontinuation of the *bracero* program. This program was launched in 1942, when the U.S. and Mexican governments agreed to allow the temporary migration of agricultural workers due to a labor shortage during World War II. The program continued in various guises until 1964, when it was unilaterally ended by the United States. The main reason given for the discontinuation was the undocumented presumption that the *bracero* program depressed the wages of U.S. natives in the agricultural industry.

The number of Mexican illegal aliens apprehended by the Border Patrol began to increase soon after the *bracero* program ended. In 1964, fewer than 100,000 illegal aliens (both Mexican and non-Mexican) were apprehended.[3] The number of apprehensions peaked in 1986, when 1.7 million Mexican and 96,000 non-Mexican illegal aliens were apprehended. In 1986, Congress enacted the Immigration Reform and Control Act, hoping to stop the flow of illegal aliens by providing amnesty to a large number of illegal aliens already here, and by setting up a system of employer sanctions designed to penalize employers who knowingly hire illegal aliens. Nearly 2.7 million illegal aliens were granted amnesty (of whom about 2 million were Mexicans). The employer sanctions, however, did not do the job. After a temporary dip in illegal border crossings, the number of annual apprehensions of Mexican illegal aliens topped 1 million annually by 1994.

The combination of large flows of both legal and illegal Mexican immigrants can have a substantial economic impact on the United States. It is instructive to begin the discussion by documenting some of the socioeconomic characteristics of the typical Mexican immigrant in the United States. Table 6-1 summarizes some of the characteristics of this population.

3. U.S. Immigration and Naturalization Service (1994), pp. 160–61.

Table 6-1. Characteristics of Mexican Immigrants in the United States

| | Immigrants | |
Variable	Mexican	Total
Number (millions)	4.3	19.8
Percent male	55.1	49.4
Median age		
Men	29.3	35.3
Women	31.0	39.3
Percent living in U.S. at least 10 years	50.1	56.2
Percent of households containing at least five persons	47.7	23.0

Source: Bureau of the Census (1993).

In 1990, the 4.3 million Mexican-born residents enumerated by the U.S. Census made up about 22 percent of the total immigrant stock in the United States. Although the Bureau of the Census made a determined effort to enumerate a large number of illegal aliens, there was probably an undercount of this elusive population. To the extent that a disproportionate number of the illegal aliens are from Mexico, the Mexican share of the foreign-born population reported in table 6-1 is an underestimate. The table also indicates that Mexican immigrants tend to be disproportionately male, relatively young, living in the United States for a shorter time, and living in relatively large households.

As noted earlier, the central distinguishing feature of Mexican immigrants in the United States is their relatively low skill level and poor economic performance. Table 6-2 reports the percentage wage differential between Mexican immigrant men and U.S. native men in the 1970–90 period. In 1970, the typical Mexican immigrant earned about 31 percent less than U.S. natives; by 1990, the Mexican immigrant wage disadvantage had grown to 40 percent. The relative economic standing of Mexican immigrants in the United States therefore declined substantially over a relatively short period.

For comparison, table 6-2 also reports the wage differential between non-Mexican immigrants and typical U.S. native workers in the United States. These statistics show that the economic experiences of Mexican immigrants differs greatly from that of non-Mexican immigrants. In 1990, the typical Mexican immigrant in 1990 earned 40 percent less than U.S. natives, whereas the wage disadvantage of the typical non-Mexican immigrant was only 5 percent.

The relative economic disadvantage of Mexican immigrants cannot be attributed to the fact that Mexicans, on average, have been in the United States for a shorter time and hence may not have had time to "assimilate"

Table 6-2. Percentage Wage Differential between Mexican Immigrants and the Native-Born Population

Group	1970	1980	1990
Mexican immigrants	−31.1	−31.6	−39.5
Newly arrived Mexican immigrants	−44.2	−46.5	−52.6
Non-Mexican immigrants	4.7	−3.2	−5.3
Newly arrived non-Mexican immigrants	−13.4	−22.0	−24.5

Source: Author's tabulations from the 1970, 1980, and 1990 Public Use Samples of the U.S. Census. The statistics are calculated in the subsample of men ages 25–64 who work in the civilian sector, who are not self-employed, and who do not reside in group quarters.

into the U.S. labor market. Table 6-2 also reports the relative wage of immigrants who have been in the country for less than five years (as of the time of each of the censuses). Recent Mexican arrivals earned 53 percent less than U.S. natives in 1990, as compared with a wage disadvantage of 25 percent for recently arrived immigrants of non-Mexican origin.

The data in table 6-2, as in most studies of immigration in the United States, are drawn from the Public Use Samples of the decennial Census. These data contain *both* legal and illegal Mexican immigrants. It is also crucial to note that the Census data do not contain *any* information that can be used to determine the legal status of any particular worker in the sample. As a result, Census data on the relative economic status of immigrants— particularly of Mexican immigrants—must be interpreted carefully.

It is typically presumed that illegal aliens from Mexico are less skilled than their legal compatriots. This presumption implies that the relatively low skill level of the Mexican foreign-born population in the U.S. Census could be a consequence of the contamination of the sample of Mexican legal immigrants with large numbers of illegal aliens. If true, this conjecture has important policy consequences. The implications for *legal* immigration implied by the "raw" Census data would have to be modified substantially if practically all of the unskilled Mexican foreign-born persons in the Census data were illegal aliens.

There is, however, no convincing way of distinguishing between legal and illegal aliens in Census data. A widely cited study by the Urban Institute, for example, takes the unusual *and* highly misleading step of defining a sample of "legal" immigrants by dropping *all* Mexican foreign-born persons from the Census sample.[4] It is certainly the case that Mexicans make up the largest component of the illegal population. But it is also true that Mexicans also make up the largest component of the legal immigrant population.

4. Fix and Passel (1994, p. 34).

In my view, it is unlikely that adequate adjustments of the Census data on Mexican immigrants will fundamentally change the main implication of the empirical evidence. In particular, Mexican immigrants—whether legal or illegal—are less skilled than other immigrants and U.S. natives. To illustrate, suppose we make the extreme assumption that all the Mexican foreign-born persons who arrived in the United States since 1975 and who were enumerated by the 1990 Census are either illegal aliens or entered the United States illegally and became legalized through the amnesty in IRCA, whereas those who arrived before 1975 (and remained in the country until 1990) were legal immigrants. Recall that the wage differential between the typical Mexican immigrant and the typical U.S. native worker was 40 percent in 1990. It turns out that there is a 27 percent wage differential between U.S. native workers and pre-1975 Mexican immigrants *as of 1990*. In other words, the relative wage level of the "presumed" legal population of Mexican immigrants is very low—even after fifteen years in the United States.

Economists typically interpret relative wages as measures of underlying skill differentials. Using this interpretation, the data reported in table 6-2 suggest that not only do Mexican immigrants have fewer skills than U.S. native workers, but also that the skill gap between Mexican immigrants and U.S. natives has widened substantially since 1970. The interpretation of the trend in relative wages as a measure of the trend in relative skills, however, is problematic. After all, there were historic changes in the U.S. wage structure during the 1980s, and these changes did not affect all skill groups equally.[5] In particular, there was a sizable increase in the wage gap between highly educated and less educated workers. If Mexican immigrants are relatively unskilled, the changes in the wage structure imply that the relative wage of Mexican immigrants would have fallen between 1980 and 1990 *even if the skills of Mexican immigrants had remained constant*.

Nevertheless, there is direct evidence that the underlying skills of the Mexican-born population declined during this period, relative to those of U.S. natives. Consider, for example, the trends in a skill measure that is invariant to changes in the wage structure—namely, the educational attainment of immigrants. Table 6-3 documents the changes in the schooling distribution of the various groups between 1970 and 1990.

In 1970, 40 percent of natives were high school dropouts; by 1990, only 15 percent of natives lacked a high school diploma. Among Mexican immigrants, 82 percent were dropouts in 1970 and 74 percent were in 1990.

---

5. Katz and Murphy (1992); Murphy and Welch (1992).

Table 6-3. Relative Educational Attainment of Mexican Immigrants

Variable/group	1970	1980	1990
Mean years of schooling			
U.S.-born persons	11.5	12.7	13.2
Mexican immigrants	6.4	7.2	7.6
Non-Mexican immigrants	11.2	12.7	12.9
Percent not completing high school			
U.S.-born persons	39.6	23.1	14.8
Mexican immigrants	82.2	76.6	74.4
Non-Mexican immigrants	44.6	28.5	24.5
Percent graduating from college			
U.S.-born persons	15.4	22.9	26.6
Mexican immigrants	2.7	3.5	3.7
Non-Mexican immigrants	20.7	30.3	34.2

Source: Author's tabulations from the 1970, 1980, and 1990 Public Use Samples of the U.S. Census. The statistics are calculated in the subsample of men ages 25–64 who work in the civilian sector, who are not self-employed, and who do not reside in group quarters.

Relative to U.S. natives, therefore, Mexican immigrants were about twice as likely to be high school dropouts in 1970 but are now *five* times more likely to be high school dropouts. At the same time, the proportion of U.S. natives who are college graduates increased substantially, from 15 percent in 1970 to 27 percent in 1990. Among Mexican immigrants, however, the proportion who are college graduates remained negligible over the past twenty years—2.7 percent in 1970 and 3.7 percent in 1990.

Some of the economic consequences of the sizable skills gap between Mexican immigrants and native workers would be ameliorated if the gap narrowed over time, as Mexican immigrants accumulate job experience in the U.S. labor market. The available evidence, however, suggests that the gap between the two groups does not narrow much over the immigrants' lives. To document this fact, we can track particular cohorts of immigrants and U.S. native workers across the censuses.

Table 6-4 reports the relative wage of Mexican immigrants in a particular cohort and age group relative to U.S. natives in the same age group (so that, for example, Mexican immigrants aged 25–34 in 1970 are compared with U.S. natives ages 25–34 in 1970, to those ages 35–44 in 1980, and those ages 45–54 in 1990). In particular, consider the group of Mexican immigrants who arrived between 1965 and 1969 and who were 25–34 years old in 1970. At the time of arrival, this immigrant cohort earned 41 percent less than U.S. natives of the same age. By 1990, both the Mexican immigrant and native cohorts are twenty years older, yet the wage differential between the two groups remained at 37 percent. Over a twenty-year period, the relative wage of this immigrant cohort therefore increased by only 4

Table 6-4. Relative Wage Growth Experienced by Mexican Immigrants

Age cohort	1970	1980	1990
1965–69 arrivals			
25–34 in 1970	–41.0	–31.3	–36.8
35–44 in 1970	–45.8	–39.6	–45.4
1975–79 arrivals			
25–34 in 1980	—	–40.9	–39.1
35–44 in 1980	—	–49.3	–50.3

Source: Author's tabulations from the 1970, 1980, and 1990 Public Use Samples of the U.S. Census. The statistics are calculated in the subsamples of men ages 25–64 who work in the civilian sector, who are not self-employed, and who do not reside in group quarters.

percentage points. In other words, there is little evidence that the wage gap between Mexican immigrants and U.S. native workers narrows substantially during the first two decades after their arrival in the United States.

It is definitely worth determining if the sizable wage gap between Mexican immigrants and natives can be "explained" in terms of observable socioeconomic characteristics, such as differences in educational attainment or work experience between the two groups.[6] These types of studies mirror the voluminous literature that attempts to document the source of the wage differential between black and white workers in the United States. For the most part, studies of the black-white wage gap conclude that part of this gap cannot be explained by differences in the "observables" but can be attributed to labor market discrimination (that is, unequal pay for equal socioeconomic characteristics).

It turns out that practically all of the wage gap between the Mexican immigrants and native workers can be attributed to differences in observable characteristics between the two groups, particularly level of education. The typical Mexican immigrant in the United States has about 5.6 fewer years of schooling than the typical U.S. native worker. If the rate of return to education is about 7 percent (as implied by one survey of the evidence) *and* if this rate of return were the same in both the U.S. native and Mexican populations, the gap in educational attainment alone would generate a 40 percent wage gap.[7] If, as is likely, the rate of return to education is greater for U.S. native workers than for Mexican immigrants, the gap in education between the two groups would be responsible for an even larger wage gap. It is therefore not surprising that practically the entire wage gap between Mexican immigrants and native workers can be explained in terms of observable skill characteristics.

6. See Reimers (1983); Trejo (1995).
7. Card (1995).

As noted above, it is impossible to distinguish between legal and illegal Mexican immigrants in the Census data. As a result, only a few studies have attempted to separately analyze the economic performance of the two types of immigrants.[8] These studies typically use selected surveys of the illegal alien populations, analyzing these data to determine if illegal status *per se* has an independent impact on the earnings of Mexican immigrants. For the most part, this literature concludes that illegal Mexican immigrants earn less than U.S. native workers and also earn less than legal Mexican immigrants. However, much of the wage disadvantage associated with illegal status disappears once the studies control for differences in socioeconomic characteristics, particularly educational attainment and the number of years of residence in the United States. The limited evidence suggests that Mexican illegal aliens have even less education than their legal counterparts and have lived in the United States for a much shorter period. Both of these characteristics of the illegal alien population are associated with lower wages. Therefore, the existing (but limited) evidence does not support the conjecture that illegal aliens pay a penalty in the U.S. labor market.

Impact of Mexican Immigrants on Native Employment Opportunities

The presence of large numbers of less skilled Mexican immigrants in the United States raises a question with important social and economic ramifications: have these immigrants had an adverse effect on the employment opportunities of less skilled native workers?

The question of whether immigrants "take jobs away" from natives has dominated the debate over immigration policy ever since the founding of the United States. Despite its central role, there was little systematic study of this important question until the early 1980s.[9] Since then, a large and rapidly growing literature attempts to document the labor market adjustments as large immigrant flows enter the United States.

Many of the early studies in this literature estimated "spatial" correlations.[10] These types of studies typically estimated the labor market impact of immigration by comparing the earnings of U.S. natives living in cities where immigrants tend to cluster (such as Los Angeles and San Diego) with the earnings of those living in cities with few immigrants (such as Atlanta

8. See, for example, Massey (1987); Borjas and Tienda (1993).
9. See the surveys by Greenwood and McDowell (1986) and Borjas (1994).
10. Grossman (1982); Altonji and Card (1991); LaLonde and Topel (1991).

and Pittsburgh). These spatial correlations suggest that the average native wage is slightly lower in "immigrant cities," but that the numerical magnitude of this correlation is relatively small. If one city has 10 percent more immigrants than another, the U.S. native wage in the city with more immigrants is only about 0.2 percent lower.

Studies of specific local labor markets confirm the finding that immigration seems to have little impact even when the market has large immigrant flows. On April 20, 1980, Fidel Castro declared that Cuban nationals wanting to move to the United States could leave freely from the port of Mariel. By September 1980, about 125,000 Cubans, mostly unskilled workers, had made the journey. Almost overnight, Miami's labor force had unexpectedly grown by 7 percent. Card's influential analysis of the data indicates that the time-series trend in wages and employment opportunities for Miami's workers, including its black residents, was barely nudged by the Mariel flow.[11] The trend in the wage and unemployment rates of Miami's workers between 1980 and 1985 was similar to that experienced by workers in Los Angeles, Houston, and Atlanta, cities that did not experience the Mariel flow.

In short, the estimated spatial correlations between U.S. native wages and the immigrant share in local labor markets do not support the hypothesis that the employment opportunities of U.S.-born workers are strongly and adversely affected by immigration. However, in recent years there has been a growing realization that the weak spatial correlations reported by these studies do not necessarily imply that immigrants have little impact on the employment opportunities of U.S. native workers. Suppose, for instance, that immigration into Los Angeles lowers the earnings of native workers in that city substantially. U.S. native workers are not likely to stand idly by and watch their economic opportunities evaporate. Many will move out of the Los Angeles metropolitan area, and those individuals who were considering moving to Los Angeles will move somewhere else instead. As U.S. native workers respond to immigration by voting with their feet (creating what has already been dubbed "the new white flight"), the adverse impact of immigration on the Los Angeles labor market is transmitted to the entire economy. In the end, *all* U.S. native workers are worse off from immigration, not simply those residing in cities where immigrants cluster.

In effect, studies using supply shifts across local labor markets to measure the impact of immigration ignore the fact that metropolitan areas in the United States are not closed economies. Labor, capital, and goods flow

11. Card (1990).

freely across localities, equalizing wage rates in the process. In fact, as long as U.S. native workers and firms respond to the entry of immigrants by moving to areas offering better opportunities, there is no reason to expect any spatial correlation between the wage of natives and the presence of immigrants. There is already some evidence that the internal migration patterns of U.S. native workers in the United States are indeed responsive to immigration.[12] As a result, the comparison of local labor markets may be masking the macroeconomic effect of immigration.

A number of recent studies provide some evidence of this macroeconomic impact.[13] Weak negative correlations found between the native wage and the immigrant share in the local labor market become substantially stronger when the geographic scope of the labor market is expanded beyond a city—say, to a state or a Census geographic region. This pattern in the spatial correlation is precisely what we would expect to find if the internal migration of native workers "transmits" the adverse impact of immigration from the affected localities to other parts of the country. Moreover, the evidence reported recently by myself and others suggests that the negative correlation between immigration and native wages may be numerically important at the region level: the wages of U.S. native workers in a particular skill group might fall by as much as 2 percent if immigrants in that group increased by 10 percent.[14]

Recent empirical studies have also linked immigration to the sizable increase in wage inequality that occurred in the United States in the 1980s. In particular, the wage gap between workers without a high school diploma and those with more education rose substantially. Both the studies by myself and others and by Jaeger suggest that 20 to 40 percent of the decline in the relative wage of high school dropouts can be attributed to the less skilled immigration flow.[15] Immigration, however, accounts for a much smaller part of the declining relative wage of high school graduates. There is some controversy about these findings. In particular, some of the studies estimate the impact of immigration by "simulating" the labor market's response to the shift in the supply of different factors of production implied by immigration. In other words, for a given elasticity of demand, these exercises essentially state that a shift of x percent in the ratio of skilled to unskilled workers must have shifted the relative wage of the two groups by

---

12. Filer (1992); Frey (1994).
13. Borjas, Freeman, and Katz (1992, 1996); Jaeger (1996).
14. Borjas, Freeman, and Katz (1996).
15. Borjas, Freeman, and Katz (1996); Jaeger (1996).

y percent. The validity of these results is obviously affected by the validity of the parameters underlying the simulation.

Although there is a growing recognition that the entry of large numbers of less skilled immigrants have had an adverse impact on the labor market opportunities of less skilled U.S. native workers, the literature has not yet "apportioned" the impact across the various national origin groups within the immigrant population. However, Mexican immigrants make up the bulk of less skilled workers among foreign-born individuals in the United States. In 1990, 52 percent of the foreign-born workers lacking a high school diploma were of Mexican origin. It is therefore not unreasonable to suspect that Mexican immigration (whether legal or illegal) has probably had a sizable effect on the economic opportunities of less skilled native workers in the United States.

Impact of Mexican Immigrants on Welfare Expenditures

An additional consequence of the migration of less skilled workers—a consequence that plays an increasingly important role in the debate over immigration policy—is the impact of immigration on expenditures in welfare programs. Table 6-5 illustrates the extent to which Mexican and non-Mexican immigrants use welfare programs. The data are drawn both from the decennial Census, which provides information on the receipt of cash benefits (such as Aid to Families with Dependent Children and Supplemental Security Income) as well as from the Survey of Income and Program Participation (SIPP), which provides detailed information on the receipt of benefits from any means-tested entitlement program. As before, it is important to note that these data cannot distinguish between legal and illegal immigrants.

The data document a number of important trends. In 1970, non-Mexican immigrants were less likely, on average, to receive cash benefits than U.S. natives, whereas Mexican immigrants were substantially more likely to receive cash benefits than U.S. natives. By 1990, both groups have higher welfare participation rates than U.S. natives. In particular, 9 percent of non-Mexican immigrants and 11 percent of Mexican immigrants received cash benefits in 1990 compared with only 7 percent of U.S. native households.

The evidence also shows that once we include the means-tested programs that are not cash benefits (such as medicaid, food stamps, and housing assistance), the gap between Mexican immigrants and the other groups widens substantially. In the early 1990s, nearly 36 percent of Mexi-

Table 6-5. Welfare Use among Mexican and Non-Mexican Households

Group	1970	1980	1990
Census data: percent of households receiving cash benefits			
U.S.-born persons	6.0	7.9	7.4
Mexican immigrants	14.7	12.4	11.3
Non-Mexican immigrants	5.3	8.2	8.6
SIPP data: percent of households receiving any means-tested entitlement program			
U.S.-born	—	—	14.1
Mexican immigrants	—	—	36.0
Non-Mexican immigrants	—	—	16.7

Source: Author's tabulations from the 1970, 1980, and 1990 Public Use Samples of the U.S. Census, and the 1990 and 1991 panels of the Survey of Income and Program Participation (SIPP). The statistics are calculated in the subsample of households where the household head is at least 18 years of age. The statistics calculated in the SIPP data refer to welfare participation in the 1990–93 period. The programs included in the SIPP statistics include cash benefits, medicaid, vouchers such as food stamps and energy assistance, and housing assistance.

can households received some type of government aid, compared with only 17 percent of non-Mexican immigrant households and 14 percent of native households.

The disproportionately large use of welfare programs by the immigrant population has generated intense public interest on whether immigrants "pay their way" in the welfare state. These studies typically compute the cost of servicing either the entire immigrant population or a particular subgroup (such as Mexican illegal aliens living in California), and then compare the costs to the taxes that the groups contribute to various levels of government. Unfortunately, existing estimates of the national fiscal burden of immigration (defined as the difference between the taxes paid by immigrants and the cost of the services provided to them) vary widely. Some studies claim that immigrants pay $27 billion more in taxes than they take out, whereas other studies blame immigrants for a $40 billion fiscal burden on U.S. natives.[16]

However, a closer look at these studies raises important, difficult questions that have yet to be addressed. In fact, I doubt that any of these studies accurately calculates the gap between the taxes paid by immigrants and the cost of services provided to them. Studies claiming a beneficial fiscal impact typically assume that immigrants do not increase the cost of most government programs, other than education and welfare. Even though we do not know by how much immigrants increase the cost of roads, cleaner air, and perhaps even national defense, we do know that the cost of providing many of these services to a larger population increases in the long run.

16. Passel and Clark (1994); Huddle (1993a).

At the other extreme, studies claiming a large negative fiscal impact often overstate the costs of immigration and understate the taxes paid.

Despite the ambiguity inherent in these accounting exercises, practically all the studies conclude that the illegal alien population in California (which is predominantly Mexican) has created a fiscal burden for California's taxpayers. The General Accounting Office recently reviewed the evidence on the fiscal impact of illegal aliens on California, concluding that illegal aliens imposed a fiscal burden on California's taxpayers of at least $1 billion annually.[17] Part of California's fiscal burden arises because a large fraction of the taxes paid by the illegal aliens are federal taxes, collected by the federal government and used to fund federal programs. In contrast, a large number of the social programs provided to the illegal aliens are state programs paid for with state revenues. Therefore, even though the evidence is inconclusive on whether Mexican immigration has created a fiscal burden at the national level, Mexican immigrants may well be responsible for fiscal dislocations in the most affected localities.[18]

The Economic Impact on the United States and Mexico

The large-scale movement of less skilled Mexican workers to the United States alters the productivity of workers and of capital both in the United States and in Mexico. If we abstract from the fiscal impact on government expenditures, these productivity effects generate a net economic gain for the United States.

Mexican immigrants increase the number of workers in the economy. Because of the additional competition in the labor market, the wages of U.S. native workers fall. At the same time, however, American firms benefit, because they can now hire workers at lower wages. Many American consumers also gain, because the lower labor costs lead to cheaper goods and services. It turns out that the gains accruing to those who use or consume immigrant services exceed the losses suffered by U.S. native workers. As a result, the United States as a whole is better off.[19]

Although no study has attempted to calculate how much the United States benefits from Mexican immigration, the existing evidence suggests that the economic gains may not be substantial. After all, standard economic models suggest that the net gain generated by *all* immigrants is

17. U.S. General Accounting Office (1994, p. 2).
18. Parker and Rea (1993); Clark and others (1994); Huddle (1993b).
19. See Borjas (1995) for a technical analysis of the gains from immigration.

relatively small. The United States has more than 20 million foreign-born residents. I estimate that U.S. native workers have lost about $133 billion as a result of this immigration (or 1.9 percent of gross domestic product [GDP] in a $7 trillion economy), mainly because immigrants drive down the wages of competing workers.[20] At the same time, employers and other users of immigrant services, such as owners of large agricultural enterprises, have gained substantially. These gains are about $140 billion (or 2 percent of GDP). The net gain is only about $7 billion (or 0.1 percent of GDP). The available evidence therefore suggests that the increase in per-capita income of natives is small (less than $30 per year per U.S. native) but that this small increase masks a substantial redistribution of wealth.

However, it should be noted that these calculations assume that the immigrant and U.S. native populations are equally skilled. This assumption is clearly incorrect when attempting to estimate the productivity effects of Mexican immigration. The skill distribution of Mexican immigrants differs greatly from the skill distribution of the native-born work force, as well as from the skill distribution of other immigrants. These skill differentials suggest that the redistributive effect of Mexican immigration on the U.S. income distribution might be particularly large on some segments of the population. Skilled U.S. natives, for example, have much to gain when less skilled persons enter the United States. They can now specialize in performing relatively technical tasks, whereas the immigrant work force complements the U.S. native work force by taking on a variety of service jobs. Similarly, firms that use less skilled workers in the production line gain substantially from the immigration of less skilled workers. However, the gains experienced by skilled workers and by the firms that hire less skilled workers carry a price: the earnings of unskilled U.S. native workers will fall. The immigration of less skilled workers from Mexico may therefore be responsible for a sizable redistribution of wealth in the United States—from less skilled to skilled workers, and from labor to capital.

The migration flow between Mexico and the United States has effects on productivity not only in the United States but also in Mexico. But these effects on the Mexican economy have not been studied systematically. The standard economic model of a competitive labor market with full employment would suggest that the less skilled workers who remain in Mexico are made better off because the Mexican labor market has been "drained" of large numbers of competing workers. Employers of less skilled workers in Mexico lose out because they now have to pay higher wages to their

20. Borjas (1995).

workers. However, unemployment in Mexico is quite high, and the impact of Mexican emigration on the wages and employment of less skilled workers will likely differ from those predicted by the standard competitive model.

It is also important to recognize that the productivity impacts of immigration on the Mexican economy might be dwarfed by the potentially important effects of remittances. Mexican immigrants in the United States remit a substantial amount of money back to Mexico. In 1990, these remittances totaled $3.2 billion, or 1.5 percent of Mexican GDP.[21] Because 4.3 million Mexican-born residents were enumerated by the 1990 Census, the remittances amount to about $750 per Mexican immigrant in the United States. However, the economic benefits generated by these remittances have not yet been fully documented.

Summary

This chapter has surveyed the empirical evidence documenting the economic impact of Mexican immigrants, mainly on the United States. The available evidence suggests a number of potentially important implications:

—The Mexican immigrant population in the United States has relatively low levels of skills. As a result, Mexican immigrants in the United States earn substantially less than U.S. native workers, with most of the wage gap being attributable to the gap in educational attainment between the two groups.

—Less skilled immigrants have an adverse effect on the earnings of less skilled U.S. natives. Because more than half of all immigrants in the United States who lack a high school diploma are of Mexican origin, Mexican immigration probably has had an adverse impact on the earnings of less educated U.S. native workers.

—Mexican immigrants have relatively high rates of welfare recipiency, primarily because of their relatively low skill levels. In the early 1990s, 36 percent of Mexican immigrants received assistance from some means-tested entitlement program, compared with 14 percent of native-born households.

—Mexican immigration generates economic gains for the United States, but these gains are probably small.

Most of the empirical evidence summarized in this chapter is based on studies emphasizing the economic impact that Mexican immigration has

21. Ascencio (1993).

had on the United States. Unfortunately, the literature assessing the economic impact of this migration flow on Mexico itself is less comprehensive. Most of the empirical studies in the literature also ignore the distinction between legal and illegal status in the Mexican immigrant population. This empirical strategy is mandated by the fact that there is little information in the U.S. Census (the data most often used in immigration studies) that can be used to differentiate between the two groups.

The existing evidence has important implications for the impact of Mexican immigration on the economic opportunities facing less skilled native-born workers in the United States and for the costs of social insurance programs that provide a safety net for less skilled workers. In view of these adverse effects, it is not too surprising that the political debate over U.S. immigration policy has moved toward minimizing these costs. For example, California voters enacted Proposition 187 by a wide margin in 1994. This proposition, a watershed event in the history of immigration policy in the United States, prohibits illegal aliens living in California from receiving many social services and welfare benefits. The recently enacted welfare reform legislation continues this trend by making *legal* noncitizens ineligible to receive most types of social benefits, and by giving states the right to deny most kinds of social assistance to illegal aliens (with the exception of emergency medical care and public schooling).

However, economic research teaches us that the problems created by the large-scale immigration of less skilled persons go far beyond the impact on welfare expenditures. This type of immigration probably alters the shape of the U.S. income distribution, worsening the economic opportunities of workers at the bottom. If a political consensus indicates that economic factors should play an important role in the setting of immigration policy, it seems that the United States would be better off by "screening" visa applicants—not only for family connections with current residents (as the current policy mandates), but also for their skills or potential economic contribution to the United States. Such screening commonly occurs in other countries that take in immigrants, such as Australia, Canada, and New Zealand. It is likely that the ongoing debate over the future of legal immigration policy will increasingly focus on the question of which criteria the United States should use in awarding entry visas.

Comment by Jeffrey S. Passel

George Borjas is a creative economist who has done much of the definitive work concerning the economic impacts of immigration. Unfortunately, this chapter overlooks much of the existing research on immigration (including some of his own), mischaracterizes many of the economic impacts of Mexican immigration, and is not up to his usual excellent standards. In drawing on what economists refer to as "stylized facts," Borjas's descriptions of the impacts, particularly those in Mexico, are at odds with the existing literature and research.

General Comments

One would not expect the impacts of Mexican immigration to be particularly great on either the United States or Mexico, given the magnitude of the migration, as Borjas correctly notes. Mexicans living in the United States in 1995 amount to 6 or 7 million persons, representing 2 to 3 percent of the U.S. population. This figure includes several million people who came to the United States more than ten years ago. At the same time, the Mexican-born population of the United States may represent 5 percent of the Mexican population. The principal impacts are probably redistributive.

Borjas concludes that the overall economic impacts of Mexican immigration on the United States, although small, are generally positive. My reading of the evidence is roughly the same, but Borjas omits some significant factors in the analysis. Furthermore, some of the "facts" he describes are not well established and are contradicted by the available evidence. It should also be noted, however, that some impacts at the *local* level appear to be large on both sides of the border. (Many of these are probably negative in the United States and positive in Mexico.)

Within Mexico, Borjas argues that economic theory predicts workers are better off and employers worse off because of U.S. migration, but that the actual situation may differ because of high unemployment. I would argue that Mexican families with migrants in the United States and Mexican rural areas that send migrants experience significant positive impacts and there are few, if any, apparent losers.

Mexicans in the United States

Mexican immigrants earn substantially lower wages than U.S. natives; indeed, their wages are lower than almost any other population group. This deficit is due, as Borjas notes, primarily to the very low educational levels of Mexican immigrants. The earnings deficit of Mexican immigrant families is mitigated only slightly by high labor force participation rates. In assessing the impacts of Mexican immigrants on the U.S. economy, two additional factors must be taken into account. One of these—the illegal status of so many Mexican immigrants—is discussed by Borjas, but discounted. The other—the geographic concentration in California—is seldom, if ever, explicitly discussed by any analysts.

Undocumented Immigration

Mexico is the largest source of legal *and* illegal immigrants to the United States. During the 1980s, about 700,000 Mexicans came legally to the United States. This figure is about 30 percent larger (not nearly three times) than the second largest source country—the Philippines (not Korea). However, the 1990 Census shows about 2.2 million Mexican immigrants who came to the country during the 1980s. Thus, about 70 percent of the most recent entry cohorts from Mexico arrived in the United States as illegal immigrants. Characteristics of these cohorts provide an excellent approximation to those of undocumented immigrants.[22]

The undocumented status at entry of the vast majority of Mexican immigrants has implications for the immigrants themselves and the policy responses to the migration. Contrary to Borjas's assertions, there are studies demonstrating that undocumented immigrants pay a wage penalty in the labor market for their legal status.[23] In addition, undocumented Mexican immigrants are channeled into certain industries and jobs because they must work with fake documents or without any documents at all.

Concentration in California

The extreme geographic concentration of Mexican immigrants in California is the other factor affecting their impacts on the U.S. economy—one which is seldom, if ever, dealt with explicitly. About 60 percent of Mexican immigrants reside in California versus roughly one-quarter of non-Mexican immigrants and about 10 percent of U.S. natives. Thus, the role of the California economy and the California welfare system, for example, on the resulting characteristics of Mexican immigrants is obviously quite impor-

---

22. Fix and Passel (1994).
23. U.S. Department of Labor (1996); Borjas and Tienda (1993).

tant but is rarely considered. A number of studies conducted in the 1980s used data from the 1980 Census to assess the impact of immigration and Mexican immigrants on the U.S. economy. In 1980, the California economy was doing quite well—booming, in fact. The studies generally found that Mexican immigration had positive effects on the economy and generally served to create an optimistic attitude toward the migration.[24]

By 1990, the California economy had entered a deep and long recession that has still not completely run its course. Not surprisingly, studies using the 1990 Census to assess the impacts of Mexican immigration are tending to be more pessimistic than the 1980 round of studies. Perhaps both views are wrong and the actual impact overall is less extreme. Alternatively, the impact may in fact be positive in healthy economies and negative in less robust times—a finding in line with some research. Other impacts that may affect California differentially include welfare use and fiscal "costs," which I discuss briefly below.

Current Research

Low-Skilled/High-Skilled Wage Gap

Borjas reports that low-skilled immigrants account for about 30 percent of the increase in the wage gap between low-skilled and high-skilled workers in the United States. This figure seems quite large, and the mechanism by which this would occur seems obscure. Changing technology and international trade have generally been cited as the dominant factors in the increasing wage gap, with declining unionization, mergers, and immigration as other significant but less important factors.

The numbers of people involved suggest a more moderate impact. New immigrants arriving in the 1980s without a high school diploma—new high school dropout immigrants—account for less than 10 percent of the high school dropouts in the labor force. Moreover, the number of native high school dropouts in the labor force actually declined 25 percent during the 1980–90 period. It is difficult to see how such a small group could have such a large impact, particularly given the other factors involved.

Outmigration of U.S. Natives

Borjas cites several recent studies claiming that immigration is "pushing" natives, particularly low-skilled natives, out of the traditional migrant-

---

24. See, for example, Muller and Espenshade's (1985) study of southern California.

receiving states.[25] Whereas this movement is well documented in the late 1980s, the role of immigration in causing the migration is less well established. Other factors, especially economic factors, undoubtedly played a major role.

Nevada was the fastest-growing state in the 1980s, with Oregon, Idaho, and Arizona also experiencing substantial population and job growth. With California experiencing a major recession and these western states experiencing booming job growth, it is only natural that U.S. natives would move to them, especially since natives have more options than the largely undocumented Mexican immigrant population. Illinois and New York have been experiencing outmigration for decades. In these states, immigrants actually reversed the population declines of recent decades. The story is more complicated in Texas, but the recent post-1990 economic upturn has been accompanied by a migration turnaround. Although immigration is undoubtedly a factor in affecting native migration patterns, the story is much more complex than simply a "push" toward racial and ethnic separation.

Welfare Use

Overall welfare use among immigrants is higher than among U.S. natives, as Borjas notes. However, this simple statement obscures a welter of relationships among age groups, eligibility/legal status groups, national origin groups, and structural groups. A full understanding of welfare use and construction of policy response requires a more careful consideration of specific groups and programs.

Usage rates for immigrants are driven up by two main groups, refugees and elderly immigrants. Refugees arrive in the United States after fleeing their home countries, often with little in the way of material or family resources. They are immediately eligible for welfare. Refugee-serving agencies, either private or governmental, direct refugees to the welfare system to facilitate their transition to American society.[26] With time in the United States, the rates of welfare usage decrease for refugee groups.

For elderly immigrants, welfare usage rates are extraordinarily high. Enrollment in Supplemental Security Income (SSI) and medicaid substitutes for social security and medicare, which are almost universal among U.S. natives. Since the latter programs require long periods of employment

25. See, for example, Frey (1994).
26. Although the wisdom of directing refugees toward welfare is subject to question, it nonetheless occurs.

in covered jobs, recently arrived elderly immigrants tend to be ineligible. Long-term residents who are elderly Mexican immigrants (that is, those arriving in the 1970s and before) also have usage rates much higher than those of U.S. natives and higher than those of other long-term immigrant groups. Such high rates probably arise because Mexican immigrants, even more so than other immigrants, may have spent much of their early employment in jobs not covered by social security (for example, farm and private household service jobs).

Borjas reports welfare usage rates by households rather than individuals. For households headed by Mexican immigrants, usage rates declined between 1980 and 1990 but remained above those headed by natives.[27] However, because Mexican immigrants are much more likely than natives to live in extended-family households, some portion of the difference must be attributable to welfare receipt by household members other than members of the household head's nuclear family.

Finally, the geographic distribution of Mexican immigrants has a direct effect on differences in welfare usage. California has substantially higher usage rates than other states and, as noted earlier, has a much higher concentration of Mexican immigrants than other states. Welfare usage rates for Mexican immigrants in the Midwest are far below those of Mexicans in California and even below those of U.S. natives in the Midwest.[28]

Redistributive Effects

Mexican immigration does have many of the redistributive effects Borjas describes. Redistribution from less-skilled workers to skilled workers and from labor to capital is occurring. However, it is clearly affected by many factors other than Mexican immigration, which may play only a small role. Borjas describes redistribution from "persons who pay the taxes required to service the immigrant population" to "consumers who purchase the goods and services produced by the less-skilled Mexican immigrants." While such redistribution is likely to exist, the two groups are, by and large, the same population. Thus, this "redistribution" effect is negligible, but consumers are often not aware of their benefit while taxpayers generally understand the "burden."

The fiscal impacts of immigrants are part of the redistributive impacts of immigration since immigrants and native both pay taxes and use services.

27. Bean and others (1994).
28. Passel (1996).

The various studies available all have problems, as Borjas correctly notes. Although measurement problems abound, deeper issues include definitions of costs, taxes, and benefits. All of the studies find that the biggest "cost" attributable to immigrants is the money spent on primary and secondary education of the children of immigrants. Yet much of this money is spent on salaries for U.S. natives (but is not counted as a benefit for natives as a group). Furthermore, virtually all economic assessments of education show significant returns to education, so that it is possible to conceptualize these "costs" as "investments."

The various studies of fiscal impacts virtually all find a similar redistributive impact. At the federal level, revenues exceed costs. The largest sources of revenue from immigrants are federal income taxes and Federal Insurance Contributions Act (FICA, or social security/medicare) taxes, whereas there are few direct federal costs for immigrants. The largest cost, primary and secondary education, is borne by states and localities that seldom collect sufficient revenue from immigrants to meet these costs.[29]

The beneficiaries of Mexican immigration, including those mentioned by Borjas, seldom pay the costs either directly of indirectly. The employers of Mexican-born labor, particularly illegal immigrants, benefit from low-cost workers. Landowners who employ illegal workers in agriculture have generally seen their land increase greatly in value as a result of the capitalization of available profits. Neither this increase in wealth nor the increased income from agriculture are taxed sufficiently at the local level to make up for impacts on local schools. Native-born workers in firms employing immigrant labor comprise an often overlooked group of beneficiaries. The somewhat diffuse character of the benefits, plus the more apparent governmental costs, account for much of the political reaction against immigration (particularly illegal immigration) in some of the major receiving areas.

Impacts on Mexico

Borjas's assessment of the impacts of Mexican immigration to the United States on Mexico is not consistent with understanding of the situation in Mexico or with the research on the topic. He derives this conclusion

29. It should be noted, however, that natives also pose a fiscal burden for these lower levels of government (for example, Clark and Passel [1993]). Borjas cites the burden on California from *undocumented* immigration, a burden widely trumpeted by the state's politicians. However, in the most recent fiscal year, the state of California actually ran a budget surplus, suggesting that the major source of California's fiscal problems has been the recessionary economy of the state rather than immigrants.

from classical economic theory based on assumptions that clearly do not apply to Mexico. The key assumption is that the removal of a significant share of the Mexican labor force through migration leads to higher wages for those workers who remain behind. The higher wages lead, in turn, to lower profits on the part of employers. This model is surely not valid in an economy such as Mexico's where underemployment and unemployment combined may reach 50 percent (or even higher in some rural areas). Under such conditions with a massive oversupply of labor, migration aids the migrants without hurting the remaining labor force.

Although the relative importance to Mexico of remittances is decreasing with increases in trade, their role remains important in many areas. This role is known to be much more positive than Borjas reports. A number of studies find significant differences between Mexican villages that send migrants to the United States and those that do not.[30] The migrant-sending communities are much better off in the private sector, certainly, and even in the public sector, to some extent. At the individual and family level, some research reports huge marginal effects on family income from remittances, substantial impacts on asset accumulation, and large local multipliers.[31] According to this research, migration to the United States serves as a substitute for local banking, social security, and welfare systems in many areas of rural Mexico.

There is little institutional impetus in Mexico from any quarter to impede migration to the United States. If the effects were significantly negative, one would expect some movement to control migration from the Mexican side.

Conclusion

There is no discounting the negative reaction against illegal immigration, particularly from California. Although there are large numbers of illegal immigrants (particularly illegal Mexican immigrants) in the state, much of the response is based on the erroneous perception that all or most Mexican immigrants are undocumented. Since the Immigration Reform and Control Act of 1986, this is no longer true. Local impacts of migration can indeed be large—the burden on many school systems is quite real. Furthermore, the beneficiaries of the migratory flow generally do not contribute an

30. Massey and others (1994); Taylor and others (1996).
31. Taylor (1992).

appropriate share towards offsetting the costs; in addition, federal help is insufficient.

However, the role of California's politics and recession in shaping the national attitudes toward illegal immigration tend to be understated. The concentration of illegal immigrants and Mexican immigrants in California affects not only the research results, but also the policy response. Outside of California, the impacts of Mexican immigration are probably more diffuse, employment impacts may be less, and welfare use is lower. Yet the national debate on *all* immigration seems to me to be driven largely by the situation in California and of Mexican immigrants.

Borjas does not deal with any potential policies to control Mexican immigration and mitigate its impacts. The appropriate policy responses to Mexican immigration are not at all clear. What is clear, unfortunately, is that none of the measures undertaken by the U.S. government to control illegal Mexican migration has had much impact.[32] Studies of migration from Mexico show that virtually everyone who wants to get into the United States does.[33] Attempts to control access to employment through employer sanctions have not met with success. Furthermore, measures taken to deter border crossers have driven up the costs of migration to the United States, but not to the point where the flow has decreased. The increased cost does seem to encourage more lengthy stays in the United States. The potential gains to migrants and to their families and communities in Mexico are well worth the effort to try to overcome any barriers the United States has thrown up so far.

32. Passel (forthcoming).
33. Donato, Durand, and Massey (1992).

Comment by Marta Tienda

The past decade has witnessed numerous attempts to reform and to revamp the criteria used to admit immigrants to the United States. Although recent immigrant cohorts represent more than 140 countries, two-thirds of all immigrants originate in just thirteen nations, and Mexicans alone account for approximately 25 percent of all immigrants admitted legally during the last two decades. The social visibility of Mexicans is augmented by their residential concentration in just a few states, particularly California and Texas. Whether the ultimate policy emphasis settles on reducing the size of the illegal or the legal flow, or strengthening the link between immigration and labor policy, recent policy debates point in two clear directions. One is toward more restrictive admission criteria; another is toward less generous social benefits to those admitted. On both counts, the greatest impacts will be experienced on Mexican immigrants. As such, Borjas's chapter 6 on Mexican immigrants is timely for current policy discussions.

One reading of this chapter is that the impact of Mexican immigration is benign. Yet this hardly squares with public perceptions that immigrants take jobs away from native workers and drain the public coffers through their reliance on means-tested benefits and the school system. He is correct in acknowledging how local and national impacts differ, particularly since most taxes paid by immigrants accrue to the federal coffers while most costs incurred by immigrants are relatively localized. This disjuncture between the local and federal costs and benefits raises a major philosophical question bearing on assessments of economic impacts, namely whether it is productive to seek, much less to derive, an empirical estimate of *the* economic impact of Mexican immigration. A net impact for the nation as a whole is virtually meaningless given that more than 2.5 million Mexican immigrants lived in California in 1990 out of 4.3 million in the country as a whole. In California, the impact is surely great, whereas in Nebraska it is trivial. Given the dedicated focus on Mexican immigration, we are likely to learn more about Mexican immigration by studying impacts in California, Chicago, Texas, and selected cities in Arizona, New Mexico, and Colorado than by deriving national averages that conceal more than they reveal. Failure to disaggregate "impacts" by region and/or industry or public sector distorts understanding of economic impacts.

A second major reservation is concerned with the "value added" from Borjas's discussion. Given the explosion of empirical studies about immigration in general, and Mexican immigration in particular, it is fair to expect new insights. If this expectation is unfair, it is fair to expect a balanced synthesis of the economic impacts of Mexican immigration. Instead, the assessment provided is essentially a distillation of Borjas's prior papers with little regard to contradictory evidence. Given his heavy reliance on his previously published work, at a minimum, the current assessment should be reconciled with earlier conclusions. For example, earlier studies concluded that the greatest substitution effects from immigration occur between recent and earlier arrivals. How does this inform the current policy debate, particularly regarding immigrants from Mexico? Do recent immigrants compete with their native-born or foreign-born cousins?

A related inconsistency with prior work concerns possibly differential labor impacts for men versus women. This is not a trivial issue. Borjas's conclusions about labor market impacts are based on analyses of men, to the exclusion of women; yet women make up a disproportionate share of the recipients of public assistance. Furthermore, in earlier work, Borjas concluded that the greatest negative impacts on the wages of domestic male workers can be traced to women, not to immigrants. Given the dramatic rise in female employment since 1960, this issue must be factored into future assessments of labor market impacts. Not to do so risks blaming immigrants for changes in the gender composition of employment.

A third issue warranting further discussion concerns the issue of "skills," measured in this case by educational attainment in country of origin. That Mexican immigrants have low levels of education is undisputable. There is also ample compelling evidence that unskilled workers have experienced the greatest erosion in relative wages since 1973. But if Mexicans have such inferior skills relative to most native workers, why do Mexicans continue to receive job offers in the United States at higher rates than black Americans? This human capital anomaly is skirted by Borjas, because the comparison categories with the U.S. population are too coarse to be meaningful. This issue deserves analytic confrontation to inform the current policy debate about the value of educating the children of Mexican immigrants (future generations of workers) and about the economic "opportunity costs" of curtailing immigration from Mexico.

Finally, I would like to raise four additional issues that invite interpretive judgment and require elaboration to inform policy debates. One concerns the analyses of wage gaps. It was unclear whether the wage gaps were education adjusted. Rather than attribute the observed differences to educational differentials by assuming a 7 percent rate of return, would it not be more direct to perform a formal decomposition? This is a fairly straightforward calculation. What is more difficult is deciding the appropriate standard for the decomposition and, I would add, the appropriate level of disaggregation for these wage gap analyses. National comparisons of the type provided beg the question. Furthermore, because it is impossible to disentangle age, period, and cohort effects with cross-sectional data, some might be impressed that the wages of Mexican immigrants did not deteriorate more during the 1970s and especially the 1980s. It is well established that inequality increased during these periods, particularly among "skill" groups. But I question whether individuals are the appropriate unit of analysis to assess the "economic mobility" of Mexicans (or any other immigrant group, for that matter). If Mexican immigrant families spread the work among a greater number of adults, the welfare of individual household members can also be improved.

A second issue requiring further attention because it is central to the current policy debate, yet given short shrift by Borjas, is the matter of internal migration. Do we have evidence that Mexican immigration triggers outmigration of native workers from labor markets where Mexicans are residentially concentrated? This prediction from economic theory may or may not occur. In some places, such as Chicago, it is the Mexican immigrants (and some native-born Mexicans) that are residentially displaced as urban gentrification unfolds. In other Chicago neighborhoods, residential density has increased, as have incomes of immigrant families, who leave their immigrant communities for suburban neighborhoods in search of better schools and social amenities. In other words, rather than trigger out-migration of U.S. natives, it is reasonable to suppose that Mexican immigrants would have a higher probability of moving again (given that they moved already). My reading of the remigration literature suggests this is so, but perhaps Borjas has some additional evidence to bring to the Mexican experience in particular.

A third quibble concerns the tabulations of welfare participation based on the Survey of Income and Program Participation. As an analyst of SIPP, I am confused about whether the welfare participation rates presented refer to monthly time periods or whether the measures refer to "ever use" over the period covered by the four surveys. It is annoying to see the rich detail available in SIPP aggregated crudely to reproduce and exaggerate the imperfections of decennial census data. SIPP permits detailed disaggregation of welfare participation by type of assistance, duration of benefits, and amount received, and it is crucial to set the record straight on these dimensions. Doing so is the minimal requirement of responsible reporting. It is also necessary to indicate whether immigrant families who receive public assistance are eligible for such benefits because they include U.S. children, or whether they are potential "abusers" of the welfare packages available in the United States. The policy implications of these two scenarios are quite different. But, as presented, the current tabulations about welfare participation distort and confuse more than they clarify.

My last of four points returns to the generalized theme of economic impacts that Borjas suggests occurs through consumption multiplier effects. I would add the need to consider economic effects through business activity of immigrants, but the paucity of data makes this topic even more tenuous than others considered by Borjas and other immigration experts. It is high time that serious estimates of economic impacts of immigration through the consumption channel of influence were provided. The sheer volume and residential concentration of the Mexican flow allows for economies of scale, which are usually ignored in assessments of economic impacts.

When all is said and done, whether the economic impacts are small or large, positive or negative is less important to policymakers than how these impacts are perceived. In the final analysis, unfortunately, it is the perceived and not the actual effects that drive the current hysteria about immigration—Mexican immigration in particular. Perhaps this explains the ambivalent tone that pervades Borjas's discussion.

General Discussion

Much of the discussion focused on the recent threats to restrict services to immigrants, and in particular, on threats to bar illegal children from U.S. public schools. Nora Lustig argued that most assessments overstate the net benefits from such a policy change, because they ignore hidden costs, such as those related to possible increases in crime. Jeffrey Passel cited recent work that finds much higher pregnancy rates for girls who drop out of high school (53 percent) than for those who complete high school (10 percent), suggesting another hidden cost of forcing significant numbers of illegal youths out of school. He also noted that existing studies focus on average (not marginal) schooling costs and argued that the average costs overstate the marginal saving from keeping illegal immigrant children out of school. However, Barry Bosworth contested this view. Empirical studies have found no significant economies of scale in education, implying that marginal and average schooling costs are likely to be similar over the long run.

A number of discussants stressed that the way public schools are funded in the United States implies that the regional concentration of immigrants imposes very real, large burdens on a few localities. However, as argued by Bosworth, Lustig, and Passel, any such burden should be distributed nationally, and perhaps viewed as an investment. Indeed, Marta Tienda pointed out that the drop-out rate among those of Mexican origin, at roughly 30 percent, is already significantly higher than the drop out rate for blacks (12 percent) and non-Hispanic whites (8 percent). Lustig noted that keeping illegal immigrants out of school may increase the relative supply of less skilled workers, exacerbating any adverse effects on the relative wages of less skilled U.S. natives. Bosworth suggested that threats to bar illegal immigrant children from schools be seen as a means of focusing national attention on a legitimate concern of these affected communities. Conference participants hoped that the result would be a more constructive solution to the problem.

More generally, Lustig posed the question of whether restricting immigrants from receiving education and other social services would actually reduce the flow. Her own expectation was that such a policy change would have little effect on the desire of Mexicans to come to the United States.

Susan Collins raised questions about George Borjas's assessment of the net economic impact from Mexican immigrants. She noted that his discussion did not make clear which alternative situations were being compared, or the time frame for the analysis. Finally, Collins asked whether available data included Mexican immigrants who were living in the United States only temporarily. Passel responded that most studies focused on relatively settled populations, and that existing evidence suggested that much of the circular flow of Mexican migrants eventually does stay in the United States.

References

Altonji, Joseph G., and David Card. 1991. "The Effects of Immigration on the Labor Market Outcomes of Less-Skilled Natives." In *Immigration, Trade, and the Labor Market*, edited by John M. Abowd and Richard B. Freeman, 201–234. University of Chicago Press.

Ascencio, Fernando. 1993. *Bringing it Back Home: Remittances to Mexico from Migrant Workers in the United States*. La Jolla, Calif.: University of California, San Diego, Center for U.S.–Mexican Studies.

Bean, Frank D., and others. 1994. "Welfare Recipiency Among Immigrants: Implications for U.S. Immigrant Policy." Immigrant Policy Program. Washington: Urban Institute.

Borjas, George J. 1994. "The Economics of Immigration." *Journal of Economic Literature* 32 (December): 1667–1717.

Borjas, George J. 1995. "The Economic Benefits from Immigration." *Journal of Economic Perspective* 9 (Spring): 3–22.

Borjas, George J., Richard B. Freeman, and Lawrence F. Katz. 1992. "On the Labor Market Impacts of Immigration and Trade." In *Immigration and the Work Force: Economic Consequences for the United States and Source Areas*, edited by George J. Borjas and Richard B. Freeman, 213–244. University of Chicago Press.

Borjas, George J., Richard B. Freeman, and Lawrence F. Katz. 1996. "Searching for the Effect of Immigration on the Labor Market." *American Economic Review* 86 (May): 246–51.

Borjas, George J., and Marta Tienda. 1993. "The Employment and Wages of Legalized Immigrants." *International Migration Review* 27 (Winter): 712–47.

Bureau of the Census. 1970/1980/1990. *Public Use Samples of the U.S. Census.* Government Printing Office.

_____. 1993. *The Foreign-Born Population of the United States.* 1990 CP-3-1. Government Printing Office.

Card, David. 1990. "The Impact of the Mariel Boatlift on the Miami Labor Market." *Industrial and Labor Relations Review* 43 (January): 245–57.

_____. 1995. "Earnings, Schooling, and Ability Revisited." *Research in Labor Economics* 14: 23–48.

Clark, Rebecca L., and Jeffrey S. Passel. 1993. "How Much Do Immigrants Pay in Taxes? Evidence from Los Angeles County." Policy Discussion Paper PRIP-UI-26. Washington: Program for Research on Immigration Policy.

Clark, Rebecca L., and others. 1994. *Fiscal Impacts of Undocumented Aliens: Selected Estimates for Seven States.* Washington: Urban Institute (September).

Donato, Katherine M., Jorge Durand, and Douglas S. Massey. 1992. "Stemming the Tide? Assessing the Deterrent Effects of the Immigration Reform and Control Act." *Demography* 29 (May): 139–57.

Filer, Randall K. 1992. "The Impact of Immigrant Arrivals on Migratory Patterns of Native Workers." In *Immigration and the Work Force: Economic Consequences for the United States and Source Areas*, edited by George J. Borjas and Richard B. Freeman, 245–69. University of Chicago Press.

Fix, Michael, and Jeffrey S. Passel. 1994. *Immigration and Immigrants: Setting the Record Straight.* Washington: Urban Institute.

Frey, William H. 1994. "The New White Flight." *American Demographics* 16 (April): 40–48.

Greenwood, Michael J., and John M. McDowell. 1986. "The Factor Market Consequences of U.S. Immigration." *Journal of Economic Literature* 24 (December): 1738–72.

Grossman, Jean Baldwin. 1982. "The Substitutability of Natives and Immigrants in Production." *Review of Economics and Statistics* 54 (November): 596–603.

Huddle, Donald. 1993a. "The Costs of Immigration." Rice University, Department of Economics.

_____. 1993b. "The Costs of Immigration to California." Rice University, Department of Economics.

Jaeger, David. 1996. "Skill Differences and the Effect of Immigrants on the Wages of Natives." Bureau of Labor Statistics.

Katz, Lawrence F., and Murphy, Kevin M. 1992. "Changes in the Wage Structure, 1963–87: Supply and Demand Factors." *Quarterly Journal of Economics* 107 (February): 35–78.

LaLonde, Robert J., and Topel, Robert H. 1991. "Labor Market Adjustments to Increased Immigration." In *Immigration, Trade, and the Labor Market*. Edited by John M. Abowd and Richard B. Freeman, 167–99. University of Chicago Press.

Massey, Douglas S. 1987. "Do Undocumented Migrants Earn Lower Wages than Legal Immigrants?" *International Migration Review* 21 (Summer): 236–74.

Massey, Douglas S., and others. 1994. "International Migration: The North American Case." *Population and Development Review* 19 (September): 431–66.

Muller, Thomas, and Thomas J. Espenshade. 1985. *The Fourth Wave*. Washington: Urban Institute.

Murphy, Kevin M. and Welch, Finis. 1992. "The Structure of Wages." *Quarterly Journal of Economics* 107 (February): 285–326.

Parker, Richard A., and Rea, Louis M. 1993. "Illegal Immigration in San Diego County: An Analysis of Costs and Revenues." Sacramento, Calif.: California State Senate Special Committee on Border Issues (September).

Passel, Jeffrey S. 1996. "Recent Immigration to the United States and the Midwest." Paper prepared for a conference, "The Changing Face of Rural America," Iowa State University, Ames, Iowa, July 11–13.

_____. Forthcoming. "Recent Efforts to Control Illegal Immigration to the United States." Paris: Organization for Economic Cooperation and Development Working Party on Migration.

Passel, Jeffrey, and Clark, Rebecca. 1994. "How Much Do Immigrants Really Cost? A Reappraisal of Huddle's 'The Cost of Immigrants'." Washington: Urban Institute.

Reimers, Cordelia W. 1983. "Labor Market Discrimination Against Hispanic and Black Men," *Review of Economics and Statistics* 65 (November): 570–79.

Taylor, J. Edward. 1992. "Remittances and Inequality Reconsidered: Direct, Indirect and Intertemporal Effects." *Journal of Policy Modeling* 14 (2): 187–208.

Taylor, J. Edward, and others. 1996. "International Migration and National Development." *Population Index* 62 (2): 181–212.

Trejo, Stephen J. 1995. "Why Do Mexican Americans Earn Lower Wages?" University of California, Santa Barbara, Department of Economics.

U.S. Department of Labor, Bureau of International Labor Affairs. 1996. *Effects of the Immigration Reform and Control Act: Characteristics and Labor Market Behavior of the Legalized Population Five Years Following Legalization*. Government Printing Office.

U.S. General Accounting Office. 1994. *Assessing Estimates of Financial Burden on California*. GAO/HEHS-95-22 (November).

U.S. Immigration and Naturalization Service. 1994. *Statistical Yearbook of the Immigration and Naturalization Service*. Government Printing Office.

Index